Barask Paraskevopoulos was born in Athens, Greece, and migrated with his parents from one year of age to Melbourne, Australia. Six years of studying medicine at Monash University, a science degree in cell biology and pharmacology at Monash as well as a Bachelor of Arts degree in English Literature and Criminology at Melbourne University together with a lifelong interest in biology and biochemistry put him in good stead to tackle the difficult scenario of life's origin.

CHARLES DARWIN

CARL WOESE　　　　　　SIR DAVID ATTENBOROUGH

This book is dedicated to the memory of the great Charles Darwin and Carl Woese who discovered the Archaean domain of life.

Barask Paraskevopoulos

From Chemistry to Life on Earth

Austin Macauley Publishers™
LONDON · CAMBRIDGE · NEW YORK · SHARJAH

Copyright © Barask Paraskevopoulos 2024

The right of Barask Paraskevopoulos to be identified as author of this work has been asserted by the author in accordance with sections 77 and 78 of the Copyright, Designs and Patents Act 1988.

All rights reserved. No part of this publication may be reproduced, stored in a retrieval system or transmitted in any form or by any means, electronic, mechanical, photocopying, recording or otherwise, without the prior permission of the publishers.

Any person who commits any unauthorised act in relation to this publication may be liable to criminal prosecution and civil claims for damages.

The story, the experiences, and the words are the author's alone.

A CIP catalogue record for this title is available from the British Library.

ISBN 9781035821389 (Paperback)
ISBN 9781035821396 (Hardback)
ISBN 9781035821419 (ePub e-book)
ISBN 9781035821402 (Audiobook)

www.austinmacauley.com

First Published 2024
Austin Macauley Publishers Ltd®
1 Canada Square
Canary Wharf
London
E14 5AA

Every scientist who worked on the 290 references employed in substantiating this work.

Table of Contents

What Is Life on Earth?	11
Introduction	13
Evolving Stardust	15
The First Protocells	31
Further Protocell Biochemistry	42
Convergent Evolution into Life	52
Sources of Energy	58
Combating Catabolism	65
More Polypeptide Catalysts	73
Advent of the Protogene	78
Crucial Phosphoryl Transferase	92
Membrane Evolution	99
Protoribosomes and Polymerases	104
Reverse Translation? Really?	116
tRNAs and Their Aminoacylators	121
Metaribosomes and tRNA Evolution	128
Specialising into DNA and RNA	139
Need for Start and Stop Codons	153
Viruses and Introns	158
Advent of De Novo Nucleotide Synthesis	162
Continuing Evolution of the Codon	174

On Past the Eukaryotes	192
Perplexing Collagen and Silk	239
Epilogue	244
References	246

What Is Life on Earth?

A coding polymer, catalysed in its synthesis, with or without accompanying chemical system (group of chemicals or chemical pathways) which uses substrates in its environment to grow and reproduce relatively accurately by a templating mechanism, actively or passively, subject to aqueous physicochemical conditions and molecular evolution.

This definition may seem far-fetched to some but in polymer chemistry, a polymer is termed as "living" if it has repeating monomers with no terminating or chain transfer mechanism and whose initiation rate is faster than its propagation.

Additionally, the polymer has limited dispersity, that is, the monomers in the chain are roughly similar in size and chemical structure. In a 2018 article (*Nature Communications*), Zhang C.J. concludes 'the use of thioureas and benzyl-alkoxide led to living/controlled carbonyl sulfide (COS)/epoxied co-polymerisation…' Faster initiation than propagation simply means enough catalyst and monomers need to be present so that the reaction is initiated faster than the growth of each polymer.

In their infancy, catalysed polynucleotide polymers propagated as slowly as 1 substrate per minute thereby making the initiation rate potentially faster. A self-perpetuating chemical systems-based concept of life based on metabolism and a plentiful environment is viable for short periods of time but not on a geological time scale. It could grow and divide by evolving systems that break into two compartments upon reaching a certain size as demonstrated by Krishna Bahadur.

They could even evolve into alternative systems by natural selection pressures in their environment terminating certain variants of cells. They could increase in complexity by adding metabolic cycles to the existing ones but they would not be recognisable as life on Earth by lacking the selfish archive that codes for catalysts: the archive that RNA or DNA and in the Eoarchean, proteinoids represent.

This deficit would make it too slow and lacking in direction to be viable during environmental perturbations: it lacks an archive of alternative catalytic products to maintain cellular homeostasis and is destined for extinction. A budding metabolic cell may have ample oligopeptides to begin a polymer archive chemistry but could not survive long enough to synthesise ribonucleotides in adequate quantity. There is no selective driver for this synthesis. The tendency is for concentration to decrease and thus when the energy wanes it will extinguish.

Polypeptides were a plausible alternative coding molecule for life on Earth but were marred by not always having the side chains facing in the same direction away from the "backbone" of the polymer thereby being less competitive than RNA for this role whilst threose nucleic acids, peptide nucleic acids and other plausible polymers were marred by 1. unreliable availability (concentration), 2. unreliable variety of monomers with stereochemical affinity for each other or amino acids or 3. Low survival value.

IN: Viruses and viroids.

OUT: Cells without polynucleotides, e.g., mature human erythrocytes.

DIAGRAM OF AN RNA VIROID –

Similar in morphology to this viroid shown, the Cadang Cadang coconut viroid is the smallest living thing on Earth at minimum 246-7 ribonucleotides long, codes for no genes, is devoid of lipid or protein, uses the coconut cells' RNA polymerase11 to replicate itself and is spread by the wind in pollen, moisture or by direct contact including via workers' tools.

Introduction

This analysis represents an integration of research by thousands of scientists over many decades in order to provide a plausible scenario up to the stage of a biotic cell with over 50 protein-coding genes plus tRNA and ribosomal RNA coding genes as well as ribozymes.

The final chapter begins the journey beyond the eukaryotes by touching on issues of nutrition, predation and endosymbiosis. A lead up to binary fission follows with an acceptance that meiosis and sexual reproduction, mitosis, apoptosis and multicellularity are still in the future of our biotic cell when control and feedback circuits can become more sophisticated with DNA in the loop and involving reaction cascades. These complex processes are still dependent on a sound background of sustaining metabolic and genetic biochemical pathways.

It is based on many scholarly articles but fills in gaps in the research with some hypotheses of what probably occurred based on sound first principles, that is, knowledge of how molecules can react based on the literature, the force of electromagnetism, the laws of chemistry and the prevailing conditions. This is integrated with a study of extant biochemistry and genetics across the three domains of life.

All possible starting locations, the "where" as well as the compositions, the "what", are accepted as possible origins of the protocell, as they are irrefutable, to focus on the more important question of "how" Earth's brand of life came about. There are many clues about the "when" but this is a lot more uncertain due to the fossil record of the Archaean being marred by weathering and subduction of tectonic plates as well as the common presence of convincing artifacts. The "how" is often suggested by the extant compositions and range of reactions integrated with some estimates of Eoarchean conditions.

This strategy also admits that the "where" and the nature of the very first protocells will never be known due to the great passage of time and the lack of fossil evidence.

Many origins: coacervates, aerosols, liposomes, micelles, rock pore contents and proteasomes, all from different locations have merged and reacted by simple physicochemical means at first towards liposome-proteasome hybrid protocells, then biotic cells of some variety on towards a range of modern cells with our recognisable nucleotide code before continuing to diverge into the enormous variety we see today.

This analysis mimics life by always looking for plausible alternative chemical pathways. These alternatives, together with abundance, are what made a seemingly impossible pathway towards life inevitable.

From Hess's Law, we know that the total enthalpy change of a particular reaction involving specific reactants to specific products is independent of the sequence of steps taken, which means they are no dearer from a thermodynamics viewpoint. There is enough research and archival factual knowledge to assemble a plausible scenario of how inorganic and organic chemistry could have become Earth's varied biochemistry and to propose an elegant, simple solution to the evolution of the genetic code and the ribosome.

Carbonaceous Chondrites rich in organic chemicals for lifes'. Origin supplemented those created by reactions on Earth. A Chixculub sized meteorite would deliver billions of Kg of organic chemicals with the impact itself inestimably evolving them further.

Evolving Stardust

Approximately, 4.6Gya the Earth was formed from accretions of condensing cosmic dust clouds that were themselves formed by the products of supernovae and neutron star mergers. Subsequently, towards the end of the Hadean period that followed, carbonaceous chondrite meteorites delivered billions of kilograms of organic and inorganic chemicals to the Earth 4.1–3.8 billion years ago, that is during the late heavy bombardment.

Strong evidence for this assertion is the analysis of the 100kg Murchison meteorite and others (Orgueil, Lake Tagish, Allende), which have been shown to contain amino acids, alkanes, alkenes, carboxylic acids, phosphonic acids, purines and pyrimidines, kerogens and a host of other organic chemicals (Philippe Schmitt-Kopplin PNAS 2010).

Thousands of different organic molecules have been identified by sensitive spectroscopy but 70% of the organics were kerogens, that is large, unreactive, polycyclic aromatic Hydrocarbons. Bandurski, E.L. et al. (1976) achieved a graded pyrolysis (150C–600C) of the kerogens from the Orgueil meteorite to produce alkanes and alkenes up to C8 as well as alkylbenzenes, thiophene, Benzothiophene, acetonitrile, acrylonitrile, benzonitrile, acetone and phenol. The alkylbenzenes are ideal protocell membrane constituents.

The following year, 1977, Hayatsu, R. et al. produced these compounds as well as phenanthrene, naphthalene and their methylated derivatives with oxidising agents such as HNO3 or O2/UV. Naphthalene is an ideal chemical to penetrate protocell membranes and act as a stabiliser, thereby mimicking the effects of sterols. Nitric acid and nitrous oxide are powerful oxidisers and were plausibly synthesised near volcanoes from ammonium nitrate, sodium nitrate and ammonium sulfates.

As a backup mechanism, the Diels Alder reaction and variants of it activated by heat, organocatalysis (i.e., Evans oxazolidinones, imidazoline, oxazaborolidines) or Copper chelates of bis-oxazoline allowed dienes and dienophiles to bond thereby forming cyclic products in such a rate, variety and stereochemical bias that some purines, pyrimidines, lactones, terpenoids and aromatic amino acids would inevitably be synthesised from the evolved products.

As a backup mechanism, the Friedel Crafts alkylation or acylation reactions can add alkane or acylium side chains to benzene or other aromatic molecules with only aluminium chloride (AlCl3) as a catalyst.

Table 1.
Murchison Meteorite 100kg

Amino acids	17–60 ppm
Aliphatic Hydrocarbons	>35 ppm
Aromatic Hydrocarbons	3319 ppm
Fullerenes	>100 ppm
Carboxylic Acids	>300 ppm
Hydrocarboxylic Acids	15 ppm
Purines/Pyrimidines	1.3 ppm
Alcohols	11 ppm
Sulfonic Acids	68 ppm
Phosphonic Acids	2 ppm

Pavel Machalek Review, 2007, Johns Hopkins University.

These organic chemicals were formed by the high pressures and temperatures generated by collisions amongst asteroids (R Hazen et al. CSHPB 2010) and by cosmic and UV rays acting on ices containing H2O, N2, CH4, HCN, Phosphorus and Sulfur (Allamandola, L. et al. (2008) *ACS Symposium Series 981*) over millions of years as well as by complex synthesis in dust clouds formed by supernovae. Comet impacts with the Earth and dust from the vapour trail of comets was another likely source of the raw materials.

Even today, approximately 30,000 tons of cosmic dust fall to Earth annually and the heat-pressure of entry into the Earth's atmosphere needs to be taken into account as a driver of chemical reactions.

Z Martins in 2018 reported by review a number of N heterocycles found in carbonaceous chondrites including pyridines, pyrimidines, piperazinediones, quinolines, lactams, lactims and proline. Proline has been found to be a weak organic catalyst for the Aldol reaction that favours certain isomers over others.

Additionally, the mode of synthesis was judged to be low-temperature synthesis in meteorites from the action of UV light on ices containing simpler chemicals. One could hypothesise that on Earth they are the breakdown products of kerogens as they mixed with zeolite (AlSiO4) clays resulting in long chain cracking to produce shorter alkenes, alkanes, olefins and possibly fatty acids and terpenes.

Other heteropolymers called Tholins which are thought to coat Titan, Triton and many comets are formed by UV and cosmic rays acting on simple interstellar gases such as methane, H2S, N2, hydrogen cyanide and frozen CO2. These are ready sources of phenols and amino acids upon lysis. Their infall as cometary dust trails is hypothesised by accomplished scientists such as Carl Sagan and Bishun Khare, after years of experiments, to have provided organic molecules for the origin of life.

Together with the chain cracking effects of zeolite (Aluminium Silicate) and UV light (<340 nm wavelength UV photons have enough energy to break C-C bonds of 347 kcal/mol) on kerogens a "heteropolymer world" of great variety could plausibly be envisioned before molecular evolution guided the process down the pathway to life as we understand it guided by concentration x stereochemical affinity x functional advantage to a cell. The chain cracking effect of zeolite (AlSiO4) together with the ready bonding of Al with silicate may be major reasons for the exclusion of Aluminium from the metabolism of life on Earth.

Once the Earth's crust had formed to a depth of 50 metres or more, together with some oceans, it could undergo the same transformations that occurred in asteroids upon impact with smaller bolides, namely to produce organic chemicals CH4, amino acids, formaldehyde, formamide, etc., from prebiotically deposited carbonate minerals (CO3, of which there were 75 different types at this time according to Robert Hazen), Hydrogen and Nitrogen.

Inorganic carboxylations can routinely occur by CO2 and Sodium Hydroxide carbonylating a phenol with subsequent carboxylation catalysed by acid such as H2SO4. Carboxylations using CO2 catalysed by silver salts such as AgCl2 are also common.

These reactions point more towards a Calvin-like cycle driven by hyperbaric CO2 (but devoid of the complex RuBisCo enzyme) and hence, high bicarbonate levels that was capable of synthesising great varieties of both fatty acids and ketoacids leading to a domination of life by bacterial ancestors. Hundreds of inorganic catalysts available in chemical company compendia today were present and available to catalyse organic chemistry in the Eoarchean. Palladium is an example of an inorganic metal hydrogenase of alkenes to help form alkanes.

The lack of significant free gaseous oxygen on the Eoarchean Earth meant there was no ozone layer to impede the ultraviolet light from the Sun. The resulting photochemistry with organic chemicals and mineral catalysts would have been significant. Even though the intensity of the Hadean Sun is estimated to be 75% of the present day intensity, the ultraviolet component was considerably higher.

Magnetite (Fe^{2+} [Fe^{3+}]$_2$ O_4) is known to promote NH_3 formation from H_2 and N_2 under high temperatures and pressure. Nitrates, nitrites and ammonia have been regularly detected in meteorites in reasonable quantities with J.D. Buddhue in 1942, finding an average of about 0.002% in eight different meteorite samples. This may seem insignificant until the enormous mass of some meteorites is considered. Ammonia is important in the synthesis of purines and pyrimidines as it reacts with hydrogen cyanide (HCN) to produce important organic chemicals such as Adenine.

Primordially, NH_3 could be produced by the Haber process (N_2+ $3H_2$ —> $2NH_3$) involving 450 degrees C, 200 Bar and Fe as a catalyst in blocked volcanic fumaroles and lava basins pre-eruption. It could also be produced in great quantity by the pyrolysis (>185 degrees C) of amino acids near volcanoes which also produces hydrogen sulfide, water and a range of poorly characterised amines.

Hydrogen cyanide itself can form from Sodium Cyanide (itself formed by lava heat acting on kerogens near seawater), in acids. With the transition metal catalyst Rhenium found in molybdite minerals and as rhenium sulfide (ReS_2 rheniite) mineral in a volcanic fumarole in Russia, it is possible that Adenine was expelled in significant quantity from volcanic fumaroles. Furthermore the industrial bulk synthesis of Adenine involves heating formamide, a simple molecule, at 120 degrees C for 5 hours in a sealed beaker. Nature could mimic the conditions of this process in blocked volcanic fumaroles. Interconversion into the other nucleobases is thence plausible.

Ruthenium ions can catalyse the oxidative deamination of amines to produce carboxylic acids using H_2O as oxidiser and releasing H_2. This excess of amines and amino acids can thus add to the pool of fatty acids and carboxylates.

A second great significance of nitrate availability in the environment is their existence as metal nitrate solids which upon heating typically produce metal oxides, nitrous oxide (NO2) and oxygen thereby providing a source of oxygenated micro-environments for protocells to develop certain aerobic metabolic alternatives parallel to anaerobic metabolism. This likelihood brings into question the severity of the "oxygen catastrophe", once oxygen levels rose sustainably following the Great Oxidation Event ~2.4Gya since cells of that era probably had alternative metabolic pathways and were probably less specialised and delicate.

Iron, Cobalt, Ruthenium and Nickel can catalyse the formation of alkanes (Methane, Ethane, Butane etc) from CO, H2 and H2O with Nickel favouring Methane production. This is the Fischer-Tropsch reaction which requires temperatures of 700 degrees Celsius (volcanic proximity) and can also produce lesser quantities of alcohols and alkenes. Nickel itself at temperatures of about 200 C is a competent dehydrogenase. Mg^{2+} ion has been demonstrated to facilitate phosphorylation reactions by chelating terminal phosphate molecules (Gull, M. (2014) *Challenges*).

SO2 and CO2 dissolved in H2O produce acids that can exergonically corrode iron sulfides and native Fe by adding hydroxyl groups which then dissolve readily, thereby creating free Fe^{2+} and Fe^{3+} ions and energy for further chemistry.

Ammonium cyanide chemistry is known to produce amino acids (Strecker synthesis) and upon heating up to 200 degrees Celsius for several hours can result in yields of Adenine, Guanine, Cytosine, Thymine and Uracil (Hammer, P. G. et al. 2017). Even though the yields are very low, one must ask what the concentrating effect of drying would achieve. The de novo synthesis of nucleobases is known to occur by ammonia reacting with hydrogen cyanide (in laboratory and possibly in meteorites) but nucleotide synthesis de novo is far more problematic, especially the pyrimidines which are unreactive with ribose in prebiotic conditions.

J. Sutherland and M. Powner (*Nature* 459, 239–242) demonstrated pyrimidine nucleotide synthesis to be prebiotically plausible, in a multi-step process from concentrations of Cyanoacetylene, Glycolaldehyde, glyceraldehyde and cyanamide with phosphate as pH buffer and substrate. Some scholars say these high concentrations are prebiotically implausible but they are possible in coacervates (Bahadur, K. et al. 1954).

Juan Oro in 1960 demonstrated the synthesis of Adenine from hydrogen cyanide and ammonia and later produced amino acids from HCN and ammonia. The HCN could plausibly form by volcanic heat acting on methane and ammonia to produce HCN + H2.

C Ponnamperuma et al. 1963 *SAO Special report* #128 reported Adenosine, AMP, ADP and ATP synthesis by the action of UV light on a solution of Adenine, ribose and ethyl metaphosphate. Possible fault with this experiment was the addition of some ATP into the original mixture thereby making the origin of the energy, (UV or ATP hydrolysis) debatable. The authors may well have proved their point with the stoichiometric and thermodynamic analysis of the reactions.

In 2017, Ferus M et al. (PNAS USA) produced all four RNA nucleobases as well as urea and glycine by passing an electric current through a mixture of NH3, CO and H2O to simulate lightning and meteorite impact. These experiments were inspired by the famous Miller-Urey experiments of 1959 which produced amino acids and kerogens (Miller S L and Urey H C Science, 1959).

Becker S et al. in 2016 and 2019 reported extensive work employing wet-dry cycling and a one pot synthesis of purines and pyrimidines as well as a dynamic variation in temperature and pH to simulate dynamic environmental variations. Purines were synthesised by mixing formate, amidopyrimidine and ribose whilst pyrimidines were formed by mixtures of cyanoacetylene, hydroxylamine, hydroxylurea, ribose and borates in the presence of ferrous ions and thiols. These chemicals were all assessed to be plausibly available in a prebiotic environment with amidopyrimidine being synthesised from the simpler chemicals.

A spectroscopic analysis of products of a 1958 spark discharge experiment by S Miller that was rich in H2S found 23 amino acids, four amines, six Sulfur containing amino acids and one Sulfur containing amine (Parker, E. T. et al. 2011). This suggests that terrestrial reactions were also important in providing the raw substrates for life to take hold.

Several methods including the Biginelli reaction can produce pyrimidine bases from combinations of urea, benzaldehyde, thiourea, ethyl acetoacetate and other chemicals.

The seemingly impossible problem of prebiotic pyrimidine nucleoside (nucleobase + ribose) synthesis, a thermodynamically uphill reaction, remained until an article in 2018 by Inho Nam et al. in *PNAS* USA demonstrated the abiotic synthesis of purine and pyrimidine ribonucleosides in microdroplets in reasonable yields (1.7–2.5%) by spraying a mixture of aqueously dissolved nucleobases, ribose, phosphoric acid and Mg2+ and allowing the electrochemical characteristics of the aqueous microdroplets to overcome the uphill thermodynamics of the reaction (Nam, I. et al. *PNAS* 2018 Jan 2). The mechanical spraying action was also an input of energy into the solutions. Pertinent to this process the Graham Cooks laboratory at Purdue University in 2022 reported the synthesis of oligopeptides up to hexapeptides by an identical microspray process involving an amino acid mixture of glycine and alanine.

It is plausible that in hot volcanic pools containing sugars, cyanide and amino acids that the Maillard reaction would cause a direct reaction between the carbonyl of the sugar and the amine of the amino acid followed by cyclisation into the nucleoside by the Amadori rearrangement of the unstable glycosylamine.

This reaction sequence is well known today to produce hydroimidazolone plus many other poorly characterised aromatic compounds from reactants as simple as glyoxylate (C2H2O3). The imidazolones and pyridines are organocatalysts that doubtless worked alongside inorganic catalysts to enhance the progress of life.

The phosphorylation of nucleosides by cyclic Sodium Trimetaphosphate to produce nucleotides has been demonstrated with a 15% yield (Gull, M. *Challenges* 2014). This slowness made the way forward precarious due to a battle with degradation but also made it open to various alternatives.

The meteorites were also composed of a large variety of extra-terrestrial minerals whose effects are unknown, as well as minerals found on Earth. Often some photocatalysis or inorganic catalysis such as by hydroxide base, phosphates, heat or metal ions can occur. Sulfuric acid can catalyse both hydrogenation and hydratase (water addition) reactions on phenols and alkenes. In addition organocatalysis, Lewis acid catalysis and self-catalysis added to the rate of prebiotic chemical evolution.

Importantly the meteorite organic chemicals included over 70 types of amino acids and 1.3 ppm of purines and pyrimidines. This latter figure translates to billions of kilograms of nucleobases in a carbonaceous chondrite such as the Chicxulub bolide (1×10 to the power of 15–16 kg). Even with a 90% destruction rate by heat, the quantities are enormous.

On Earth, those nucleobases that were not destroyed could have been chemically modified in solution with the remaining organic chemicals to possibly produce over 300 different types of nucleobase. An extant molecular clue to this possibility is the post-transcriptional modification of RNA molecules that results in over 300 different nucleotide molecules in RNA, both mRNA and tRNA (Cantara, A. N. et al. *N Acids Res*. 2011).

Most interesting is the observation that many of the extant modifications have no known enzymes which catalyse them which is consistent with this hypothesis over the hypothesis that all modifications have a specific coded enzyme. This phenomenon could be explained by the presence of non-specific methylating or formylating catalysts such as pterins or pyridines in the Eoarchean.

In extant biology, it is almost certain that non-specific or promiscuous methylating or formylating enzymes catalyse many post-transcriptional modifications since the slow uncatalysed rates would be catastrophically inadequate.

In one yeast phenylalanine tRNA (Sussman, J. L. et al. 1978), found 15 different nucleobases out of 76 nucleotides in total whilst the average number of modifications per tRNA molecule is 13. The Eoarchean Earth could have had this tremendous availability of nucleobases from the vast natural organic chemistry that occurred during and shortly after the Late Heavy Bombardment 4.1-3.8 Gya.

Sussmans' results showed a "ribosylthymine", that is, an unreduced thymine at position 54 which has subsequently been found to promote polysome (multiple ribosomes translating a single mRNA strand) efficiency in several eukaryote species compared to Uracil at position 54 of tRNA which slowed the process down (Dingermann, T. et al. *Eur. J. Biochem*. 104, 1980).

This finding is a significant exception to the dogmatic "rule" that Thymine is only found in DNA (albeit unreduced in this case) and also a significant example of a post-transcription modification of tRNA that clearly influences its function. Candidates that don't appear in the MODOMICS post-transcriptional modification database add to this list and include appropriate chemicals such as the lactones, the methylxanthines caffeine, theobromine, theophylline and the xanthine uric acid to push the grand total to over 300 nucleobases in 2022.

The Nicholas Hud lab has published work supportive of this hypothesis with melamine and barbituric acid as base candidates.

More than 70 amino acid varieties were found in the 100 kg Murchison meteorite (17–60 ppm) so one can imagine the possible variety and quantities in the Chicxulub carbonaceous chondrite that was up to 10 km wide and ten trillion times as massive. Whatever this number and variety was, subsequent reactions could potentially push the number closer to the extant biological number across the three domains of life, over 400. This does not mean they were all available to each protocell, maybe across a large number of protocell colonies at the edges of shallow pools and rock pores in a volcanic region.

The inference from this scenario is that different protocells absorbed and used different sets of nucleobases in their earliest reactions, which were nevertheless related to the extant canonical nucleobases A, C, G, T and U, which often comprised their core molecule.

The kerogens and organic chemicals of the Chicxulub meteorite have plausibly been consumed, diluted or otherwise chemically recycled over 65 million years.

The extant aromatic proteinogenic amino acids phenylalanine, tyrosine and tryptophan are currently formed by a complex biosynthesis in the Shikimate pathway but the primordial synthesis was more of an industrial chemical process with phenylalanine and tyrosine delivered serendipitously by meteorites (Pizzarello, S. and Holmes, W. (2009) *G C Acta* 73(7)), tryptophan and histidine produced by condensation reactions between 1. serine and indole for tryptophan and 2. serine and imidazole for histidine.

Indole and imidazole were both potentially available from kerogen catabolism as were benzene and phenol that could react with serine in a condensation reaction, catalysed by microscopic aluminosilicates (zeolite) to produce phenylalanine and hydroxyphenylalanine (tyrosine) respectively here on Earth. Zeolite with added Mg^{2+} and Boron has been found to catalyse the reaction of benzene with ethanol to produce alkylbenzene + H_2O (Emana, A. N. and Chand, S. (2015) *Applied Petrochemical Research* 5, 121–134).

There is no reason to doubt that serine which has a hydroxymethyl side chain could substitute for ethanol in this reaction to produce phenylalanine when it reacts with benzene, tyrosine when it reacts with phenol. Furthermore, dozens of non-canonical aromatic amino acids were produced by short-chain additions to the phenol, benzene or imidazole groups with supporting evidence coming in a 2020 article by Tharp, J. M. et al, *Ang. Chemie Int. Ed*. 59(8), which indicated 17 different non-canonical aromatic amino acids could be incorporated into proteins in the first or second position with slight alterations to the sequence of initiator tRNA Meth.

Some of these non-canonical amino acids were from cellular sources and others had been synthesised chemically by the supply company. This finding suggests that many different aromatic amino acids may have been included in early proteins.

The Diels Alder reaction, catalysed by heat, provided a backup supply of cyclohexenes for further synthesis into aromatic amino acid varieties. These processes sustained the aromatic amino acid supply until the evolution of parts of the Shikimate pathway whose first step is a reaction of phosphoenolpyruvate and erythrose 4 phosphate, two prebiotically plausible chemicals. Histidine, which technically does not classify as an aromatic amino acid, was alternatively synthesised from prebiotically available starting substrates phosphoribosyl and an AMP analogue AICA-R (aminoimidazole carboxamide ribotide) to result in the imidazole ring structure.

The great significance of amino acid availability was demonstrated by Fox, S. W. and Harada. *Science* in 1958 when "proteinoids" were produced from solutions of amino acids by moderate heating (70 degrees C) and drying cycles with some phosphoric acids as a catalyst. These compounds could not be proved to be standard polypeptides but had catalytic activities and upon lysis produced amino acid solutions again. These experiments were later repeated in the field with volcanic ash deposits with similar results and again some "proteinoids" were found to have catalytic activity.

Proline alone has been found to catalyse an Aldol reaction in which a more complex aldehyde or alcohol is produced by the reaction of two simpler ones with this work contributing to the Nobel prize in chemistry being awarded to Benjamin List in 2021.

Another significant finding in 2019 was a report by Cornell, C. E. et al. *PNAS* 116(35) of a range of amino acids, mainly those with a neutral charge, binding to 10 micrometre decanoic acid vesicles with a triple effect of increasing their resistance to ocean salt levels or significant Mg^{2+} concentration as well as promoting multilamellar vesicles that were more resistant to lysis.

These effects were assessed to be caused by binding of the amino acids to the carboxyl of the fatty acids and all three effects are greatly beneficial to protocell stability and evolution. The spaces between the lamellae of the multilamellar vesicles would be fertile regions for polynucleotide or polypeptide synthesis due to the water excluding effect, which is also seen between salt crystals or even ice crystals.

Kerogens in the organic component of the chondrite dust and rock would likely have been heated and pressurised on the Hadean Earth from the impact to the point of decomposition to smaller organic molecules found in crude oil and natural gas. In 1976 Bandursky, E. L. et al. reported products of stepwise pyrolysis of the kerogens in the Orgueil meteorite to include alkanes and alkenes up to C8, an extensive series of alkylbenzene isomers as well as acrylonitrile, benzonitrile, phenol and others (*Geochim. Et Cosmochim. Acta* 1976).

Of these, the terpenes could have been released in great quantities to react with other chemicals and thereby acquire functional side chains, hence producing vast quantities of terpenoids. The absence of significant atmospheric oxygen meant terpenes and kerogens could be destroyed by pressure and heat (turned into carbon rich by-products) but not fire, which requires a minimum of about 14% oxygen. The hyperbaric CO_2 conditions would make fire even less likely.

Permanganate was formed on the early Earth by manganese containing meteorites reacting with hot acidic water in an exergonic reaction sequence involving native manganese reacting with nitric acid to produce manganese nitrate.

The dissolved Mn^{2+} and NO_3^- ions can then react with potassium peroxydisulfate (also known as persulfate, which can be formed by oxidising of KSO_4-with Fluorine produced as HF from lava) to form permanganate. As an oxidising agent, it would tend to break kerogens down into smaller aromatic compounds, as demonstrated by Hayatsu, R. et al. in 1977. Permanganate can also react with hydroxide bases to produce manganate, water and oxygen.

Zeolite $(Al\ SiO_3)_n$ is a mineral known to facilitate long-chain cracking in the catalytic breakdown of terrestrial kerogens and consideration of the reverse, ligation of alkanes and alkenes, needs to be accepted through basic equilibrium laws.

Grignard reagents (R-Mg-Halide) formed by Bromobenzene reacting with native Magnesium in the presence of diethyl ether or tetrahydrofuran would form substantial quantities of aromatic compounds from amino acids to nucleic acids and terpenoids via various pathways.

The carboxylic acids in the meteorite dust comprised up to 300 ppm of the carbonaceous chondrite bolides and included vast quantities of fatty acids which could be released in aqueous environments by the action of acidic pH in the form of vesicles and micelles.

Profuse quantities of ketoacids reacting with ammonia could produce more amino acids de novo on Earth. Ketoacids such as 2 ketooctanoic acid also formed vast numbers of stable vesicles by self-assembly (Huifang et al. 2017). Self-assembly occurs via the hydrophobic regions of the molecules being unreactive with water or ions but subject to Van der Waal electromagnetic forces and the Casimir effect.

Ketoacids have been found to be more resistant to salt and temperature variations than fatty acids. Amongst the terpenoids, carotenoids (carotenes and xanthophylls) could take part in membrane formation to add vibrant photochemistry but could not form whole membranes due to their limited rate of synthesis and they went into accessory pigment, protective and metabolic roles. Availability issues meant fatty acid/ketoacid membranes dominated by some isoprenyl phosphate based membranes also present.

Ammonia is a chemical which some thought was not present in significant quantities on the early Earth but recent inorganic chemistry simulation has indicated a ready prebiotic source from NO_3-and NO_2-(nitrate and nitrite) on pyrite (FeS_2 or FeS) surfaces under hydrothermal vent conditions of high temperatures and pressure (Stirling, A. et al. Inorganic Chemistry. 2016) and also from volcanic fumaroles. Lightning is known to break nitrogen gas triple bonds to help form nitrates and nitrites upon reacting with water vapour, thereby adding to the supply of usable nitrates for protocells.

Sugars have been synthesised by oligomerising formaldehyde with glycolaldehyde in a self-catalysing formose reaction (additionally catalysed by sodium hydroxide) that produces threose and ribulose sugars (Butlerov A., 1861). Formaldehyde in cosmic dust clouds readily polymerised into glycolaldehyde and paraformaldehyde. Glycolaldehyde can subsequently enter glycolytic pathways to produce energy. Glyceraldehyde forms part of the Butlerov reaction and the diphosphate form could enter the glycolytic pathway catalysed by Archaean ocean conditions to produce energy that activated nucleotide diphosphates to NTPs.

The steps of the Formose reaction were described by Breslow, R in 1959 in Tetrahedron Letters being facilitated by Calcium Hydroxide but the mechanism of the first step that involves dimerization to glycolaldehyde remains unknown. In 2017, Steer, M. et al. *Chem Commun*. produced glucose from a similar group of starting chemicals to Butlerov, with amino nitriles as catalysts.

Simpler sugars glyceraldehyde and glycolaldehyde have been reported by Ritson and J Sutherland produced from hydrogen cyanide in the presence of cyanometallates by photochemistry. Glycolaldehyde has been detected in cosmic dust clouds. Glyceraldehyde 3 phosphate is an important component of the Calvin cycle, the pentose phosphate pathway and glycolysis. High concentrations of this small molecule could have driven the synthesis of sugars catalysed by Fe^{2+}.

Threose sugars (4 carbon) have been postulated to have provided a pre-RNA sugar phosphate backbone for nucleic acids due to their stability and their demonstrated formation of in vitro polymers, TNA. The possible prebiotic presence of TNA is irrefutable but to say it came first or was more stable and prevalent in prebiotic chemistry is insupportable when the stabilising effects of borates on the ribofuranose isomer have been demonstrated and the microspray formation of nucleosides from ribose, Mg^{2+} and nucleobase solutions were demonstrated in 2018 by Nam, I. et al.

Furthermore, the frequent location of sassolite (boric acid mineral) in volcanic fumaroles and sediments suggests boron was in the right place at the right time to stabilise the ribofuranose isomer. If TNA ever existed it went extinct as ribose was favoured for nucleic acid synthesis and the threose went into metabolic cycles.

Further evidence of the prebiotic plausibility of sufficient D-ribose comes in a 2017 article that produced significant yields of 2-deoxy-D-ribose (4–5%) from glyceraldehyde, glycolaldehyde, acetaldehyde and formaldehyde mixtures promoted by proteinogenic amino esters and aminonitriles (Steer, A. M. et al. 2017). This combination of starting ingredients is similar to those of Sutherland and Powner in the abiotic synthesis of pyrimidine nucleotides.

In 2004, Lambert, J. B. et al. found silicate gels (H_2SiO_4) to chelate readily with furanose forms of monosaccharides, including ribose in a 2 ribofuranose:1 silicic acid chelation ratio (Lambert, J. B. et al. *J. Am. Chem. Soc.* 2004). The dehydrating effects of silicic acid make their likely presence in prebiotic environments a favourable condition for concentration of the vital molecules of life around protocells. Extant hydrolysis reactions have been known to be catalysed by test tube glass (SiO_2) which was freely available in the environment as sand to catalyse both hydrolysis and the back reaction, condensation.

Furthermore, the dissolution of sodium metasilicate into sodium ions and polymeric metasilicate polyanions could serve to provide a physical template lacking in coding significance for either amino acids or nucleobases to polymerise on.

The electron transporting Iron-Sulfur cuboid forms were freed from montmorillonite or hydrothermal vents by dissolution and fracture, allowing them entry to primordial protocells by the lysis and reformation caused by waves and tides. These later bound proteinoids formed by wet–dry cycles to constitute abiotically formed ferredoxins in protocells.

Large quantities of alpha keto acids in meteorites means that the simplest of these, pyruvic acid and pyruvate were likely available in great quantities to form carbohydrates, alcohols and amino acids using mineral catalysts (especially $Fe2+$) and photochemistry thereby beginning some steps of future metabolic pathways even before protocells had use for them. This "gift" of pyruvate from meteorites was additional to that formed in protocells by glycolysis of glucose, a process that can be catalysed by Archaean ocean conditions (Keller, M. A. et al. 2014).

Photochemistry is known to produce isomer conversion of alkenes so ketoacid vesicles with retinal in their matrix had a ready source of proton pumping and alkene isomer formation.

V Srinivasan and H Morowitz found (*The Biological Bulletin* 2009) that all 20 proteinogenic amino acids and the four major nucleobases have their synthesis begin with just a few prebiotically available organic chemicals: Acetyl CoA, oxaloacetate, pyruvate, phosphoenolpyruvate and 2-oxoglutarate thereby suggesting a plausible start to the subsequent complexity. Unfortunately, Acetyl CoA is far too complex to be plausibly included in such a list, possibly replaced by acetyl chloride, acetic anhydride or acetyl phosphate.

Even earlier in molecular evolution, Ritson, Sutherland and Patel demonstrated a possible common origin of RNA, protein and lipid precursors by photochemistry acting upon hydrogen cyanide and its derivatives with H2S as an electron acceptor (*Nature Chemistry*, 7, 2015, 301-7).

With phosphates being an essential part of life, the 2 ppm of phosphonic acids in the Murchison meteorite translates into more than a billion kilograms of phosphonic acids in a carbonaceous chondrite meteorite such as the Chicxulub bolide. Subsequent reactions and heating in Hadean conditions could have produced the crucial polyphosphates and phosphates necessary for life (Yamagata, Y. et al. *Nature*, 1991).

Arsenic is an element whose concentration on the primordial Earth is estimated to be 200x its present levels due to ongoing subduction of crustal plates. Arsenic is a very similar element to phosphorus and could have provided the most primitive protocells with an alternative to phosphorus for nucleotide backbone formation as well as structural molecules, redox reactions and ADP-arsenate that may have provided some energy for the protocell (Wolf-Simon et al. *Science,* 2011).

The secondary ester products of Arsenic reactions are less stable than those of Phosphorus, which may account for its depletion in primordial biotic cells, as does the fact that arsenate does not significantly release from rocks upon weathering and oxidation.

Additionally, Arsenic was far less prevalent in the Earth's crust than Phosphorus: even at x200 greater than its present levels it was 1/3 as available as P. Despite these drawbacks, ADP-arsenate forms as efficiently as ATP and then hydrolyses rapidly in an enzyme independent way thereby precluding the need for a primordial ATPase to release the hydrolysis energy. Rapid, spontaneous hydrolysis thence results in abundant energy release from the enthalpy of bond formation (Gresser, M. J. (1981) 'ADP-arsenate', *Journal of Biol. Chem.*, Vol. 256, No. 12, 5981–3).

Lebrun et al. 2003 postulated from phylogenetic studies that arsenite oxidase is an ancient enzyme that preceded the divergence between the Bacterial and Archaean domains. This divergence probably predates the period of the modern cell by many millions of years and interaction of coacervates and liposomes of terpenoid, fatty acid, ceramide or ketoacid together with proteinoids and aerosols probably predated any subsequent evolution into the two prokaryotic domains of life.

Despite the ample quantities, however, concentrations and pressure-temperature conditions in the various environments were the most important factors for chemistry to occur. A significant proportion of organic chemicals were altered in unknown ways by the high temperatures and pressure of impact events and lava. The simple condensation of organic chemicals in aerosols followed by evaporation at the edges of bodies of water, both salty and fresh, either acidic or basic, could provide a fortuitous concentration of life's organic ingredients as could the presence of silica gels in rock pools.

Since all of the earliest genesis scenarios are speculative, one ought not ignore the significant fullerene content of the Murchison meteorite and the amazing geodesic carbon spheres (1–2 nm) and nanotubes they form. These micro structures could have stabilised the earliest protocells and pores, whether fatty acid, ketoacids, isoprene or protein based, to greatly improve their survival. More research is warranted in this field, with the practical value of fullerenes also providing a conduit for targeted treatment delivery for tumours and infections (Goodman, G. et al. 2012).

Furthermore, the uncanny resemblance of extant (180kD) clathrin triskelion proteins involved in endocytosis and exocytosis to the geodesic shapes of fullerenes suggests that tiny abiotic proteinoid molecules, unrelated to clathrins, could have been moulded onto such structures from the most primordial phases of protocell self-assembly and wet-dry cycling. With the scaffold of fullerenes and no demand for speed and efficiency, the process could be independent of nucleotide triphosphates at this early stage.

Heat and pressure in lava basins and fumaroles, UV light from the sun, lightning (plasma) with gamma rays, ice to concentrate solutes, mineral & organic catalysts, microwaves (hot rocks), organic substrates H^2, N^2, CO^2, S, rock pores and pools at the volcanos' base all contributed to lifes' origin along with meteorite contents

The First Protocells

This scenario proposes that protocells existed in great numbers on the Hadean Earth 4.1 billion years ago, only to be mostly destroyed by the Late Heavy Bombardment 4.1-3.8 G years ago. This date provides more than enough time for condensation and cooling to solidify the Earth's surface from the Thea moon forming scenario and for erosion to provide some gravel, sand, dust, clay and bodies of water.

Furthermore, protocells could have been varied in their origin and chemical composition at first; aerosols, coacervates, micelles, liposomes and proteasomes only to converge in their evolution by the time of the first biotic cells (with catalysts and templates) due to the constraints of thermodynamics and the forces of gravity and electromagnetism on their chemical evolution.

This convergence was at first totally physicochemical and independent of polynucleotides but still included them in the processes. It could not occur in deep-sea hydrothermal vents due to the tremendous dilution that flowing seawater causes and most likely occurred at the edges of hot (40–70 C), acidic pools and the adjoining rock pores near volcanoes that were periodically inundated with basic or salty inflows.

Since heat, volcanoes, tides, rock pores and water were ubiquitous, this inference is obvious but the benefits of wet-dry cycling have been deduced by thinkers such as Sidney Fox over decades.

A look at the effect of increased temperature in Le Chateliere's principle and the Van t' Hoff equation indicate that exothermic reactions such as polymer formation would favour reactants over products in prebiotic climates whilst exothermic reactions would favour reactants. Furthermore, more reactions would become spontaneous in high-temperature conditions. This subtle difference could be very significant in the battle against degradation.

Smaller carbonaceous chondrite bolides striking the crust would be pulverised and then partially dissolved in the hot, acidic conditions. Quintillions of fatty acid, proteinoid proteasome, ketoacid, terpenoid (isoprene-5,carbon based) or sphingosine (a C18 amino alcohol) membrane bound protocells containing combinations of these organics exuded into puddles, muds and oceans by the action of acids, manganates and nitrates on the dust and small rocks formed from the meteorite impacts.

The coacervate (including micelles) and aerosol paths to protocell formation were blocked by the fatal flaw of not being able to maintain homeostasis and discreteness but their evolved chemical products were made available to protocells. These products would have included di-and tripeptides due to the ubiquitous presence of carbonyl sulfide to facilitate their formation from amino acid mixtures (Leman, H. and Orgel, L. *Science* 2004). The resultant ubiquitous presence of weak organic catalysts as short as one residue such as proline then follows.

Even though kerogens are resistant to acids, they are subject to potassium permanganate reactions, the pressures and high temperature of earth above them and to C-C chain cracking by UV light or aluminosilicates (zeolite). Following this step, concentrated sulfuric acid would oxidise the organic products to many useful chemicals for a protocell to ingest or encapsulate during its formation.

The meteorite impacts could have separated the macromolecules into component molecules, including terpenes. With further reactions to add side chains, the terpenoids could be formed. Large quantities of dust and small stones from pulverised meteorites and basalt provided the Earth with a soil and a mud in which some of the microscopic vesicles could have formed from the self-assembling nature of fatty acids and terpenoids which derives from Van der Waals' force and the Casimir effect.

Even though a proportion of liposome vesicles would have eventually collapsed into micelles, they would still be available to interact chemically with vesicles. The mass extinctions of protocells by meteorite strikes, lava and a host of other factors were balanced by their mass formation in the Hadean conditions. Even with a fatal flaw, enough could have evolved to be more resistant to the degradation. The division at this stage was achieved by the violent tides, waves and rains, which shook the protocells apart and scrambled them so that some divided and some internalised others whilst resisting the dilution.

These forces, together with constraints on cell size by molecular content, produced a diameter range of 0.2–10 microns. This natural origin of endosymbiosis and cell division is a recurring theme, as life mimics many of the physicochemical processes that brought it into being.

Importantly, alpha keto acids such as 2 ketooctanoic acid have been demonstrated to be more stable in salt water and heat variations than fatty acids, thereby providing a backup system to fatty acids and terpenoids in the molecular evolution towards life (Xu, H. et al. 2017). More complex polymers (oligopeptides, oligonucleotides and short peptidoglycans) were quickly formed by:

a) the meteorite impact (Blank, J. G. et al) and, separately, carbonyl sulfide acting on amino acid solutions to form oligopeptides (Leman, L., Orgel, L. et al. 2004 *Science* Vol. 306).

b) lightning strikes through volcanic emissions and meteorite dust (Miller, S. and Urey, 1959) to form amino acids and kerogen.

c) wet–dry cycles causing condensation reactions of amino acids into proteinoids of varying length and bond type at the drying edges of small bodies of water(Fox, H. and Harada, 1960; Yanagawa, H. et al. 1990 [up to 4KDaltons]).

d) montmorillonite clays facilitating 1. polymerisation of activated nucleotides (J. P. Ferris 2006) up to 50 bases or 2. isoprenyl phosphate molecules (Nakatani, Y. et al. *OLEB* 2014).

e) UV light acting on coacervates or aerosols of formaldehyde and formamide with metal ion catalysts (Molybdenum) and citrate (Bahadur, K. et al. 1954) to form amino acids and nucleobases and f. polymerisation of activated NTPs into polynucleotides of 90–150 bases in length on volcanic glasses as demonstrated by Benner, S. et al. 2022, Astrobiology 22(6).

As proposed by Leslie Orgel nucleotides may have been activated by imidazole ring additions at the phosphate leaving group at this early stage to enhance their uncatalysed polymerisation rate. The common presence of imidazolides and pyridines in carbonaceous chondrites was confirmed in a review by Z Martins in *Life* (2018) who provided an inventory of meteoritic N heterocycles together with a careful assessment of the delta C13 content in order to confirm their extra-terrestrial origin. Imidazolides and pyridines are both organocatalysts that tend to favour the catalysis of a certain stereoisomer.

The Jack Szostak lab also demonstrated the robust retention of ribozyme activity with 5' to 2' RNA polymerisation instead of the usual 5' to 3' polymerisation. Furthermore, the Benner lab. has demonstrated the plausible synthesis of polynucleotides with sulfone (R-SO2-R) backbones replacing phosphate, resulting in less efficacious templates due to folding problems.

All of the technical problems conscientious scientists have encountered were overcome in nature by the vast number and variety of conditions in which the organic chemicals and minerals relevant to life were situated, namely in quintillions of protocells.

Where phosphate was unavailable, arsenite or arsenate could substitute by binding to fatty acid-glycerol molecules, terpenoid molecules, amino acids in oligopeptides or to nucleosides to form the nucleic acid backbone (Wolf-Simon Science 2011). This molecular natural selection was won by Phosphorus as the secondary arsenic compounds have much faster rates of degradation (Kulp, T. R. 2014), they do not release from rocks upon weathering as well as P and Arsenic availability was greatly less than phosphorus and steadily reducing due to tectonic plate subduction.

Another possibility is that borate esters derived from bicarbonate by cosmic ray spallation were a second backup to phosphate that also doubled as a stabiliser of the correct ribofuranose isomer for nucleotide formation. Although boron is unreactive with carbon in nature, it could still potentially form a diester backbone via the oxygen moieties of the borate.

A recent review has found boron compounds ubiquitous and essential to animal and human health in such a broad and difficult to define way that it can be hypothesised that it stems from the maintenance of the cytosolic ribofuranose isomer essential for efficient nucleotide triphosphate synthesis (Bialek, M. et al. 2019. *Journal of Animal and Feed Sciences*-Poland-28, 2019, 307–320).

Silicon is the second most abundant element in the Earth's crust and is highly reactive with oxygen. The resulting formation of silicon dioxide (quartz) rock and sand led to its reaction with water to produce silicic acid (H_4SiO_4) solution which has always been in adequate supply to act as an alternative to phosphate but is hampered by being unreactive with hydroxyl groups.

Its usefulness as a chelate of the ribofuranose monosaccharide, amongst others (Lambert, H. C. et al. 2004), suggests its plausible role as a prebiotic matrix that served to concentrate intercellular organic chemicals with its hygroscopic nature. Silicic acid would also react vigorously with native Aluminium to form the hydroxyaluminosilicate thereby effectively removing Al from proto biology, a phenomenon that persists to this day.

Silicon polymers based on siloxane are all man-made today. This was not the case in the Eoarchean but their involvement in protocells was marred by their hydrophobicity. Silicon compounds are reactive with carbon to produce silicon oils to potentially provide an alternative prebiotic cell membrane.

In aqueous solutions, silicon is unreactive with carbon except for the unusual case of an Icelandic hot spring prokaryote with a cytochrome C that can catalyse the formation of organosilicates with C-Si bonds as reported by Frances Arnold in her Nobel lecture. Was this more common in the Archaean and did the polymeric metasilicate polyanion or polyphosphate polyanion form the first template, albeit meaningless regarding coding but helpful regarding polymer production?

The prominence of 3'-phosphoadenosine 5'-phosphosulfate in the metabolism of Sulfur oxidising bacteria and 5'-phosphosulfate adenosine in Sulfur reducing bacteria is evidence that it was available for incorporation into polynucleotide polymer backbones in place of phosphate. Steven Benner has demonstrated this possibility with sulfone (SO_2), sulfoxide and dimethyl sulfide backboned polynucleotides.

Glycol, peptide, arabinoside and threose backbones have already been demonstrated in the laboratory. The earliest Nucleic Acids could have had a significant variation of the phosphate moiety as well as the base and the sugar, with the eventual uniformity being a product of environmental supply, stereochemical affinity, reactivity and molecular evolution of catalysts. Albert Eschenmoser first investigated this hypothesis decades ago.

The self-assembling nature of some organic chemicals was caused by attractive Van der Waal's forces, which can become repulsive at shorter distances due to electron shell proximity. Others were caused by London dispersion forces (induced dipole between two atoms by transient electron positions), Debye forces or Keesom force all of which are more transient and delicate in nature than permanent dipole moments, e.g. between water molecules.

It meant that protocells took one of two paths with regards to membrane composition. Those with fatty acid, ketoacid (e.g. 2 Keto octanoic acid) or Sphingosine membranes would eventually evolve into bacteria and those with membranes composed of isoprenyl phosphate derived compounds would evolve into the archaea. Some support in the literature for this claim comes from a phylogenetic molecular clock study that puts archaea between 3.1–4.1 Gya (Battistuzzi, F. U. et al. 2004).

The latter figure predates the modern cell and is also the figure the authors use for the advent of methanogenesis. Their "tree of life" depicts bacterial ancestors and archaea to be separate from all the way back to 4.1Gya. Potential fault with the Battistuzzi results lies in the assumption that mutation rates and the extant genetic code are relevant at a time when the code for life was not fully evolved.

Additionally, their placement of identifiable bacterial origins after the time of the mythical LUCA begs the question of how they or any of us, define bacteria or archaea at this early stage of evolution. The earliest distinction was cell membrane composition alone thereby placing the separation all the way back to 4.1 Gya.

A simple molecule like coenzyme M ($HSCH_2CH_2 SO_3^-$) methylated by methyl chloride and bound to the simplest abiotically formed oligopeptides could have taken part in the essential methyl transferase reaction, together with coenzyme B, required for methanogenesis. An elegant deletion of six of the seven Wolfe cycle dehydrogenase genes of an archaeon methanogen demonstrated that only one was necessary for the cycle to complete (Lie, T. J. et al. (2012) *PNAS* USA) and three of the reactions are exergonic which means they could potentially have occurred spontaneously in the Eoarchean.

The single step that requires catalysis could have been driven by high substrate concentrations. More likely is that the Wolfe cycle, named in honour of Ralph S Wolfe (1921–2018) is too evolved for our protocell since F420 and formylmethanofuran are complex molecules. Methanogenesis probably emerged around the time of the modern cell as NTPs and coenzymes that were produced by the energy forming glycolytic and pentose phosphate pathways fed into other, now catalysed, catabolic pathways that produced methane as a by-product of organic molecule cleavage yielding energy for the cell.

The simplest and therefore most likely protocell metabolic pathways were glycolysis, the Krebs cycle, Sulfur redox reactions and the Calvin cycle (originally lacking the extant rubisco enzyme). If glyceraldehyde was in great supply, these cycles could have been driven to produce glucose, citrate, cysteamine (in lieu of the more complex Acetyl CoA) and ribulose bisphosphate as well as a cyclic arabinose that could feed into a primitive Shikimate pathway for aromatic amino acid synthesis.

The phylogenetic analysis by Lebrun et al. in 2003 that arsenite oxidase predated this archaea-bacteria divergence is more consistent with a primordial divergence hypothesis. Lebrun et al. 2003 deduce a "pre LUCA" origin for arsenite oxidase and also an origin before the divergence into bacteria and archaea.

Even though Archaea are the only extant methanogens, this may not have been the case in the Archaean since there are bacteria that produce methane as a by-product of metabolism but do not need the Wolfe cycle for adequate energy conservation (Buan NR 2018).

Further evidence is the convergent evolution of the shape of release factor 1 of archaea and release factor 1 of bacteria to mimic the shape of a tRNA molecule even though they are phylogenetically different protein molecules. If bacteria and archaea diverged after the modern cell, then RF1 of bacteria and archaea should more likely share phylogeny since the mythical LUCA is purported to possess "modern" translating molecular machinery and 350+ genes.

Millions of years of evolution meant that protocells developed synthesis pathways for those abundant membrane forming chemicals by simple reaction reversals embodied in equilibrium laws. It also meant that some chemical systems coevolved in an almost identical way whilst others took a different path and sharing of polynucleotide material by the forced conjugation caused by violent tides and by absorption through pores of the membrane itself meant similarities were common.

Those that had fatty acids, Sphingosine, glycerol, proteinoids and a little isoprene in their membranes were more stable and resistant to lysis from the shock of concentration variations but it is not observed that hybrid membranes of equal amounts of fatty acids and terpenoids should self-assemble. The great numbers and the great passage of time meant that the liposome membrane molecules could evolve in situ by reacting with acetylators, glycerol, phosphates and with each other.

The presence of acetyl chloride, (CH_3COCl), O-Acetyl serine, cysteamine, acetic anhydride and benzoyl chloride meant the membranes had a backup prebiotic source of acylium ion available for the binding of the fatty acids and terpenoids to a glycerol molecule.

Glycerol itself could plausibly form prebiotically from propylene by chlorination to allyl chloride, then with hypochlorite to Epichlorohydrin and then hydrolysed by silicon dioxide to glycerol or else formed by the glyceraldehyde-3-phosphate from the pentose phosphate pathway all steps of which are weakly catalysed by Fe^{2+} ion (Keller MA et al. 2014) and the transketolase step is enhanced by cyanate ion with equal efficacy to the extant coenzyme, thiamine pyrophosphate (Breslow et al. *PNAS* March 2013).

The primordial production of glycerol in volcanic fumaroles or where lava meets water from the reverse of the highly exothermic redox reaction $KMnO4+ C3H5(OH)3$ (glycerol) needs investigation. That is $K2CO3+ Mn2O3+ CO2+H2O$—> glycerol + permanganate. Furthermore, glycerol has been reported to be synthesised at -250C (asteroids) by H2 reacting with carbon monoxide ice and other products of CO+ H2, namely methanol, formaldehyde and glycolaldehyde (Fedoseev, G. et al. *The Astrophysical Journal* 2017).

Glycerol greatly enhanced the stability of membranes in hot environments by binding to the fatty acid or amino alcohols. Simultaneously, the fatty acids and terpenoids were subject to some prebiotic phosphorylation by soluble polyphosphates (known to take part in prebiotic membrane pore formation along with poly beta-(R)-3-isobutyrate (Reusch, R. N. 1999 *PMSB* vol. 23).

These abiotic channels, which have been found in extant bacteria, together with ionophore channels such as neutral proteinoids formed in wet–dry cycles, gave the protocells a flexibility of intake and output that gave molecular evolution something to work on. Furthermore, hydrothermal environments that contain phosphoric acids, boron, metal salts, heat and pressure produce borophosphates which may have helped to favour the ribofuranose isomer crucial for nucleoside synthesis.

Alternatively, to polyphosphate channels C2 ceramide (sphingosine + fatty acid) or c16 ceramide composition of some membrane sections have been demonstrated to form channels (0.8–11 nm) and be permeable to large molecules (Siskind, L. J. and Colombini, M. *J Biol Chem* 2000).

They are found in many extant bacteria, including the Bacteriodetes, Chlorobi, Deltaproteobacteria (Myxococcus, Bdellovibrio) and Alphaproteobacteria (Panevska, A. et al. *BBS* 2029 Vol. 1861:7, 1284–92). The authors concede that little is known about their metabolites or the genes involved in their biosynthesis or metabolism other than the first enzymatic step, serine palmitoyltransferase.

In the lab of Eric Klein phosphate starvation of Caulobacter resulted in a synthesis of ceramides, detected in the membranes which suggests that a complex feedback loop involving non-specific acylators and methylators may be involved and also demonstrates a complex cells' alternative responses to nutritional depletions. Klein may well have demonstrated how eukaryotes turned to amino alcohol membranes during a rapid size increase that deprived them of adequate phosphate.

The proteinoid derived channels have probably evolved and persisted as the holin group of extant prokaryotic superfamilies that can be as little as 50 amino acids long (average ~100 residues) that act as active membrane pore formers directed by the genome of bacteriophage viruses.

Prebiotic synthesis pathways for C10-C30 isoprene (C5) based molecules have been demonstrated on montmorillonite clay and prebiotic synthesis of isoprene from ethylene, isobutene and formaldehyde have been demonstrated (Nakatani et al., 2014). Together with natural absorption from terpenoid micelles exuding from pulverised chondrites, these supplied the Archean ancestors with membrane constituents until they developed enzymes.

It is highly likely that protocell membranes were of bilayer fatty acid or isoprenyl phosphate sections until increasing catalytic activity by proteinoid enzymes and ribozymes coded on the protogene (Ch. 9) resulted in the biosynthesis of enough fatty acids, isoprenyl phosphates and phosphokinase to result in a stable phospholipid bilayer by the protoribosome stage.

Within the protocells were collections of smaller protocells of varying size that interacted with the more protected primordial "cytosol" of the larger protocell until possibly merging with the outer membrane to enlarge it or providing a backup system in the event of cell lysis. Where membranes apposed each other, the activity of water to hydrolyse polymers fell to negligible levels, thereby making polymer formation more likely.

Outside and within the protocells, in rock pores, drying muds and clays, a great number of "experiments" took place (10 to the power of 54 estimated by R Hazen).

Another rich source and location of prebiotic chemistry was the vast aerosol mixture of acidic water vapour mixed with meteorite dust and volcanic ash. Vast updrafts from a generally hot Earth surface maintained the aerosol in the atmosphere where it was exposed to the powerful energy source of UV light and lightning strikes (which release gamma rays) whilst rain brought the evolved molecules in the aerosols to the Earth.

Some of these molecules could have formed coacervates before falling to the Earth and others contained nucleosides from the action of Magnesium divalent ion on nucleobases, ribose and phosphoric acids in the aerosols (Nam, I. 2018 *PNAS,* USA).

Some people feel that hot, acidic conditions would preclude formation of life forms but this notion is falsified by the acidothermophilic prokaryotes that have enzymes with their acid vulnerable, hydrophobic regions on the interior of the molecule, have more disulfide bonds between protein chains and more charged side chains on their surface thereby resisting an acidic cytoplasm (Reed, C. J. et al. Archaea 2013).

These evolved controls that are DNA coded were not available in the Eoarchean so serendipity played a large part until proteinoid catalysts and ribozymes with their active centres on the interior were coded for on protogenes thereby being subject to natural selection.

In 1954 and 1958 K. Bahadur produced coacervates, (cell like microscopic structures first studied in 1932 by H G Bungeberg de Jong) from formaldehyde, paraformaldehyde, citric acid, ammonium molybdate and ammonium chloride with ferric chloride and molybdenum as catalysts. With periodic shaking and ultraviolet light, these changed and produced amino acids and nucleobases and were observed budding.

The main criticism of this possibility for life's origin is that the contents of the coacervates could diffuse away and be diluted, thereby failing the "self-contained" requirement for life's definition. A phase transition may slow diffusion and reaction rate but not contain it.

Furthermore, the fine detail of how one set of chemicals reacted to form another is not explained. If a proportion of the coacervates were to produce enough terpenoids or fatty acids to form an outer membrane, then the coacervate possibility for life's origin would be plausible. Oparin was an ardent proponent of the coacervate theory of life's origin and favoured the idea that polypeptide and polysaccharide mixtures were the most likely first coacervates.

The idea that a deep sea alkaline hydrothermal vent could manufacture de novo, retain, assemble and evolve all the chemical ingredients of life except for minerals is preposterous. Conceivably, some coacervates could have fused with vesicles emerging from meteorite dust to form membrane enclosed structures that could potentially bud under the physical forces of tides and waves.

Propionic acid, one of the simplest fatty acids, when subjected to salty solutions, forms a film that could potentially form regularly on the exterior of coacervates or organic chemical laden raindrops in seawater to form protocell membranes that could evolve into more complex ones. Some experimental evidence for this scenario is provided by Dora Tang (Dora Tang, T. Y. et al.

(2015) *Nature* Chem 6), who assembled multilamellar fatty acid membranes around coacervates and demonstrated growth and resistance to ionic flux in such conditions.

The benefits of water exclusion in decreasing the activation energy of reactions was simulated and discussed in great detail in 2016 (by Deamer, D. and Ross, D. S. *Life*, 6, 28) with D Deamer also demonstrating a novel lysis of protocells in drying test tubes with subsequent formation of multilamellar structures that concentrated the protocell contents between them to produce polynucleotides before reforming into protocells during a wet stage.

Rock pores are fertile places to find living prokaryotes and single-celled eukaryotes today and there is no reason to doubt that these rock pores, especially zeolite, were just as much a haven for protocells of the Eoarchean for a variety of reasons.

Rock pore contents, proteinoid bodies, liposomes, micelles and aerosols converged in their evolution by physicochemical means into protocells of immense number (say 5×10^{18}) and variety.

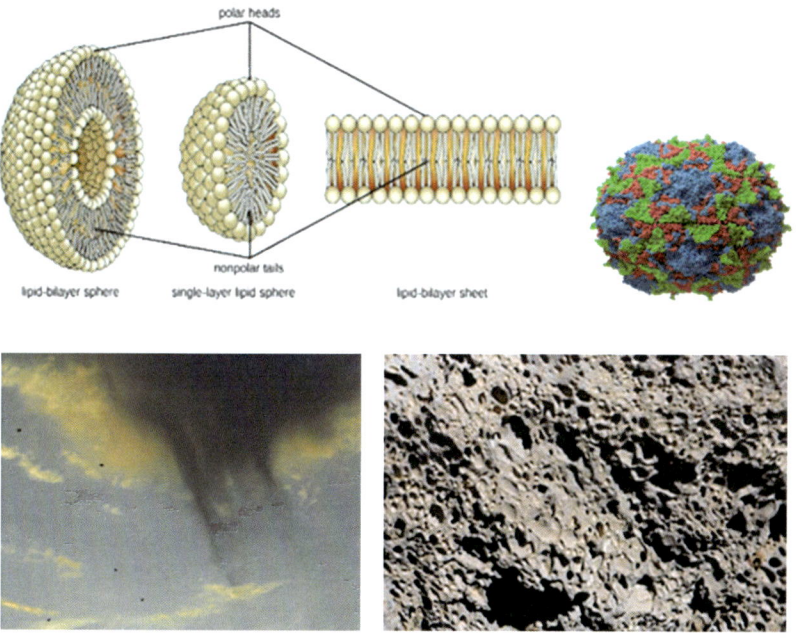

Further Protocell Biochemistry

Rather than dull micro vesicles, the protocell already had a vast array of simultaneous chemical reactions with pyruvate, glyceraldehyde, pentose phosphate, glycolaldehyde, glyoxylate and glucose at their core.

Whatever their length oligopeptides together with minerals and organic chemicals were able to react in an enhanced way by the space constraints within protocells that had taken up microscopic clay particles in their assembly or those that had a smaller liposome in their cytosol from the violent shaking of tides and waves.

With the Earth spinning faster and the moon closer, the diurnal tide was much higher than today since one is caused mostly by the moons (and Suns) gravity and the opposite tides are caused by centrifugal force and the force of the moon on the Earth being greater than that on the distal ocean, all limited in their effect by the rate at which the tides can flow.

Many dipeptides were formed by the high pressures and temperatures of meteorite impact (Blank, J. G. et al.) or the effects of carbonyl sulfide and these dipeptides have been demonstrated to enhance affinity for free fatty acids after binding to a membrane thereby enhancing protocell growth (Adamala, K. and Szostak, J. W. (2013) *Nat Chem,* 5(6)).

Amino acid amides could be formed by the action of hydrochloric acid on alpha aminonitriles in the presence of alcohols (Johnson, H. E. and Crosby, D. G. 1961). The alpha aminonitriles themselves could be synthesised efficiently from aldehydes and amines in the presence of trimethylsilyl cyanates and cyclic ketones (Baeza, A. et al. *Synthesis* 2007).

More directly, the vast quantities of amino acids could be acted upon by a halogenating agent in the presence of methanol to produce the methyl ester and then in the presence of ammonia, the amino acid, amide is produced (Palle, V. R. *Acharyulu* 2004 patent EP 1566376A1). All these substrates and reactions are prebiotically plausible and their great significance comes in the work of H. Yanagawa who, in 1990, produced polypeptides up to 4 kDaltons (approximately

37 average amino acids) with some alpha spiral and beta sheet shapes by using microwave heat to create repeated wet-dry cycles on a solution of amino acid amides.

Criticism came from his use of microwaves for the heating process but these would be present in the blackbody radiation coming from volcanic rocks. Accepting Yanagawas' methods and results, evidence exists for catalytic action from the short polypeptides he produced. These include weak hydrolase, oxidoreductase and esterase activity (Masahiko, I. et al. 1990). Importantly a phosphatase can often catalyse a phosphorylase reaction in the presence of high phosphate concentration.

Any criticism aimed at his use of L, alpha amino acid amides would have been defeated in the real world by the greater number and variety of chemical reactions and organic substrates. Yanagawa and Masahiko in 1988 used wet-dry cycling and prebiotic ocean conditions to produce proteinoid protocell membranes from amino acids or amino acid amides as well as lipid-protocell membranes and combinations of them by varying the temperature and starting chemicals (*OLEB* 18, 179–207). For the lipid membrane self-assembly they used egg lecithin, dialkyl phospholipids and fatty acids in different combinations.

A polypeptide of 32 residues has been demonstrated to catalyse a thiol ester ligation of two smaller fragments of its own molecule (Lee, H. D. et al. *Nature* 1996).

Ribose-5-phosphate may have been available from the pentose phosphate pathway. Sceptics have suggested that ribofuranose was too rare an isomer of ribose to be available for nucleotide synthesis on the early Earth but strong evidence exists that borates in the primordial soup bind and selectively stabilise the appropriate ribose isomer (Furukawa, Y. et al. 2013) over the other aldopentoses.

The propensity of borates to be preferentially sequestered into clays following hydrothermal alteration of rocks is a good indicator that borates, precious to life for their ribofuranose stabilisation, were in the right place at the right time to facilitate nucleoside formation (Ataman, G. et al. 1978). In hotter, acidic conditions they are readily soluble with Ataman, G. et al. finding fifteen different types of borates and Mg^{2+} montmorillonite as a significant component of the large deposits in Turkey.

Boron is an element created almost entirely by cosmic ray spallation in the upper atmosphere and in the Earth's crust down to about 10 metres. A most direct ubiquitous source on the early Earth is the creation of Carbon11 (6 protons, 5 neutrons) from Carbon 12 (6 protons, 6 neutrons) in CO2 by cosmic ray collisions causing neutron expulsion with an almost immediate beta+ decay of the nucleus by positron emission to form Boron 11 (5 protons, 6 neutrons) since C11 has a half-life of 20.3 minutes.

Carbon 11 could also enter the protocell as bicarbonate (HCO3-) and be converted to borate by the beta+ decay that cosmic ray spallation and subsequent positron (and neutrino) emission represents.

Aluminium Silicates (zeolite) in those clays would provide a catalyst for kerogen breakdown and organic chemical synthesis.

A combination of rain, weaker sun intensity (70% of today but higher UV component), escaping Hydrogen, Helium, methane and the presence of atmospheric ash and water vapour cooled the Eoarchean Earth's atmosphere to temperatures close to the present day thereby creating convection currents of varying intensity in bodies of water and in the atmosphere.

These convection currents provided a cyclic energy source for the protocell by separating small polymers which then exergonically reanneal by electrostatic bonds in cooler parts of the aqueous environment. Monster tides caused by the moon being a lot closer and the Earth spinning faster added great disequilibrium and dilution to environments not compartmentalised in protocells, coacervates or aerosols.

In general, conditions were hot and acidic which helped to replenish the aqueous environments with protocells and micelles from the ubiquitous meteorite dust. Importantly guanine can dissolve in hot, acidic conditions to then become available for ribonucleotide synthesis.

The matrix of the fatty acid, ketoacid or isoprene membranes could have contained sulfates, phosphates, porphin, heme c, oligopeptides, sterol analogues, glycerol, amino acids, quinones, carotenoids, retinal and amino alcohols such as sphingosine in varying quantities. The presence of heme is apparently far-fetched but a similar urobilinogen based molecule could have plausibly formed from four pyrrole (5-membered ring) molecules.

These additions reacted in various ways with the main self-assembling molecules, with any proteinoids that had been trapped in the membrane upon assembly and with each other thereby making the protocell membrane more robust and reactive with respect to its cytoplasm and its extreme (by today's standards) environment.

The porphin and retinal could easily bond to a hydrophobic proteinoid trapped in the cell membrane thence potentially responding to light with a conformational change to pump protons in or out of the protocell (depending on their orientation) and thereby create a proton pump powered entirely by light. Directionality and worth as a selective advantage of the pumps to the protocell were dubious at this stage but it gave natural selection variations to work on.

Furthermore, the benzene ring based quinone group of chemicals could have been trapped in the protocell membrane to start off the electron transport and Sulfur oxidation (exergonic) activities of the cell. Indeed ubiquinone is a simple benzene ring based molecule with isoprenyl side chains also known as Coenzyme Q10. Potentially, the quinones could be produced by the action of potassium permanganate (KMnO4) on kerogens in the meteorite dust or by cyclisation of isoprene (C5) molecules to start with Limonene (C10).

High sulfuric acid levels from acid rain and volcanic emissions may have resulted in alkyl sulfonates and alkyl benzenes of great variety to enter protocell membranes and act as a backup to phospholipid, fatty acid or isoprenoid constituents.

Theoretical analysis in self-assembling membranes of fatty acid composition has been achieved (Scott, K. A. et al. 2008 *Science Direct*) to propose a self-assembly of phospholipid molecules around proteins of known structure normally found in the plasma membrane. There is no reason to think plain fatty acids, ketoacids, terpenoids or sphingomyelins would not self-assemble in the same way around primordial proteinoids of neutral, hydrophobic nature, some of which had catalytic or ionophore activity.

It is conceivable that from this early phase the peptidoglycan building block N-acetyl glucosamine was formed from glucosamine and acetic acid and subsequently reacted with lactic acid to produce the second building block N-acetyl muramic acid. These molecules could react with oligopeptides on the protocell membrane to act as stabilising compounds long before they could bond with each other or via oligopeptides to form cell walls.

Indeed, a full cell wall could have blocked interactions with the environment. This peptidogycan molecule along with silicic acid matrices and abiotically formed molecules of hyaluronic acid (from repeating disaccharide beta 1,3-glucuronic acid and beta 1,4-glucosamine) could have helped to bind small communities of related progenotes in such a way that the protocells in that community could share nutrients more efficiently.

This important concept was first proposed many decades ago by C Woese and GE Fox and reflects extant prokaryotic colony behaviour. The colonies of the Eoarchean were physically thrown together as they lacked the large extant cell adhesion molecules or motility systems and the extracellular matrix was enhanced by the contents of lysed protocells which should include short peptidoglycans.

Small polymers of cellulose (repeating glucose chain), hyaluronic acid, peptidoglycan or even chitin and lignin could potentially form inside the protocell to strengthen and protect it from physicochemical perturbations. These substances are all formed from very simple glucose or amino acid-based polymers. Again, the cycles of temperature variation, rain-evaporation and ionic flux including pH were powerful factors in driving reactions by creating disequilibrium.

These organic chemicals were further evolved by reacting with the profuse amounts of minerals such as the iron sulfur rich Mackinawite ($[Fe.xS]$) or Greigite ($[Fe3.S4]$) found in meteorites, serpentinised rock beneath hydrothermal vents and clays including Montmorillonite.

Nickel bound to Iron-Sulfur cuboids and oligopeptides containing cysteine were able to take part in early redox reactions which released small amounts of energy at each step to contribute to uphill reactions within the protocell. What may have begun as internalised iron sulfur cuboids upon protocell formation was later achieved by assembly of the cuboids on scaffold polypeptides with iron binding sites, by photochemistry or both. Molybdenum or Tungsten were also present in some cysteine-Iron-Sulfur clusters to acquire this role.

In the distant future, some of the primordial ferredoxin containing electron transport chains acquired a nitrogenase capability whereby they could form NH_3 from N_2 and Hydrogen ions in a thermodynamically uphill reaction that opportunistically used nearby exergonic reactions until the ATP currency system of energy supply evolved. This fixation of nitrogen was an important advance in the origin of life as NH_3 contributes greatly to the formation of the amino acids, amino acid amides and precursors to the nucleotides.

Indeed, ammonia is used by some extant bacteria in the de novo formation of nucleotides in place of the glutamine that eukaryotes use. This is another example of a de novo acquired synthesis pathway by living cells mimicking an abiotic natural reaction ($NH_3 + HCN \rightarrow$ Adenine). As cyanide became toxic molecular natural selection led to more indirect pathways for essential chemicals to be synthesised and for chemicals like NH3 and HCN to be excreted safely before they reach toxic levels.

Pterins which form the basic structure of the flavins, including riboflavin could conceivably have been in some coacervates or membrane bound protocells from reactions between breakdown products of kerogens thence to acquire benzoic acid side chains and ionic bonds with Zn2+ or Mo2+ and thence to take part in methylation and formylation reactions.

Pyridoxal 5 phosphate (vitamin B6) and its other active forms have been synthesised by Waddell et al. 1999 by heating dilute solutions of NH3 with glycolaldehyde. These pyridine derivatives facilitated methylation, transamination and phosphorylation reactions, albeit less efficiently than enzymes, since pyridine is a known organo-catalyst. Furthermore, the pyridines include the invaluable nicotinic acid also known as niacin (vitamin B3) which is a precursor to NAD and NADH, invaluable hydrogenators and dehydrogenators of intracellular chemicals and employed in electron transport chains.

The possible formation of D ribose in significant yield (5–6%) from glycolaldehyde, acetaldehyde, formaldehyde and glyceraldehyde has been demonstrated (Steer, A. M. et al. 2017) and the similarity of this group of substrates to those of Sutherland and Powner who produced pyrimidine nucleotide is striking. If it was available to a protocell, then the weak catalysis by ancient ocean conditions of the pentose phosphate pathway becomes plausible.

With pyridines and pterins available, the prebiotic methylation of Uracil to form Thymine (5 Methyl Uracil) is plausible thereby making its apparent absence in meteorites immaterial. If researchers had more than a few grams of meteorite material to work with, through no fault of their own, Thymine may have been found more often in meteorite samples. A 2022 article details a novel technique that uses neutral, cool, aqueous agents over longer periods of time resulting in extraction of all five canonical nucleobases as well as ribose from meteorite samples (Oba, Y. et al., *Nature Communications,* April 2022).

Wet–dry cycles (Yanagawa, H. et al. 1990), meteorite impact (Blank, J. et al.) and heat acting on the primordial soup (Oparin-Haldane hypothesis) produced amino acids, oligopeptides and proteinoids as did ketoacids reacting with ammonia (NH3) and amino acid amides within the protocells at points where membranes apposed each other. The use of both left and right-handed amino acids, however, meant that secondary shapes were not identical to extant polypeptides.

Nucleobases broke down chemically and were reconstituted as nucleotides by the pathway discovered by J. Sutherland from formamide, cyanoacetylene and glycolaldehyde. Freezing temperatures at the poles greatly reduce the hydrolysis rates of nucleobases (meteoritic origin or Earth organic chemistry), nucleosides (microspray synthesis a.k.a. Nam, I. et al. 2018) or nucleotides (nucleosides phosphorylated by Diamidophosphate and polyphosphates) to produce half-lives of tens to hundreds of thousands of years.

The significance of ice crystals in concentrating nucleotide solutions between the crystals to the point of polymerisation was demonstrated by A Kanavarioti and D Deamer (2001, *Astrobiology* 1(3)). Other nucleotides could have been formed by unknown extra-terrestrial mineral catalysts that no longer exist on Earth due to aeons of molecular evolution.

However they formed, polynucleotides were most likely a chimera of RNA and DNA due to the reducing effect of H2S on nucleotides in ultraviolet light in the presence of copper cyanate (J D Sutherland et al) and possibly by the catalytic reducing effect of Titanium hydride TiH_2.

Furthermore, they were most likely composed of many different nucleobases. There are over 300 post transcriptional modifications in RNA today (MODOMICS database) and there is no reason to believe that the synthesis of these compounds was precluded in the prebiotic world, catalysed by promiscuous methylators, formylators and phosphorylase chemicals, enzymes and ribozymes.

The great likelihood of large quantities of pyrophosphate and polyphosphates being formed by Hadean conditions acting on phosphonic acids in the meteorite dust (Yamagata, Y. et al. *Nature,* 1991) meant that polyphosphate, cyclic trimetaphosphate, phosphoenolpyruvate, acetyl phosphate and phosphocreatine were likely to be available for the development of limited nucleotide salvage pathways which in rate and volume, at this stage, greatly exceeded the practically negligible de novo synthetic pathways.

A prebiotic inorganic phosphatase such as Cu^{2+} bound to Adenine polymer resin (Srivatsan, S. G. et al. 2001 *Chemistry. A Eur. J*) may have catalysed the hydrolysis of polyphosphates or ATP to transfer the energy required to form a bond between ribose-5-phosphate and the nucleobase. This process is enhanced in acidic conditions.

Adenine has been found in carbonaceous chondrite meteorites and can also be synthesised de novo from cyanide so its presence on the early Earth is plausible. Polyphosphates or any nucleotide triphosphate could substitute for ATP. The extant de novo synthesis of purine nucleotides involves an 11 step process that synthesises the phosphoribose in the process. A primordial phosphoribosyl transferase could achieve a much shorter synthesis pathway from purine + ribophosphate, one or two steps.

A recent article has reported that Diamidophosphate formed from trimetaphosphate is an efficient phosphorylase of amino acids, fatty acids, glycerol and nucleosides without the need for a condensing agent (Gibard, C. et al. *Nature Chemistry*, 2018).

Furthermore, the authors report some polymerisation of amino acids into oligopeptides and nucleotides into oligonucleotides (requiring some imidazole). Several workers have polymerised polynucleotides by:

1. natural means (e.g. James Ferris in montmorillonite, Steven Benner on volcanic glass both with wet–dry cycles)

2. by using laboratory designed ribozyme ligases (Fujita, Y. et al. 2010. Molecules (15):9) or

3. by using enzymes such as T4 phage ligase to produce longer chains from oligonucleotides (Cheng, K. et al. *RSC Advances*, Issue 15, 2019).

Ribozyme ligase sequences as short as 18 contiguous bases long were designed by Y Nomura and Y Yokobayashi in 2019 that "catalyse template directed regio-specific RNA ligation". The greater side chain variability in the Eoarchean means a ligase would be chanced more often and with fewer bases. This expands on work done by Niles Lehman and Eric Hayden in 2006 who demonstrated a reassembly of the Azoarcus type1 intron (derived from the tRNA for isoleucine) self-splicing ribozyme from four cleaved fragments of itself.

Schreibersite (FeNi)3P is a component of iron meteorites and terrestrial basalts which when oxidised by weathering produces orthophosphate, pyrophosphate, phosphides and other phosphorus compounds thereby providing an additional supply of soluble phosphate.

In a Hadean Earth, this oxidation was limited to the action of water on the Schreibersite and the action of sunlight on polar ices to produce hydrogen peroxide (H_2O_2). Arsenate was rarer than Phosphorus in the Earth's crust and is not readily released from minerals during oxidation from weathering, thereby favouring phosphates in the molecular evolution of life as does the greater longevity of phosphates secondary metabolites.

With manganese comprising 0.1% of the Earth's crust, the 12th most common element, potassium manganate K2MNO4 would have been plentiful in the Eoarchean. Pure manganese in meteorites would react with sulfuric acid to produce manganese hydroxides and oxides, which could then react with peroxide (H2O2) to produce manganate and O2 in a highly exergonic reaction. When heated to 230 degrees C, the manganate reacts with water to produce manganese dioxide and O2 thereby providing a further method of oxidation for schreibersite.

Permanganate itself reacts with hydroxide bases to produce manganate, water and oxygen and its ability to break down kerogens to prebiotically useful molecules means that some diverse chemistry crucial for life could occur near volcanoes.

In the distant future, 3.4Gya oxygenic bacteria would employ manganese oxide and Calcium in an oxygen evolving enzyme complex that used energy from sunlight to catalyse the splitting of water to produce O2 and the protons needed for incorporation into its sugar building processes or energy on which their growth is based. Phylogenetically, these are not cyanobacteria whose origin is at 2.1Gya.

Table 2.
Catalysts

1. Physical-heat, ultraviolet light, drying, plasma (lightning resulting in gamma rays).
2. Inorganic-divalent metal cations e.g. Fe2+, Ni2+ etc, AlSiO4 (condensation reaction), AgCl2 (carboxylase), acid-base,
3. Organic-pyridines, carbonyl sulfide, proline, imidazolides.
4. Ribozymes.
5. Non-ribosomal peptides and proteinoids.

NB- > 1200 Inorganic Chemical/Physical catalysts exist in nature and in chemical company sales compendia.

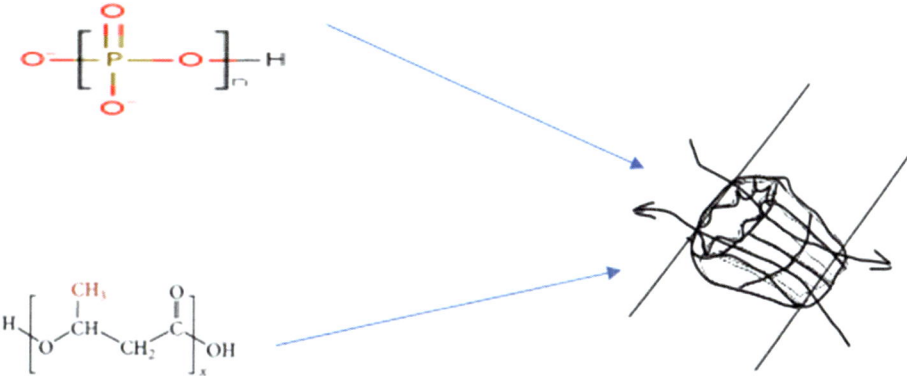

TOP- Combined in solution, The Polyphosphate – Hydroxy Butyrate polymers self-assemble into usable pores (Illustrated) Found in E. Coli, other bacteria and eukaryotes, often forming Calcium Gated Ion channels.

BOTTOM- Five C^2 ceramide molecules may spontaneously h bond (left) and then stack in layers(right - as illustrated) in hydrophobic membrane regions to form large pores.

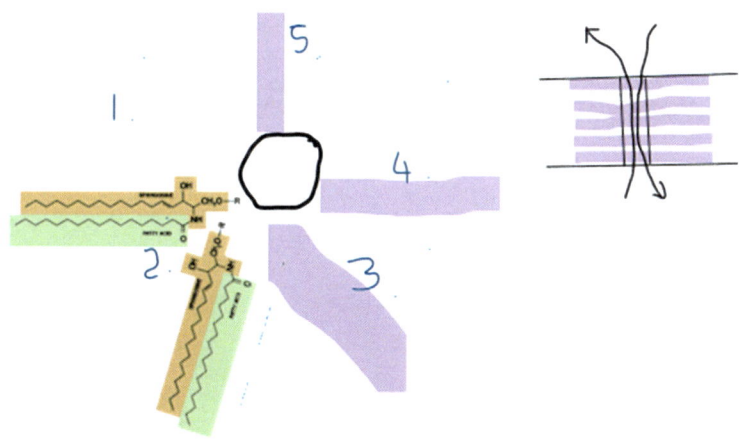

Convergent Evolution into Life

The polynucleotides described above were shielded within the protocells and a small proportion of them acquired catalytic activity (ribozyme) purely on the basis of their chemical sequence, folded shape and reactivity of their nucleobases. RNA sequences of significant length, more than 50 nucleotides long, have been achieved by J Ferris on clays using activated nucleotides as substrates and a team including Steven Benner in 2022 demonstrated the catalysed polymerisation of significant length RNA (100–300 bases) by volcanic glass at standard temperature and pressure from solutions of the main NTP's found in RNA.

The nucleotides could be formed and activated in processes already discussed. This length is adequate to achieve ribozyme activity, such as ligase or phosphodiesterase after entering protocells through polyphosphate pores. Together with the knowledge that the extant Cre-recombinase is short and ATP (NTP) independent then inferring the presence of an ATP independent primordial RNA ligase is plausible.

Those nucleotides not in protocells or their immediate matrix were greatly dispersed by currents and tides and were progressively degraded. Some of the longer ribozymes became a nucleotide polymerase that could not only form a template on which to form a complementary strand but catalyse the polymerisation of polynucleotides of significant length (~100 nucleotides) and ribozyme functionality (Wochner, A. et al. (2011) *Science,* 332, 209), (Joyce, G. F and Horning, D. P *PNAS,* Aug30, 2016., Vol. 113). Wochner et al. report the synthesis of a hammerhead endonuclease ribozyme.

Those who say ATP must be present in ample quantities to drive polynucleotide polymerisation should note in vitro PCR it is not necessary other than as a substrate although Mg^{2+} is. In any case, polyphosphate and pyrophosphate could have helped to activate the nucleotides. There was no start or stop codon and primase did not exist. Primers were not necessary for template formation or elongation. Joyce G and colleagues have also demonstrated ligase activity (which had a similar effect by ligating two or more strands to form a longer one) resulting in exponentially enlarging polymers.

Niles Lehmann et al. in 2008 demonstrated a selective spliced ligation of Azoarcus type 1 intron fragments from the tRNA gene for isoleucine in that organisms genome. Others acquired endonuclease or exonuclease capabilities and some formed peptide nucleic acids, polymers with bases that are joined by an N-2(aminoethyl)-glycine backbone (Nielsen P E 1993 US Patent) or other amino acid.

Even though no dedicated ribozyme replicase has been found in nature to date, some with limited efficiency have been produced in the laboratory and the processes described above can provide a similar result until a ribonucleoproteinoid acquired this role.

The ability of the ubiquitous tRNA acceptor stem synthesis and maintenance enzyme to add an ACC sequence without a template hints at the possibility that an ancient ribozyme or small proteinoid heteromultimer may have acted as a nucleotidyl transferase that did not require a template.

Furthermore, only one of the four domains, the "head", of this already small enzyme catalyses the ACC addition (Ya-Ming, H. (2011) *IUBMB Life*, 62(4)). This indicates that size is not crucial to the existence of a protein enzyme nucleotidyl transferase and that a template is not an absolute requirement. Further evidence is the DNA polymerase X, a terminal nucleotidyl transferase found in eukaryotes or the poly(A) nucleotidyl transferase that adds the polyA tail to mRNA of eukaryotes.

Once the protocell acquired chemical systems that included polypeptides and/or polynucleotides with catalytic activity, it follows that they therefore possessed a genotype and a phenotype albeit not reproducible in a reliable way. This would bring the protocell under the definition of life by NASA "a self-sustaining chemical system capable of Darwinian evolution".

The plausibility of the RNA-polypeptide world where polynucleotides and polypeptides are templated to each other was supported by Muller, F. and Carell, T. (2022) *Nature*, 605, 279–84 who "grew" peptides on RNA composed of non-canonical nucleosides. Here, the polynucleotides and polypeptides were not hydrogen bonded to each other and the experiment was marred by being conducted at standard temperature.

Division by budding further increased the sustainability of the protocell population as environmental or intracellular calamities that afflict one may miss another and the aforementioned progenote community living in a matrix that protected its members by simple shielding more than if they were alone also improved survival. Modern day budding is an active, complex process but the most common type of budding in the Eoarchean would have been driven by violent shaking through tides and waves or the impact of raindrops on enlarged, elongated and therefore unstable protocells. This phenomenon gave molecular evolution a progeny on which to work.

The formation of proteinoids in wet/dry cycles (Fox, S. W. and Harada, 1958;Yanagawa, H. et al., 1990) meant that they were available to many protocells making the protocell a potentially dynamic environment by virtue of the powerful combination of peptides, metal ion catalysts, organic and inorganic catalysts and polynucleotides. Much consideration has already been given by researchers into the possibility of small polypeptides binding ribozymes by electrostatic forces to function as cofactors to enhance their catalytic efficacy.

The electrostatic bonding of templated replication needed for a polymerase ribozyme to produce a molecule longer than itself need not have been a perfect fit as replicating polynucleotides are today and the lengths need not have been very great in order to be functional.

Indeed, in 2010, R. Turk and M. Yarus demonstrated the SELEX production of a five nucleotide ribozyme with aminoacylation activity, being capable of catalysing the aminoacylation of several different small RNAs with phenylalanine-AMP. Even though this experiment is far from demonstrating a promiscuous (acts on many different substrates) and fast peptidyl transferase one could imagine that such a C3 ribozyme derivative bound to a proteinoid multimer of helicase morphology and a Mg^{2+} ion could have been the earliest protoribosome.

With time, quintillions of protocells and the presence of greater varieties of nucleobase side chains the odds swing wildly in favour of evolving such a ribonucleoproteinoid.

With the availability of a great variety of nucleobases in the Eoarchean, the extreme cycling and molecular natural selection that SELEX represents was unnecessary since a functional ribozyme could be chanced more often. This hypothesis is supported by a 2018 article by Kalra, P. et al., Frontiers in Molecular Bioscience who note "the limited chemical diversity of traditional

DNA/RNA libraries (four nucleotides) is perhaps the most obvious shortcoming in traditional SELEX to evolve high affinity aptamers".

Additionally, these alternative nucleotides "stall the enrichment and sequencing steps in SELEX, due to poor enzyme recognition capabilities". This extant drawback was irrelevant in the Eoarchean because proteinoid enzymes and ribozymes were slow anyway and the diversity of the nucleotide side chains was the norm and an advantage. In effect, surviving cells are an immortal line and time was not an issue.

The inter species variability of the length of the Shine-Dalgarno sequence (full sequence AGGAGG) on mRNA in prokaryotes and the variability of the length and content of the recognition site on the 16s ribosomal RNA between prokaryotic species (typically ACCUCCUUA that acts as a "pre start" command) is a molecular fossil reflecting the "wobbly" nature of templating and sequence recognition in biotic cells of the Eoarchean.

Some prokaryotes have even lost the Shine-Dalgarno motif while others have reduced complementary bases which reinforces the strong influence of control and feedback molecules, whether protein, nucleic acid or other chemical in nature (Amin, M. R. et al., 2018) and also illustrates the flexibility of the code for life.

A second clear example of polynucleotide functional complementarity with variations are the small nuclear ribonucleoproteins of the spliceosome that recognise the distinct start and end sequence of an intron-exon boundary. Some bases are conserved, others are not.

The bubbled and convoluted shape of tRNA may be the best extant clue to the molecular morphology of ancient polynucleotides with the chaos and dysfunction of poor control balanced by the few favourable catalytic processes and the presence of large numbers ensuring some survival.

This suggests that the code for life was "wobbly" or less important to begin with and became more refined by control and feedback molecules, that is, it was secondary to catalysis and synthesis. Transfer RNA at 50 deg. C has about 50% of strands in the open "melted" configuration and at 70deg. C has about 100% of strands in the open configuration. If these were the ambient temperature ranges of bodies of water in the Eoarchean then those small RNAs are the first protogenes, able to transcribe with nucleotides, translate with amino acids and catalyse reactions in the folded form.

This templated catalyst phenomenon provided life on Earth with its first great convergence as many substrates were not available in adequate concentration, did not have adequate stereochemical compatibility to optimise hydrogen bonding-base stacking or were not functionally useful once they formed.

Some of the energy for the polymerisation of polynucleotides came from the electrostatic bonding of nucleotides to the template (21 kJ/mol in water), was topped up by some electron transport cascades within the cytoplasm or membrane (with nitrates, fumarate, arsenate or Sulfur as electron acceptors instead of oxygen) and benefited from the reduced hydrolytic activity of water in a crowded cell. The higher temperatures shifted equilibria in favour of products of endothermic reactions, as per the Van t' Hoff equation.

Partial hydrolysis of the RNA template or cleavage by random ribozymes added great variety to the emerging code for life by alternatively producing better or worse templates. Clearly, there could not be start and stop codons at this stage since the codon had not yet evolved in our scenario.

The idea that cellular life is "self-sustaining" is simple minded when one considers the essential nutrients (amino acids, sugars, lipids, vitamins and minerals) that all cells must ingest in order to survive. Clearly, this nutrient supply is totally dependent on the environment. Even chemolithoautotrophs can "incorporate small amounts of organic compounds into cellular biomass" (Chain, P. et al. 2003).

These compounds include amino acids, pyruvate, urea and methane (Prosser, J. I. *Adv Microb Physiol,* 1989). 50 years ago, in 1972, S C Rittenberg reviewed the literature and concluded that "all putative obligate autotrophic bacteria tested so far assimilate and metabolise exogenously supplied organic material" in an article entitled *The Obligate Autotroph – The Demise of a Concepts.*

The protocells of the Eoarchean had nutrients dissolved from the rocks by the acidic conditions and were supplied with abundant organic chemicals while those of today use the enzymes that millions of years of evolution has afforded them to produce most of the organic chemicals they need, supplemented by the uptake of nutrients from the extracellular matrix from the lysed contents of colony members and other sources. The notion that life could have begun deep in the Earth is misguided due to the lack of dynamic chemical fluidity and exchange at this depth.

The definition of life by NASA-"a self-sustaining chemical system capable of Darwinian evolution" has also served to exclude viruses from the family of living things and that is regrettable. A better definition would be "A distinct polynucleotide template molecule, catalysed in its synthesis, with or without accompanying chemicals or chemical pathways which can use nutrients in its environment to grow and reproduce, actively or passively, subject to the physicochemical conditions and molecular Darwinian evolution". We don't need to define life on other planets yet.

On that basis, the Cadang coconut viroid at minimum 246–247 nt long is the smallest extant living thing on Earth. "Living" because in the right environment it replicates and propagates interminably with little dispersity. What would have been an invaluable asset to a protocell is a disease bearing "predator" in a multicellular eukaryotic organism by using the cells RNA polymerase11 to replicate and then, by being degraded by Dicer and Drosha endonucleases to micro RNAs, interfere with mRNA translation and therefore gene expression of the host (Hill, J. M. et al. 2014).

This causes sickness and death to the coconut palm but a polynucleotide of even 1/4 that length would have been a boon to a protocell.

RNA VIROID – No Genes, naked RNA.

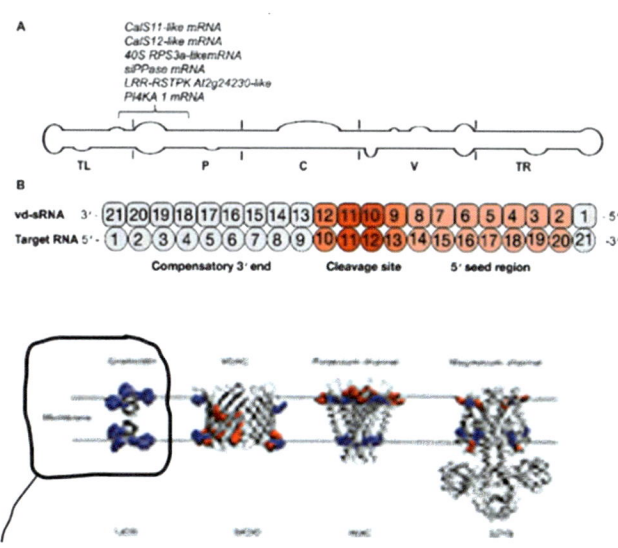

Two spiral Gramicidin A molecules (far left) forming a narrow membrane pore 0.4nm in diameter (conducts ions and small aliphatic molecules). Gramicidin A is a natural antibiotic, nonribosomal peptide with hydrophobic side chains (membrane permeable) produced by nonribosomal peptide synthetases.

Sources of Energy

The SO2 from fumaroles and volcanic craters reacts with water to produce sulfuric acid with Sulfurous acid as an imperceptibly brief intermediary. This common exergonic reaction could "donate" energy to nearby endergonic reactions, such as polymer formation.

Metallic meteorites containing Manganese and Iron delivered billions of tons of manganese which reacts with acids in water at high temperatures to produce manganese dioxide (MnO2) and Mn(OH)2 with a standard enthalpy of formation of -520 J/mol for the former. This exothermic reaction provided much energy for other endergonic reactions to use and was complemented by exothermic dissolution reactions in the hot acidic conditions.

Any sugars trapped by phosphorylation via Diamidophosphate or acetyl phosphate in the protocell could enter the glycolytic and pentose phosphate pathways poorly catalysed by minerals Fe2+, Ni2+, Co, Mo2+, PO3- and borate (BO3) to produce some energy in the form of ATP (Keller, M. A. et al. 2014). Before adequate levels of ATP were attained, pyrophosphate and polyphosphates performed the same function.

Electron transport chains involving cytosol or membrane bound Ferredoxin-like molecules and quinones produced small amounts of energy in each step with Sulfur, nitrates, fumarate or arsenate as electron acceptor in the absence of oxygen. The quinones are lipid soluble and could easily penetrate the cell membrane along with the carotenoids and neutral proteinoids to continue their electron transfer function there.

The electron transfers of methanogenesis also produced small releases of energy that could be used opportunistically in other endergonic reactions. The absence of a complete electron transport chain in the predatory Cyanobacteria Vampirovibrio Chlorellavorus (Hugenholtz, P. et al. 2015) and the loss of oxidative phosphorylation in obligate endosymbiont parasites such as Microsporidia (eukaryote) or bacteria (such as Tremblaya princeps) indicates that in a nutrient rich environment not all energy producing chemical pathways need to be operative at once(Lopez-Madrigal et al. 2013).

That microscopic iron sulfide lattices physicochemically detached from minerals could bind the cysteinyl moiety of abiotically formed peptides and then participate as primordial ferredoxin is plausible and has been approximated by Scintilla, S. et al. (2016) *Chem Comm* 52(92) in the laboratory with glutathione tripeptide and duplications of it to involve hexapeptides and dodecapeptides bound to iron sulfides.

Volcanic heat helped the formation of pyrophosphate and polyphosphates from phosphonic acids in the meteorites which then, upon hydrolysis by prebiotic acidic environments, especially in the presence of a catalyst, Cu^{2+} bound to Adenine resin, had the capability of providing energy for endergonic reactions such as polymer formation.

Pyrophosphate and polyphosphate are unstable in hot acidic conditions and can hydrolyse with a release of energy. Once formed by heating in the presence of phosphates and a condensing agent ATP will spontaneously hydrolyse to ADP and P but still needs an activation energy of ~10 kJ/mol from a nearby source resulting in a release of energy (up to 54 kJ/mol in a cell) upon hydrolysis.

In a primordial world, all the nucleotide triphosphates could release energy upon hydrolysis of the phosphate bonds. Role differentiation would come later with molecular evolution of the protein enzymes that bind them and lower the activation energy of their reactions.

The similarity of Arsenic to phosphorus opens up the possibility that there was a nucleoside arsenate mirroring the actions of the NTPs until the difficulty of hydrolysing arsenate from rocks and the higher degradation rates of secondary products of arsenate and arsenite metabolism favoured phosphate for these roles. Esters of arsenic are much more unstable than phosphate esters however a rapid and spontaneous hydrolysis of ATP-arsenate could supply energy for other useful biotic reactions in the vicinity so arsenate could well have played a useful role in life's origin whilst being phased out by molecular natural selection.

Sulfate, carbonate, borate and silicic acid were all competitors for this role but for various reasons were unable to compete with phosphate. Carbonate, for example, was bound to Na^+, Ca^{2+}, H, Mg^{2+} and Fe^{2+} and transitioned to CO_2 at the water-air interface.

Iron sulfide (FeS i.e. pyrite) formed by volcanoes and hydrothermal vents was available to react with abundant sulfuric acid and HCl in exergonic reactions to provide energy for protocells to couple with their polymer building reactions.

As complexity increased, polymers within protocells that electrostatically reannealed in cooler parts of the aqueous environment after being separated by heat provided a constant and cyclic energy source for further polymer formation by releasing about 21 kJ/mol.

Enough sugars and pyruvate could diffuse into protocells through polyphosphate-gamma 3 iso-butyrate pores to enter the glycolytic pathway or the anaerobic pentose phosphate pathway to produce some energy. These non-proteinaceous pores are found in several extant bacteria and could represent a living fossil of the earliest pores if their apertures were not too wide (Reusch et al. 1999).

Random proteinoids could have solved this potential leakage problem for the protocell only to evolve into the polypeptide pores following the advent of the protoribosome and later evolving into the holin superfamilies of small but effective pore forming proteins.

The Donnan effect caused by the polyanion oligonucleotides trapped in the protocell also favoured influx into the protocell.

Nucleotide triphosphates were certainly produced in protocells activated by any of the exergonic reactions mentioned before and once produced, were available in the hot acidic conditions to deliver both the nucleotide (e.g. GMP) and energy (hydrolysis of pyrophosphate) for polymer synthesis. ATP (and all NTP's) was so close to equilibrium with ADP that it did not readily release its phosphate and the energy of bond formation upon hydrolysis. Without the proton motive force, its usefulness was opportunistic for the protocell.

Chemolithoautotrophism as it is now understood is a "modern" capability, based on many enzymes acquired by billions of years of biotic cell evolution and such a thing could exist in the first protocells only because they were in an energy rich environment full of organic molecules in aqueous solution. Modern inorganic carbon concentrating mechanisms (in thylakoids and Carboxysomes) that actively transfer HCO3- and CO2 into cells and store it as malic acid appear to have evolved in order to maintain the Rubisco enzyme functionality in a low CO2 atmosphere (Raven, J. A. et al. 2008).

Before the oxygen producing bacteria appeared, inorganic carbon in the form of CO2 was in abundance so these concentrating mechanisms were unnecessary.

Organic carbon was the principal of several contributors to the biotic cells' energy economy and the enormous Rubisco enzyme had not evolved yet. Some extant bacteria, including some chemoautotrophs (e.g. Halothiobacillus), have microcompartments that process organic chemicals such as propanediol or ethanolamine to reduce their toxicity which is evidence that they have some access to organic chemicals in their environment (Yeates, T. O. et al. 2008).

Whatever the energy sources for the growth and evolution of the protocell they could never match the extant ATP currency system underpinned by the highly evolved ATP synthase molecular machine, so chemical processes had to be slow and more often interrupted through a lack of substrates or energy. In this scenario, ATP synthase evolved before the age of the eukaryotes by a merger, in advanced prokaryotes, of genes coding for ATP dependent helicase and others for ATP powered proton pumps or passive ion channels (Niu, Y. et al. *J Mol Biol* 2017) whose protein products merged in the prokaryotic cell membrane.

Until that point, the lack of energy meant there was a strong selection of biotic cells with catalysts for anabolic reactions in order to defeat degradation. In their favour, however, was the absence of apoptosis and the occasional "perfect storm" of favourable substrate concentrations and pressure-temperature conditions that catapulted life forward.

Some evidence for this claim comes in a phylogenetic study by VL Koumandou and S Kossida in PLoS 2014 who found that despite a variety of other horizontal gene transfers and a variety of bioenergetic modes the ATP-F synthase (bacteria) and ATP-V synthase (archaea) of prokaryotes have not been subject to horizontal gene transfer. This means they have employed their ATP synthase to fit in with their existing electron transport chains and that these two domains of life evolved this complex molecular machine independently.

The sodium pumping N ATPase, which now lacks ATP synthase ability, is thought to be the common ancestor of bacterial F ATP synthase and Archean V ATP synthase (Dibrovna DV et al. 2010).

This could be explained by a convergent evolution in both domains from a primordial proteinoid sodium and proton pump described previously (evidenced by a simple 24 residue H+/Zn2+ neutral antiporter simulation designed by W F DeGrado et al., 2014) before the advent of the protoribosome and the extant genetic code only to morph into a canonical protein Na+/H+ pump afterwards and then into the two types of ATP synthase by convergent evolution involving a merger with an ATP dependent helicase.

From this point onwards, some of the exothermic energy of ATPase reactions fortuitously maintained an intracellular temperature that was more favourable for the vital metabolic reactions of the biotic cell, as did the extracellular matrix and the close proximity of colony members.

Volcanic Pools And Their Rock Pores Receiving Acids, Bases, Uv Light, Microwaves (Hot Rocks), Aerosols, Ash, Minerals, Kerogen Breakdown Products, Other Organic Chemicals, Salt Water Inundations And Subject To Wet- Dry Cycles Were Ideal For Protocell Biochemistry.

BELOW-Proton pumps 1, 111 & 1V create a proton gradient across the mitochondrion and prokaryotic cell membrane which drives the ATP synthase via the proton motive force. Such complexity probably evolved after DNA evolved in prokaryotes. Complex 11 is succinate dehydrogenase of TCA cycle.

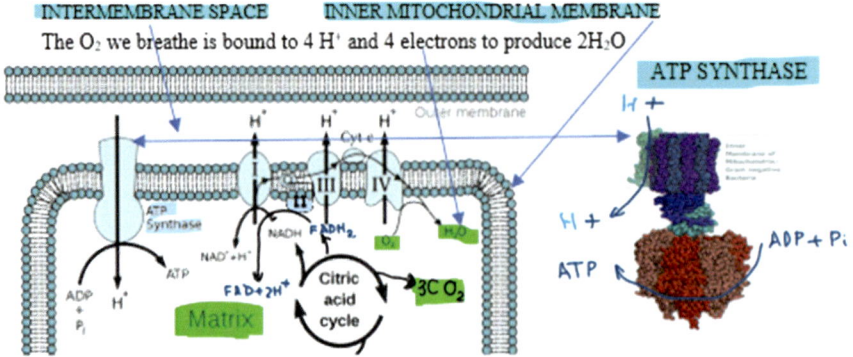

Biotic cell energy sources before Proton Pumps and ATP synthase but after the advent of the Protoribosome. Most are substrate level ADP Phosphorylations (3. is weakly catalysed by Fe^{2+} and 1., 6.,7., 8. and 9. are spontaneous)

1. Phosphoenolpyruvate + ADP ----→ Pyruvate + ATP
2. Glycolysis: Glucose ->->1,3 BPG + ADP→3 PG + ATP

3. Krebs cycle: Succinyl Pi + GDP → Succinate + GTP
4. Acetyl Pi + ADP ←-Acetate Kinase---→ Acetate + ATP
5. Arginine Deiminase Pathway

   Arginine→ →Ornithine + Carbamoyl Pi+ ADP→ CO_2 + NH_3 + ATP

6. Polyphosphate & pyrophosphate hydrolysis
7. Adenosine arsenate hydrolysis- Spontaneous, rapid & exergonic
8. Fermentation ending in Acetic Acid-------→ Methane + CO_2 Spontaneous reaction (catalysed by acetate kinase + phosphotransacetylase analogues with Co B, Co M and cofactor F430) releasing > 50kj/mol. Apply Hess's Law for a circuitous pathway (Wolfe cycle). Prebiotic Cerium-$Cu(OH)_2$ catalyst alone.
9. RNA templating by H bonds – releasing 21kj/mol- Spontaneous
10. Electron transport chains- membrane or cytosolic- energy released at each electron transfer.
11. Any exergonic reaction in proximity

Modern cell ATP sources (After Proton Pumps and ATP synthase)

1. Photophosphorylation
2. Oxidative phosphorylation
3. Methanogenesis via Wood Ljungdahl pathway
4. 1.- 10. In substrate level list with Succinyl CoA for Succinyl Pi

Combating Catabolism

The simplest plausible source of energy for protocells was by glycolysis catalysed by Archaean ocean conditions. Parallel to glycolysis, the pentose phosphate pathway has been proposed as a prebiotic metabolic pathway catalysed by ancient ocean conditions.

Even with glyceraldehyde 3 phosphate or phosphoenolpyruvate entering the glycolytic pathway some ATP can be produced and high concentrations of small molecules, G-3-P, pyruvate or PEP, can see the two pathways producing glucose, ATP, ribose 5 phosphate as well as all other substrates and products of the two pathways. Pyruvate itself can be formed as a breakdown product of amino acids.

Sintered rock pores and the edges of fresh water acidic pools near volcanoes periodically inundated with seawater waves or basic (NH_3) volcanic emissions and are also subject to drying out are the most favourable locations for life to begin. Protocells in this acidic iron-sulfide world would "breathe" Sulfur or arsenic instead of oxygen (in the sense that these were the terminal electron acceptors) and the small releases of energy in each redox pair on these pathways summated into enough energy to cause some proton and sodium pumping out of the protocell against the gradient enacted by the simplest membrane bound proteinoids with some neutral surface charge.

Some of those proteinoids could potentially contain retinal to pump protons by a photochemical conformational change. Natural selection eventually favoured those protocells that pumped protons out against the gradient for reasons of homeostasis in an acidic environment. Without dedicated enzymes, the Sulfur (S, SO_3-, SO_4-) reduction or oxidation was driven by higher ambient heat, inorganic catalysts and high concentration of substrates.

Arsenate and arsenite provided a simple backup molecule for protocells to use in redox reactions. Its role in respiration diminished with time as its levels reduced with subduction of crustal plates only to be revived in extant aqueous environments high in arsenic levels, such as Mono lake. For most organisms, Arsenic interferes with pyruvate dehydrogenase to block AcCoA synthesis, resulting in cellular apoptosis, a highly evolved method of poisoning and cell death that did not exist in life's origin.

Most likely AcetylCoA is too complex a molecule for this early stage of evolution so acyl carrier proteinoids, acetate, Acetyl chloride, acetic anhydride, pyruvate, ethanol, O Acetyl serine, mercaptoethylamine, acetyl phosphate and bicarbonate provided this early source of acylium ion or carbonyl group with the transferase catalytic function provided by pyridines of various structure including pyridoxal phosphate whose simple chemical synthesis has been demonstrated.

This pathway continued until Pantoic acid in the primordial soup that these pools represent reliably reacted with beta alanine amino acid to produce pantothenic acid (vitamin B5) which subsequently can react with cysteamine, beta mercaptoethylamine and 3' phosphorylated ADP to produce CoA, an important coenzyme in the protocell, binding alternatively to acetate, succinate, propionate or methyl malonate to take part in the Krebs carboxylic acid cycle, the HMG-CoA (Mevalonate) pathway and therefore also the anabolic pathways for the fatty acid and isoprene compounds.

The current enzymatic synthesis of Acetyl CoA is a highly evolved process requiring a series of catalysed reactions in a cytosolic membrane or outer mitochondrial membrane enzyme complex, Acetyl CoA synthase, which did not exist yet, nor did the cytosolic Acetyl-CoA synthetase. Even the CoA synthesis pathway today is different by beginning with pantothenate phosphorylation by ATP.

In the Eoarchean, phosphorylation could occur from many sources and the extant CoA synthesis pathway could only come into being when beta alanine became depleted and ATP became the predominant energy and phosphorus currency of life.

Acetate in the prebiotic world could react with Mg^{2+}-Cysteine complex to form O Acetylserine + H_2S whereby O Acetyl serine could potentially substitute for AcCoA. The Acetyl Transferase reaction could be catalysed by pyridoxal phosphate, which has now become a coenzyme in many important biochemical reactions. This means in high H_2S or cysteine solutions, OAS synthesis would be favoured.

$AgCl_2$,(silver chloride) can catalyse pyruvate bonding to bicarbonate in the presence of ATP to form oxaloacetate, thereby initiating the Krebs cycle, itself catalysed by ancient ocean conditions. In the Eoarchean, O-AcetylSerine, acetic anhydride or acetyl phosphate would react with oxaloacetate catalysed by a promiscuous hydratase encoded by free floating protogenes of the stereochemical era to form citrate.

Native (uncharged) metals Fe, Zn and Co can catalyse the formation of acetate and pyruvate from CO2 and H2 in millimolar concentrations in water over hours to days in hyperbaric CO2 at temperatures of 30-100 degrees C (Varma, S. J. et al. *Nature Ecology and Evolution,* 2, April 2018).

In the presence of Nickel coated silicates (Ni/SiO2) as catalysts and high temperature and pressure CO2 reacts with Hydrogen in the Sabatier reaction to form methane (CH4) and in similar abiotic conditions the Haber process produces NH3 from nitrogen and H2, that is, it fixes nitrogen into a biotically useful substance. Hence, previously environmental reactions, possibly in rock pores, coacervates or volcanic aerosols emanating from fumaroles and lava basins pre-eruption were subsequently catalysed within proteinoid containing protocells at more bearable temperatures of 50–70 degrees C to stave off degradation and to grow.

In the distant future, around the time of the first modern cells (~1000 genes) with replicases and two subunit ribosomes the Wood Ljungdahl pathway would use CO2 or pyruvate, hydrogen and CoA to make AcetylCoA by using the first synthase and CO dehydrogenase while the Wolfe cycle would use CO2, hydrogen and several coenzymes to produce methane by-product and energy to drive the metabolic pathways leading to de novo nucleotide synthesis and the establishment of a reliable electrochemical gradient for the newly evolved ATP synthase.

In all likelihood, coenzymes synthesised by reaction sequences that assembled small amino acids in a chelating assembly around Ni2+ or other metal ions predated protein enzymes which would have begun as proteinoid electrostatic accretions on the coenzyme. Any manganese oxides thus trapped in the protocell could have been the first catalase to catalyse the release of H2O and O2 from damaging H2O2, hydrogen peroxide. This simple, highly exergonic reaction predated the more complex water splitting of the Oxygen Evolving Complex that came later at around the time of the "modern cell", 3.40 Gya.

The AcCoA synthase was a polypeptide multimer bound to a nickel iron sulfide complex and the cell membrane and would act alone, not tethered to a CO2 dehydrogenase. The tethering would occur later by selected gene fusion. It used CO2 or pyruvate and a methyl group as precursors and over many aeons evolved and accreted with other polypeptide enzymes by increasingly controlled means to comprise four classes of enzyme composed of different combinations of the five subunits (alpha to epsilon) and modes of action, some anabolic others catabolic (Lindahl, P. A. and Chang, B. (2001) *OLEB*, 31, 403–434).

Electron transport functions in these subunits were greatly enhanced by iron sulfur complexes ([4Fe-4S] or [2Fe-2S]) binding to Ni^{2+}, Copper and/or Molybdenum ion and primordial proteinoids to form primordial ferredoxins and membrane bound transporters of ions including protons. When Molybdenum was depleted, Tungsten could be used in a similar way. Mackinawite is found in some meteorites and serpentinised hydrothermal vents and Greigite is found in clays, including Montmorillonite, thereby making the relation to prebiotic life apparent.

Rather than a macroscopic effect, these minerals had their dissolved cuboids entering cells via polyphosphate or ceramide pores to then bind with proteinoids or proteins to achieve this function. Electron transport activity releases energy, which can potentially be used for endergonic reactions by nearby substrates. The most useful endergonic reaction for the membrane bound components of the electron transport chain was the pumping of protons out of the cell for reasons of homeostasis in an acidic environment or the phosphorylation of ADP to ATP.

As the pH of the aqueous environment neutralised over aeons, these proton pumps served to maintain a proton gradient across the cytoplasmic membrane that could be used for energy or signalling when ion channels opened for any reason thereby reinstating a situation that helped to bring life into being.

The Krebs' citric acid cycle had possibly begun as a consequence of catabolism and absorption in the protocell (especially fatty acid breakdown) to produce NTP's, FADH and NADH thereby adding to the increase in entropy but achieving anabolic biosynthesis in the process.

Alternatively, the Krebs cycle began from the citrate and pyruvate found in meteorites and demonstrated in simple synthesis scenarios on Earth (Cooper G et al. PNAS 2011). Pyruvate can be carboxylated with carbonic acid in the presence of silver chloride, AgCl, catalyst to produce oxaloacetate for the Krebs cycle. Sulfate radicals generated from Peroxidisulfate and Fe^{2+} can then weakly catalyse all steps of the Krebs cycle with reasonable efficiency, except for the citrate anaplerotic step (Keller, M. A. et al. 2017).

The lack of this final step was not considered crucial by the authors who saw citrate replenished from other potential sources. Citrate may be synthesised by manganese ions Mn^{2+} reacting with alpha ketoglutarate (from amino acid catabolism), CO_2 and water to also produce permanganate MnO_4^- or may well have been synthesised from oxaloacetate and AcCoA catalysed by an extinct proteinoid citrate synthase to fortuitously complete the Krebs cycle.

Without oxidative phosphorylation $FADH_2$ and NADH could potentially enter cytosolic electron transport chains with alternative electron acceptors to oxygen (e.g. Arsenate, sulfite) and the single GTP produced per citrate molecule could provide energy for endergonic reactions.

Increasing complexity of the ferredoxins, caused by the binding of multimers of polypeptides (read off the ribozyme protogene-see below) rich in cysteine binding a Greigite derived Fe-S cuboid led to the self-assembly of a primordial CO dehydrogenase and separately an Acetyl CoA synthase that was a small fraction of its present size (310 k Daltons), say 30 KDaltons.

A phylogenetic study of carbon monoxide Dehydrogenase from many sources concluded that it was a very plastic, variable enzyme whose primordial ancestor molecules were probably in the modern cell and that furthermore some share structural and sequence similarities with ABC membrane transporter molecules (Inoue, M. et al. (2019) *Front. Microbial*. 9).

The primordial cytosolic Acetyl-CoA synthetase provided an alternative source of Acetyl CoA from acetate and CoA whilst the membrane bound AcetylCoA synthase produced it via the Wood Ljungdahl pathway from CO_2 and H^+ or pyruvate, H^+ and CoA.

The Krebs cycle can proceed in anaerobic conditions but is far less productive regarding ATP. Even though the oxidative phosphorylation pathways were undeveloped, whatever electron transport chains they did have, whether membrane bound or cytosolic, could make more efficient use of oxygen in minor oxygenation events.

An extant clue that a bacterium can survive in a nutrient rich environment without the oxidative phosphorylation pathway is the case of a bacterium with the fewest number of protein-coding genes (110 genes), Tremblaya princeps, an obligate endosymbiont of a mealybug that has lost its oxidative phosphorylation enzymes (Lopez-Madrigal (2013) *PLoS ONE*). A second example is Monocercomonoedes, a parasitic eukaryote that has no mitochondrion or ATP synthase, producing its ATP by enzymatic breakdown of amino acids, including the arginine deiminase pathway.

A phylogenetic study of Acetyl CoA synthetases, Acetyl CoA synthase and enzymes of the rTCA cycle found they were all clouded by horizontal gene transfer and the authors point out that no conclusions can be made on phylogenetic grounds before the advent of the coding and translation systems (Becerra, A. et al. 2014).

Becerra states that the five individual subunits of ACoA Synthase, alpha to epsilon, probably preceded the full enzyme as each subunit has its own function. It can be inferred that "modern" gene fusions have resulted in the ACS-CO dehydrogenase complex as well as the multi-subunit ACS hence however primitive the archaeal or bacterial species in which they are found seem they have still been evolving for more than 3 billion years and are sophisticated "modern" organisms with thousands of genes.

The original uncatalysed production from the amide of pantoic acid and beta alanine, beta mercaptoethylamine, cystamine and ADP was still possible. In the absence of ACS Coenzyme A could possibly be acetylated by acetyl chloride or by methyl chloride reacting with CO_2 and CoA. With possible further production from fatty acid beta oxidation, the protocell has several backup pathways for the production of Acetyl CoA.

Another possible consequence of the presence of primordial ferredoxins in protocells is the possibility that some may have been able to reduce ribonucleotides to deoxyribonucleotides.

The reverse tricarboxylic acid cycle is anabolic and therefore led to the ability of the protocell to grow in complexity and resist breakdown by synthesising longer molecules but was potentially energy consuming. Six of the eleven steps of the rTCA cycle, however, have been experimentally catalysed by Zn^{2+}, Cr^{3+} or Fe^{2+} in acidic conditions and may have even predated the protocell by occurring in rock pores, in drying clay soils, coacervates or in aerosols (Muchowska, K. B. et al. 2017).

If these metal cations catalyse the rTCA cycle, then they catalyse the forward cycle as well. Other steps could have been driven by high substrate concentrations or catalysed by minerals via photochemistry (Zhang, X. V. and Martin, S. T. 2006). The forward Krebs cycle used sulfates, nitrates, sulfur, H_2, arsenite, borate and fumarate as electron acceptor to oxidise the NADH and $FADH_2$ produced instead of O_2 (which was scarce on the early Earth) and was weakly facilitated by Fe^{2+} (Keller, M. A. et al. *Nature Eco Evo,* 2017).

The synthesising role of the primordial CO dehydrogenase, if it could exist so early, was greatly enhanced by the markedly hyperbaric CO_2 levels which forced CO_2 through any gas channel in the primordial enzymes to push the equilibrium towards the synthesis of longer chain carbon compounds (La Chatelier principle) in metabolic cycles analogous to the Calvin cycle.

With synthesis of more complex molecules from simpler ones, it follows that complexity will also increase. What we see as bewildering complexity are simply the alternative pathways cells utilised from the abundant chemicals around them to achieve growth and procreation of the "living" polymers within them. These alternatives now include the glyoxylate pathway, which, in an extant low CO_2 atmosphere of 0.04% compared with 70% estimated in the Archaean, is a variation of the Krebs cycle, which logically avoids two of the CO_2 releasing steps.

With potassium permanganate $KMnO_4$ producing potassium manganate K_2MnO_4, MnO_2 and O_2 upon heating at >230 deg. C and Titanium Oxide (TiO_2) a photocatalyst that splits water into O_2 and H_2 in the presence of UV light it is likely that micro environments rich in oxygen allowed the full Krebs cycle and oxidative phosphorylation (using membrane bound quinone, anthraquinone and ferredoxins as electron transporters) to evolve.

Manganese is the 12th most common crustal element and Titanium the 11th most common so this oxygen generation could have been significant. Rather than being lost during an anaerobic phase, the quinone-ferredoxin electron transport chains could exergonically oxidise elemental Sulfur to sulfuric acid using H_2O thereby providing a reliable energy source for the cell's anabolic reactions.

The work of Keller MA et al. in 2014 demonstrated glycolysis and pentose phosphate pathways catalysed by Archaean ocean conditions, 70 degrees Celsius, Fe^{2+}, Fe^{3+}, BO_3, Ni^{2+}, Co^{3+}, Mo^{2+} and Phosphate. This gave protocells a base from which to continue but was dependent on adequate substrates, with some (e.g. glyceraldehyde 3 phosphate) being shared in the two pathways. With these two pathways producing energy to activate nucleotides for the protocell, its anabolic functions were supported and substrates were produced for the advent of additional metabolic cycles.

Discussion of ancient enzymes catalysing metabolic pathways should always be open to the possibility that they had fewer steps and variant substrates with catalysts that have now become extinct and replaced by extant complex enzymes. This likelihood is evidenced in the inter-domain variations in enzymes of the

TCA cycle as well as the glyoxylate pathway in some cyanobacteria and purple sulfur oxidising bacteria as well as some plants, protists and fungi.

The possible alternative synthesis of the aromatic amino acids from serine reacting with benzene, phenol, indole or imidazole catalysed by zeolite mineral is another example. More evidence of this likelihood is the variations in glycolysis steps between the Embden-Meyerhof-Parnas pathway and the Entner-Doudoroff pathways. The latter can form pyruvate using the KDPG aldolase and even in the full ten step alternative produces one less ATP and NADH. Is this pathway more primitive as well as less efficient?

Glucose may have been a rare starting chemical to glycolysis due to its complex structure so it may have been the "glyceraldehyde 3 phosphate pathway" in the Eoarchean as a branch of the pentose phosphate pathway or primordial cycle resembling the Calvin cycle which would not require as much glucose or the early ATP consuming steps of glycolysis.

Indeed, glucose could have been a product rather than a starting chemical of this pathway since the essential irreversibility of extant glycolysis is caused by allosteric inhibition, phosphorylation and transcriptional regulation of the complex enzymes hexokinase, hosphofructokinase and pyruvate kinase which was impossible at life's origin (Berg, J. M. (2002) *Biochemistry 5th Edition*, W H Freeman). Furthermore, all steps of extant glycolysis can be reversed since pyruvate phosphate dikinase catalyses a direct synthesis of PEP from pyruvate.

Proteinoid and ribozyme catalysts of this epoch may have been promiscuous by having an effect on two or more similar substrates and reactions, a concept well accepted and understood for extant enzymes (Khersonsky, O. and Tawfik, D. S. (2010) *Annu. Rev. Biochem*, 79, 471–505).

Cori Cycle illustrating the enduring central role of Pyruvate

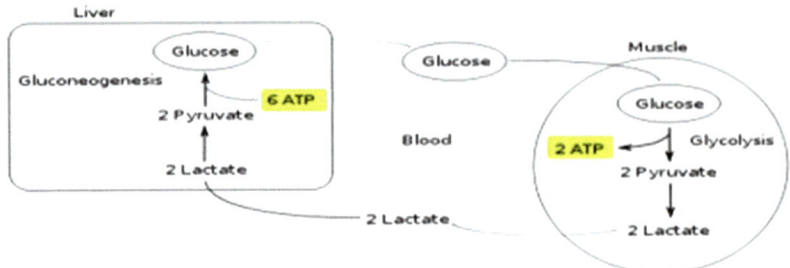

More Polypeptide Catalysts

Heating and drying of alpha amino acid solutions had been demonstrated by Sidney W Fox and K Harada in 1958 (*Science* Vol. 128 Issue 3333) to produce protein-like compounds that could be lysed back down into an amino acid mixture. The analytical tools were not available to Fox to distinguish peptide bond formation from other possible bonds so the products were termed "proteinoids".

Testing of these in the 1960s indicated catalytic activity; hydrolysis of carboxyl esters and phosphate esters (hydrolase and phosphodiesterase respectively), decarboxylation of glucose and oxaloacetate (decarboxylase) and decomposition of hydrogen peroxide (catalase) [Fox, S. W. (1973) *Pure Appl Chem*].

Amazingly, Fox reports a proteinoid composition, observed upon lysis, involving both d and l alpha amino acids when he only used l amino acid mixtures (Rohlfing, D. L. and Fox, S. W. 1969). This would suggest he produced an isomerase enzyme as well, that they spontaneously isomerise as has been observed with alanine or that there is some as yet unexplained way that chirality can spontaneously alter, possibly on quartz crystal surfaces (as proposed by Robert Hazen).

Short oligopeptide synthesis has been demonstrated in solutions containing crystal salts. It is believed that the concentration and organising as well as water exclusion causes the condensation reaction required (Schwendinger and Rode 1992). Subsequent influence of these oligomers as cofactors to ribozymes is plausible, as is their potential self-aggregation into proteinoid catalysts.

Some of the polypeptides formed in wet-dry cycles (H. Yanagawa et al. 1990) from amino acid amides achieved lengths of 30–40 residues and 4kDaltons and acquired weak hydrolase, oxidoreductase or esterase activity (Masahiko, I. et al. 1990). One of Yanagawas' polypeptides catalysed Ferricyanide ion [Fe(CN)3-] reduction with NADH and in earlier experiments his team demonstrated the formation of proteinoid protocell membranes or proteinoid-lipid chimera (using lecithin from egg) membranes with ancient ocean conditions (*OLEB*, 18, 179–207).

With the knowledge that one of the smallest epimerases, methylmalonyl CoA epimerase is only 18 kDaltons in mass it is not hard to visualise a tetramer of polypeptides formed by the Yanagawa or S Fox methods being one of the earliest abiotic amino acid epimerases that worked randomly to give molecular natural selection something to work on.

Some catalysts were potentially able to ligate polypeptides and short peptidoglycans, not always end to end (Lee HD et al. Nature 1996). This transpeptidase activity was in addition to the ability of wet–dry cycles to cause significant polymerisation from an amino acid amide mixture thereby producing strands with long primary structure and beta helices but not alpha helices (because of the use of both d and l amino acids).

With the availability of amino acids reduced to 70 or more by catalyst selectivity and shortage of supply in the environment, the majority would have the side chain remote from the alpha carbon position and the side chain composition was very varied. The resulting structures were varied in the extreme but a small proportion would by chance be recognisable as modern oligopeptides.

Some of the longer polypeptides may have acquired peptidyl transferase activity, which meant they could catalyse the formation of even longer polypeptides. As a consequence of using both l and d forms of amino acids folding patterns almost certainly did exist, such as beta helices and tertiary folding as well as multimer formation and the cyclical shapes that some of the non-ribosomal polypeptides have but not alpha helices or beta sheets.

Along with RNA or RNA-DNA chimera molecules with numerous different nucleobase types kept in the open strand by ambient heat and uncrowded protocells it was a very different biological world to the present. Apart from:

1. peptide bonds oligopeptides could be joined by
2. isopeptide bonds to lysine or other amino acid side chains containing amine or carboxyl groups,
3. thioester or
4. disulfides bonds with cysteine and

5. ester bonds. Not all of these reactions need a catalyst, since many isopeptide bonds can form spontaneously.

In the absence of a catalyst, the cyclical drying of colonies of protocells in tidal pools short of destroying them could generate a concentration and a decrease in the hydrolytic activity of water to such an extent that peptide bonds can occur more readily. These reactions lengthen the polypeptide and thereby increase the chance for it to form oligomers and multimers, however odd or non-standard they may be.

A small proportion of the unusual little domains thus formed had some catalytic activity. The uncontrolled nature of the process provided a tremendous variety on which molecular evolution could operate. Without Golgi apparatus, endoplasmic reticulum, chaperonin-heat shock proteins or ribosomes polypeptide folding and modification was limited to effects caused by the amino acid sequence and the cytosolic chemical composition that affected side chain reactions.

An extant molecular clue that short polypeptides could perform peptidyl transferase, protease and ligase functions exists in inteins that can form a peptide bond between exteins on either side of them as they separate themselves from the sequence. Inteins can be as little as 100 amino acids long, some of which constitutes the homing endonuclease. Split inteins without homing endonuclease activity can be as little as 40 amino acids long, similar to the length of some of H Yanagawas' polypeptides.

Another extant clue is the multitude of oligopeptides and short polypeptides in the literature with catalytic or signalling ability. Glutathione is a non-ribosomal tripeptide that protects cells from oxidation damage and Thyrotropin Releasing Hormone is a tripeptide released by the hypothalamus to cause the pituitary gland to release Thyrotropin.

Thyroxine itself, the thyroid hormone that stimulates cellular metabolism is an amino acid comprised of two iodinated tyrosine residues. Even though ribozymes have been created using the SELEX technique in vitro (by M Yarus and R Turk, 2010) to perform peptidyl transferase function with as little as five nucleotides (with only three nucleotides being the catalytic portion) short peptides could act as a redundancy system that made the advent of catalysts more robust.

The non-ribosomal peptide synthetases that use each one of their domains for a specific peptidyl transferase reaction and transfer the growing peptide from one domain to another may hint at a time when these domains were free floating proteinoids and catalysed one reaction in a cascade that led to the synthesis of a primordial non-ribosomal polypeptide.

Indeed, it has been shown that adenylation domains of NRPSs and aminoacyl-tRNA synthetase catalytic sites have functional similarities with each other and with aminoacyl carrier protein ligase (Jakubowski, H. 2016 FEBS) even though they have structural divergence.

Peptidyl carrier proteins are small alpha helix and primary structure polypeptides that could have competed with ancient ribozymes for free floating amino acids. A most notable extant example is the Peptidyl Carrier Protein of the large fatty acid synthases that transport elongating fatty acids from one part of the multifunctional enzyme complex to another.

There is an accepted extant clue in the modern ribosome that peptides become less folded and complex in their shape the closer they are to the peptidyl transferase catalytic site or the mRNA decoding channel with those most adjacent being almost devoid of secondary structure (Lupas, A. N. et al. (2017) *J Struct. Biol.*, Vol. 198).

This observation, together with the finding that those peptides closest to the PTC site and decoding channel are the most ancient and conserved, suggests that primordial polypeptides were likely to have been less folded. Reasons for this could have been 1) They were shorter, in general and hence were more likely to have only primary structure and 2) The uncrowded cells reduced folding proclivity.

3) A higher mean ambient temperature and significant convection currents meant the polypeptides were "melted" in their conformation 4) the use of a greater variety of amino acids and bond types could have assisted in the retention of the primary state 5) the phosphorylation of peptides that may have occurred in this environment prevented significant initial folding 6) the use of both d and l amino acids in a random order encouraged disordered folding patterns and 7) the absence of the ribosome and chaperone proteins' role in protein folding.

The random proteinoids thus formed have little relation to the coded and complex extant protein domains (more than 10,000) other than that their odd, small shapes, bound to metal ions, could potentially catalyse important reactions or provide building blocks for sub-cellular structures such as membrane components. This possibility was simulated in 2014 (Joh, N., Wang, T. and Degrado, W. *Science*, Vol 346, Issue 6216, 1520–1524) when chemists designed a 24 residue, neutral, helical peptide by self-assembly that could potentially penetrate the membrane with Zn^{2+}/H^+ antiporter functionality.

Furthermore, what may initially be an inactive oligopeptide may acquire catalytic activity upon binding another proteinoid. This has been demonstrated by Rufo, C. M. et al. (2014, *Nature Chemistry*) who formed a series of heptapeptides, allowed them to self-assemble into amyloid like proteins and then measured an esterase catalytic activity. In the primordial world, such an Esterase could have catalysed the hydrolysis of phosphoenolpyruvate to release energy and pyruvate for metabolism. Resistance to high temperature and acidity was a big factor.

Extant short peptides have diverse roles as facilitators and signallers to larger proteins but in the Eoarchean, they were in the primary functional role possibly synergising with organic and inorganic catalysts, ribozymes and long proteinoids.

Electrostatic binding of peptides to polynucleotides could also influence primordial transcription or translation (Ma, B. et al. 2010).

With the ribozyme or ribonucleoprotein peptidyl transferase core established as an efficient, promiscuous catalyst (i.e. effective on many amino acid substrates) at 22–80 bases long (Petrov et al. 2014) there was no selective pressure to replace it with a protein peptidyl transferase since these were increasingly substrate specific.

BELOW- One of more than 2000 Ribonucleoproteins illustrating the enduring close association between Proteins and Polynucleotides.

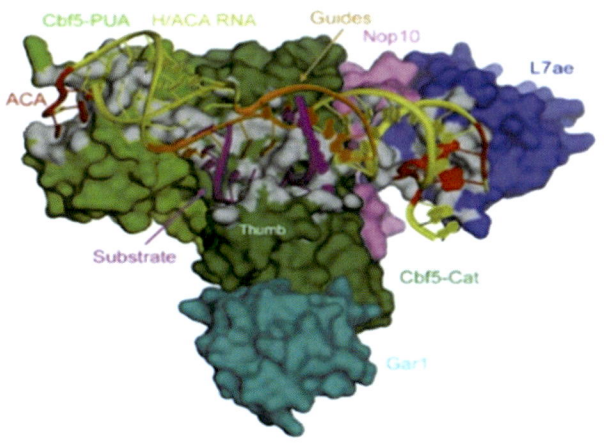

Advent of the Protogene

Citrate is a natural siderophore that served as a Fe3+/Fe2+ buffer for the protocell. These ions weakly catalyse all steps of the glycolytic, pentose phosphate and Krebs' pathways. Citrate and pyruvate have been detected in carbonaceous chondrite meteorites as well as simple scenarios found for their formation post impact (Cooper, G. et al. *PNAS,* 2011).

Cooper et al. also detected ketoacids, tricarboxylic acids and hydroxytricarboxylic acids in meteorites which they claim had previously not been detected. Free ferrous or ferric ions in higher concentrations are involved in single electron reactions that produce damaging free radicals in cells. Free Fe^{3+} ion in higher concentration can result in the formation of damaging insoluble $Fe(OH)_3$, hence the chelating effect of citrate was crucial before the advent of abiotic proteinoid ferritin-like molecules.

Subsequently, a multimer of proteinoids coded on the protogene (see below) bound Fe^{2+} to act as an iron buffer, i.e. a ferritin like molecule. The ready and buffered supply of Fe^{2+} weakly catalysed all steps of the pentose phosphate pathway that supplied the protocell with ribose 5 phosphate and NADH as well as catalysing the glycolytic and Krebs' pathway that provided the cell with pyruvate, reducing agents and GTP (Keller, A. M. et al. 2014). The extant ferritins are a superfamily of enzymes that include the ribonucleotide reductase amongst its number.

Citrate is a component of the TCA cycle, some steps of which are weakly catalysed by ZnS colloid (Zhang, X. V. and Martin, S. T. 2006) with photochemistry and it is postulated that the remainder could have been facilitated by high substrate concentrations (Morowitz, A.). Six of the 11 steps of the rTCA cycle are promoted by Zn^{2+}, Cr^{3+} and Fe in acidic aqueous conditions in two distinct 3-reaction sequences (Muchowska KB et al. 2017). Therefore, it follows that the same is true for the forward TCA cycle with Keller, M. A. et al. in 2017 finding that Fe^{2+} facilitated the Krebs cycle in the presence of sulfate radicals derived from peroxydisulfide.

Any borates in the protocell would help to stabilise the ribose molecule in the correct isomer and catalysed the ribose phosphorylation by providing a stable product (Furukawa et al. *OLEB*, 2013). The synthesis of boron is by cosmic rays acting on carbon 12 to produce unstable C11 with a 20.3 minute half-life —> Boron11 + positron + neutrino (beta + decay) so dissolved bicarbonate was often turned into borate in this manner with adequate frequency to be useful. Magnesium ion also tends to stabilise phosphorylated molecules as the phosphates chelate the Mg^{2+} ion.

Any purine and pyrimidine nucleobases that had not been degraded and were trapped in the protocell were able to bind ribose 5 phosphate (at the C1 position) formed by the pentose phosphate pathway to form nucleosides. This reaction has been demonstrated by Nam, I. et al. in 2018 by a simple aqueous microspray of the nucleobase and ribose substrates in the presence of phosphonic acids and Mg^{2+}. The protocells relied on a proteinoid ribophosphorylase for their nucleosides and ingestion through polyphosphate pores following the micro spray process outlined by Nam et al.

In the presence of Sodium Trimetaphosphate and a reducing agent such as cyanogen the nucleosides can bind phosphates with a 15% yield of nucleotides (Gull M et al. 2015). These could enter protocells through pores already described, directly through the protocell membrane or within the protocells themselves.

Other nucleotides formed by using energy from random exergonic reactions, any primordial electron transport cascades in the cytoplasm and the high energy phosphate carriers creatine phosphate, acetyl phosphate, polyphosphates and phosphoenolpyruvate to achieve activation energies and the phosphate required. The high energy phosphate bond of phosphoenolpyruvate (61 kJ/mol upon hydrolysis) formed by trimetaphosphates in hot acidic conditions could potentially act to add phosphate to sugars entering the cells thereby preventing them from leaking back out and facilitating the metabolic pathways for the cell.

The extant reaction in the glycolytic pathway PEP + ADP—> pyruvate + ATP is exothermic (-31.4 kJ/mol) so the primordial phosphorylation of ADP by PEP would also be thermodynamically favourable. The active glucose transporters of the bacterial phosphotransferase system were still in the distant future but have retained the use of PEP over other phosphate and energy sources.

Activated nucleotides in solution could subsequently be polymerised by montmorillonite clay (upon cell lysis) which acts as an organising mineral surface that encourages condensation reactions and polymer formation (Ferris, J. P. (2006) *B Biol Sci*). Polymerising of "RNA like molecules" on monovalent salt crystals, including NaCl and NH4Cl, has also been demonstrated (Da Silva et al. 2014).

In addition to this method, catalysed polymerisation of activated nucleotides into long polynucleotides (100–300 bases) on glass derived from cooling lava has been demonstrated in 2022 by the Steven Benner lab whereas quartz was found to be ineffective.

Unactivated nucleotides may have been activated by polyphosphates, pyrophosphate and cyclic Trimetaphosphate to energise the uphill polymer forming reaction (especially in the presence of cyanamide or cyanogen as condensing agents). The hypothesis that these experiments confirm were proposed by Leslie Orgel.

These extracellular processes could occur on the lysed contents of protocells only to have the evolved molecules taken up by living protocells through polyphosphate-hydroxybutyrate pores or N acetylsphingosine (C2 ceramide) pores (Peters, M. N. et al. (2012) *BBA-Biomembranes*).

Once protocells acquired polynucleotides they formed a template upon which they could potentially form ribozymes or polypeptides by electrostatically binding substrates, mainly via hydrogen bonds and Pi stacking and then covalent bonding along the phosphate-ribose backbone or the carboxyl-amino peptide bond.

At this point, any amino acids or oligopeptides that could electrostatically bind to the polynucleotides on a 1:1 basis or even 1:2 with regard to amino acid and nucleotide and then formed more peptide bonds and a useful oligopeptide would make that polynucleotide a protogene and that protocell a biotic cell.

The work of Mike Yarus in 2009 and 2017 proved a close stereochemical affinity between amino acids and cognate RNA codons but was marred by being conducted at 25 degrees Celsius. This temperature is not thought to be typical in the Eoarchean (50–70 degrees C) and resulted in most of the amino acids binding the exterior of a folded RNA molecule. Fifty to 70 degrees C would mean more than half the RNAs would be in the open conformation resulting in more useful results.

These temperatures have been shown to be tolerable for amino acids (Brautaset, T. et al. 2007) most of which start to thermally decompose between 185–280 degrees C (Weiss, I. M. et al. 2018) into H_2O, NH_3, H_2S, CO_2 and a peptide rich residue. This residual group of compounds is most interesting with the authors barely able to identify them so their usefulness to a protocell is speculative but exciting. A higher temperature in a closed system like a protocell would mean a higher pressure thereby facilitating reactions in cells that could withstand those conditions without lysing.

There are many computational studies of binding affinity and free energy calculations between protein sequences and mRNA that point strongly to an affinity between cognate amino acids and their codons. These theoretical approaches tend to support the experimental approach of Mike Yarus.

Lehmann, J. et al. (*PLoS ONE,* 2009) conducted a favourable theoretical analysis involving binding aminoacylated 25 nt long looped RNA fragments acting as adaptor molecules onto an RNA template as well as cognant amino acids not bonded to tRNA. Experiments in 2022 by Carrel et al. demonstrated a binding and polymerisation of short oligopeptides on RNA of varied non-canonical monomer composition.

Without codons on the protogene, there was no favoured reading direction. Nucleotides could also polymerise on the protogene but in this case synthesis of the new strand in the 5' to 3' was favoured for being faster and coming with its own energy source, the pyrophosphate. This means the -ve sense strand was read in the 3'–5' direction, a situation which persists to this day.

Without start or stop codons there was a variety of length and sequence (a multiple reading frame-frame shifting system) that gave Darwinian evolution a rich palette on which to work. What could have been disastrous "errors" and lack of control of such a transcriptional and translational system are now observed useful and controlled means by which a cell can enrich its genetic expression (Advani, V. M. *Bioessays,* 2016; Atkins, J. F. et al. *Nucleic Acids Research*, 2016).

Evidence of partial gene overlap is found in two versions of mitochondrial DNA coded ATP synthase and full overlap is found in bacteriophage virus phi X174 that has two examples of total gene overlap where one gene produces two different proteins with a small frame shift (Weisbeek, P. J. et al. (1977) *PNAS,* USA).

This bacteriophage gene overlap could only have evolved in the host bacteria on whose replication and transcription machinery it relies. Without metabolism and regulation biochemistry, the phage can only acquire evolved products from a host hence the total gene overlap was once a feature of primordial prokaryotes.

Despite binding the exterior phosphate backbone of the RNA molecules or non-adjacent nucleotides in RNA loops, Yarus was still able to demonstrate that hydrogen bonding was most frequent with the extant codons or anticodons of all the amino acids tested, probably due to some persistence of the electromagnetic force on an inverse square basis with the distance between the amino acid and the nucleobases and also due to the inevitable single strand overhang on many RNA segments.

This bond was not always with the side chain so in a real-world situation those amino acids that hydrogen bonded to the protogene with a side chain could polymerise whilst non-canonical hydrogen bonds including Hoogsteen bonds in oligonucleotide formation resulted in a termination of polymerisation or the formation of an odd molecule, a proteinoid as coined by SW Fox or termination of oligonucleotide synthesis.

Some hypothetical pairings are listed in the following brief table which can be extended to 300 possible nucleobases hydrogen bonding up to 400 amino acids. The idea that the existence of any of these molecules in the Eoarchean was precluded is preposterous although their concentrations are inestimable.

NUCLEOSIDE-AMINO ACID
1. 1A Methyl adenosine-lysine
2. 1G Methyl guanosine-asparagine
3. 5 hydroxycytidine-pyrrolysine
4. 2'-o-methyluridine-aspartic acid
5. Lysidine-serine
6. 5-hydroxycytidine-proline
7. Methylwyosine-isoserine
8. Queuosine-isovaline
9. Wyosine-a-amino isobutyric acid
10. Inosine-N-Methyl alanine
11. N4 methylcytidine-Djenkolic acid
12. 5-methyldihydrouridine-D lysine
13. 5-hydroxymethylcytidine-hypusine
14. 5-hydroxyuridine-citrulline
15. Cytidine-pipecolic acid

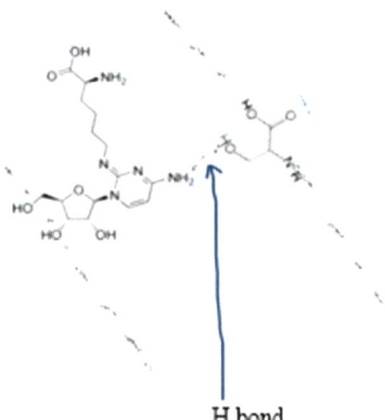

H bond

LYSIDINE COULD H BOND WITH 2 AA's

The templated polymerisation of oligonucleotides or polynucleotides that by chance had ribozyme activity also made that template a protogene. The protogenes were the preferred location for a replicase or peptidyl transferase ribozyme to work at this point but the possibility remains that the coordination of amino acids on the protogene by hydrogen bonding and base stacking brought them close enough to overcome the hydrolytic effect of water and achieve the activation energy.

Some experimental support is afforded by a 2022 article by Carell, T. and Müller, F. (*Nature*, 605, 279–84) where the scientists covalently bonded amino acids to RNA with non-canonical nucleotides and "grew" the peptides into the solution and into loops. Admittedly, this is not hydrogen bonding. Even the modern ribosome, along with initiation and elongation factors, is thought to significantly function by coordination and alignment of substrates.

Both cis and trans oligopeptides were compatible to bind with oligonucleotides since in either case a spiral oligopeptide has its side chains on the outside. The protogene provided the second dramatic reduction in amino acid choices, the first being the reduction caused by inadequate supply and therefore concentration. The protogene effectively selected for amino acids of L configuration with the side chain on the alpha carbon and nucleotides with d-ribose. A simple observation of l alanine and d alanine will show that they cannot peptide bond when their side chains are hydrogen bonded to consecutive RNA bases but two isomers will.

Modern day interpretations of the word "protogene" involve an altered or de novo formed polynucleotide that may have an open reading frame but still contains codons (Carvunis, A. R. et al. *Nature*, 2012 Jul 19). The authors define the proto gene as a novel gene that codes for a translational product, whereas previously that region was non-coding and therefore is a transition state leading to a gene selected for survival by natural selection.

The protogene in our scenario is a polynucleotide but to begin with, the molecular transcription and translation machinery is yet to be developed in order to create the need for a codon or to make use of it. The protogene in this scenario has a multiple reading frame (but still an open reading frame) no codons including start or stop codons and no intron-exon system due to the infancy of splicing hence it is very different from the modern use of the term protogene.

The choice of many nucleotides, nucleotide analogues and odd aromatic molecules like toluene also makes it quite different but it could code for both useful and inactive products whether polynucleotide or polypeptide. Odd molecules like toluene could cause a break in the templating. The non-canonical bases and the non-canonical hydrogen bond configurations such as the Hoogsteen hydrogen bonds were a hindrance to "modern" gene coding but provided nature with many alternative pathways and potential genesis scenarios as well as many points of interruption-termination.

These alternatives to the canonical choices were all selected against by not meeting the selective pressure of Available Concentration x stereochemical affinity x Functional Advantage and the genetic code was constantly morphed by these factors as polynucleotide polymerases, whether ribozymes or enzymes placed demands on the first two components of the equation and natural selection a demand on the third. The 400 or so amino acids and 300 nucleotides therefore rapidly and greatly diminished in this function to create a great convergence in the coding molecules of life.

There is no directionality to the nucleotide templating, it can start anywhere and go in either or both directions, however the 3' to 5' synthesis is more problematic as it requires an extra energy source.

One may argue that this does not represent a code for life but it began a molecular environment in which there existed a proclivity of one nucleotide to hydrogen bond and base stack with another nucleotide or with a particular amino acid and thereby allowed biotic cells with catalysts and control molecules to be selected for over other protocells.

The templated catalysis continued a molecular natural selection that operates inexorably to this day with the 23s rRNA of extant E Coli being found to code for a pentapeptide, including having a Shine Dalgarno motif before the gene and a Stop codon at the end, that confers resistance to erythromycin antibiotic by blocking its binding to the PTC (Tenson, T. et al. (1996) *PNAS,* USA, vol. 93).

The actual DNA gene for the pentapeptide is on the circular plasmid of the E Coli, which may have occurred by an accurate splicing event and has had the effect of conferring erythromycin resistance to the particular ribosomes that have the motif. This is further evidence for the ancient existence of spliceosomes in prokaryotes which could accurately splice the mRNA from this gene into the rRNA of ancient bacteria for the purpose of defeating an attack by erythromycin (a non-ribosomal polypeptide antibiotic) producing bacteria.

The aqueous (and to a lesser extent non-aqueous liquid) environment of the Earth allowed the individual organic components of meteorites to react in a multitude of ways as if the wobble base pairing was the rule and included amino acids. The variety of amino acids present precluded polynucleotides from forming with an amino acid backbone other than those demonstrated in vitro with the N-2-amino ethyl glycine backbone (Nielsen, P. E., USA Patent, 1993).

If they ever existed, the peptide nucleic acids went extinct due to the templated polymerisation of nucleotides and polypeptides on the protogene depriving them of substrates. This scenario suggests the code for life's phenotypes were less important than the catalysis, control and feedback molecule products of the protogene which overcame degradation processes, that is, sequence was important but not always crucial.

It is possible that primordial riboswitches began to evolve as soon as some ribozymes evolved since ribozymes could inadvertently bind substrate molecules such as glucosamine 6 phosphate, which then may have inhibited the efficacy of the ribozyme. Extant glucosamine 6 phosphate binds a riboswitch on a non-coding section of the mRNA and inactivates glucosamine 6 phosphate synthase translation by blocking ribosomal access to the ribosome binding site.

The simplicity of such a feedback mechanism in the protocell suggests it could have to precede the ribosome and is a possible reason why it is not present in most eukaryotes today, it may be too simple and has been replaced by more complex small interfering RNAs bound to RISC proteins that do the same job.

The biotic cell had a great advantage over the protocell that relied on minerals alone or abiotically formed peptides and ribozymes for their catalytic processes due to the template providing both a primordial code (1 amino acid:1 +1nucleotide) and possibly a catalyst whilst the electrostatic bonds themselves released some of the energy that could be used for the polymerisation.

Separation of the polymerised oligopeptide from the protogene template could occur by the ambient heat of convection currents or ATP independent helicase at this early stage and was made much easier if the fit between the two types of polymer was looser. A melting temperature (Tm) of 70 degrees C would ensure 50% or more of the polynucleotides were in the single strand shape and low salt conditions (fresh water) or solutions rich in formamide or urea would lower this temperature requirement since these two chemicals tend to denature nucleic acids (i.e. separate the folded strands). Effects of sequence and ribose reduction were so random and varied at this stage as to be an inestimable chaos.

A proportion of polynucleotide strands themselves were often in the open strand conformation due to hot conditions (more than 50 degrees Celsius) long enough to transcribe and translate whilst in colder conditions, say nightfall or a prolonged volcanic cloud, they were in a conformation in which they could catalyse reactions.

The first useful oligopeptide or polypeptide formed on the protogene could have simply been a structural peptide such as a membrane binding peptide that conferred stability or nutrient transport to the protocell. Others could have formed proteinoid multimers of helicase morphology and function. Those that bound metal ions could have been catalysts of varying efficacy. Looser fit means less electrostatic bonding to overcome.

The most likely first fit for protogenes and forming polypeptides was the classic single strand RNA-DNA chimera B helix on the exterior and the alternating d and l amino acid beta helix of a Gramicidin like polypeptide molecule on the interior.

Additionally, later in evolution, when the molecular machines self-assembled, the alpha helix (which in variable temperatures can transition from spiral to helix and back) could represent a template fitting into the interior of a polynucleotide B helix strand. Indeed, the outer diameter of a protein alpha helix (12 Angstroms) fits perfectly into the groove of the single strand DNA helix.

W.T. Astbury in 1947 found with X Ray crystal studies of nucleic acids that the 3.3A distance between bases was identical to the distance between side chains in an extended polypeptide. He believed it to be not an accident but a "stereo chemical correlation of deep significance".

Bayesian inference would suggest that these two aforementioned experimental findings, together with the work of Mike Yarus, who demonstrated hydrogen bonding proclivity between some amino acids and their mRNA codons swing the probabilities in favour of close primordial hydrogen bond interactions between polynucleotides and alpha amino acids.

Further evidence exists in the occasional non-enzymatic or non-ribozyme covalent ester bond formation between an amino acid and an Adenine on spiral RNA (Tamura and Schimmel, 2004) and the conserved hydrogen bond pairing of lysine on eukaryotic release factor 1 with the Uracil of the STOP codons (Lind, C. et al. 2017) on mRNA as it traverses the ribosome.

Additionally, the biochemistry of inteins is so close to that of autonomous retrotransposons that they represent the "mirror" of these polynucleotides and a molecular living fossil of a protein-RNA stereochemical era.

Stronger evidence for the described protogene is the demonstration by several teams of uncatalysed templating of short peptide nucleic acids, some with lysine side chains, onto DNA. This uncatalysed binding reflected a stereochemical compatibility between the polymers without the influence of a polymerase (Kleiner, R. E. et al. (2008) *J Am Chem Soc.*, 130(14)).

These experiments demonstrate that aromatic amino acid side chains could hydrogen bond and base stack with an oligonucleotide chain. That they do with each other was demonstrated by Wilson K. A. et al. (2014) who examined crystallographic structure and found 344 Pi-Pi nucleobase-amino acid contacts out of 428 DNA-protein Pi-interactions with energies >25 kJ/mol for each of the three aromatic amino acids phenylalanine, tyrosine and tryptophan as well as histidine bound to nucleotide bases.

Complementing this work Kondo J and Westhoff E (2011) found five of the twenty standard amino acids Asn, Gln, Asp, Glu and Arg. are able to orient with nucleotide bases in a coplanar fashion through two hydrogen bonds which Seeman, N. C. et al. (1976) deduced was necessary to adequately fix one base-amino acid pair. This brings the total current amino acid-nucleobase pairings to 9 with Kondo J qualifying that electrostatic, Van der Waals, cation-Pi and CH-O contacts were not considered.

A computational approach in 2003 by Cheng, A. C. et al. found 32 possible pairs, 19 of which were bifurcated H bonds and 13 were pseudo pairs, that is, bond with the Hoogsteen edge of the base. These findings are highly supportive of the stereochemical era that Astbury, Woese, Orgel and Yarus envisioned and strongly support the hypothesis that given a broader range of possible nucleobase-amino acid choices there is hydrogen bonding and base stacking of enough strength and variety to make the stereochemical era more probable than plausible.

In this scenario, polypeptides of the beta or alpha helix type provided a template for polynucleotides to form and when separated, those polynucleotides formed a direct template on which polypeptides could form. The universal nature of the trans peptide configuration was not present yet but trans polypeptides could have been part of the protein milieu.

These 70 or more amino acids paired with a decreasing variety of nucleobases, say 25 and reducing rapidly on a per cell basis as biotic cell numbers increased with budding.

With time, a small proportion of polypeptides formed in this way had nucleotidyl transferase activity and helped to make longer ribozymes and protogenes. Conversely, some protogenes randomly acquired weak peptidyl transferase activity and initiated bona fide polypeptide formation.

Again, this catalysis would begin a natural selection for amino acids that a. were available in adequate concentration and b. the correct stereochemical fit to the ribozyme leaving the rest to disperse and be potentially degraded or enter signalling and metabolic pathways. It is possible that polynucleotides that form with multiple varieties of nucleobase do not fold and self-anneal so easily, thereby conferring a predilection for the open strand. This hypothesis is supported by the tRNA molecules' shape and melting temperature (75-80 degrees Celsius for nearly 100% strands melted).

Biotic cells that had ribozyme or polypeptide based nucleotidyl transferase activity were more likely to provide the cell with protogene templates.

The small proportion of ribozymes, that developed peptidyl transferase activity, made polypeptide enzyme synthesis more efficient and provided extant ribosomes with a molecular fossil of the "polynucleotide-polypeptide" world. One may ask why the ribosomal ribozymes are composed of RNA and not mixed RNA-DNA if they truly are a relic of this undifferentiated world. Since they are currently synthesised by "modern" polymerases, they have to be made of one or the other and the modern ribozymes (post 3.6 Gya) are nearly all RNA. Primers and primase are the exception since primers are often mixed NTPs and dNTPs further supporting this hypothesis.

The proteinoid analogues of the ribozymal peptidyl transferase were the molecular ancestors of the transaminases, the aaRSs and the individual domains of the non-ribosomal peptide synthetases but the evidence suggests that they were always precluded from a potential role in the ribosome by being substrate specific whereas the peptidyl transferase has been shown to work on at least 90 different alpha amino acids (Hartman, M. C. T. et al. (2007) *PLoS One*).

Experiments that test the naked 23s rRNA peptidyl transferase activity are potentially marred by altering its tertiary and quaternary structure and thereby losing the water excluding effect of the PTC and catalytic side chains thus bringing its catalytic activity to zero.

Being read off the protogene the primordial proteinogenic amino acids give some credence to the Thioester world hypothesis proposed by Christian deDuve since the use of aminoacylated CoA-SH as a tRNA-like adaptor in non-ribosomal peptide synthesis and in carrier protein ligase persists (Jakubowski H 2000 JBC) with the amino acid binding the pantothenate moiety.

Without start and stop codons, with inaccuracies and the use of multiple reading frames and frame shifting the same protogene could produce many different products, both nucleic acids and polypeptides. Ribozymes which cleaved polynucleotides added great, seemingly random, variations to the sequence of the protogenes as did any proteases to the polypeptides.

Ribozymes that ligated polynucleotides allowed the formation of longer polymers, probably RNA-DNA chimera that were more likely to have catalytic activity. Synthesis of substrates in the required quantities was impossible at this stage and absorption together with salvage pathways and nucleotide interconversions was the way protocells could make their catalysts work. Primordial micro RNAs binding to protogenes could have acted as random stop points to produce immense transcript variety.

Evolution favoured those protocells with RNA polyanions and oligopeptides for their chemiosmotic advantage via the Donnan effect. The increase in size caused by the Donnan effect was hypothesised by J Szostak to cause an increased likelihood of division by budding for those protocells, thereby providing a numerical advantage in the competition for nutrients in the environment. Acidic Eoarchean conditions combined with protocells containing polyanion polynucleotides meant a natural proton motive force was available to the protocell.

All that was required was an ion channel that opened in response to chemical stimuli and a source of energy was available to the protocell without energy cost. Paradoxically, degradation of large polymers was an opportunity for the cell to sustain its metabolism due to the consequent supply of smaller substrates. This natural selection on a molecular level has continued to this day with a bewildering array of pre and post transcription as well as pre and post translation suites of molecules controlling synthesis of the ribosomal RNA and proteins.

The post transcriptional modifications on ribosomal RNA number over 100 in budding yeast, with fifteen individual nucleotide variations and over 200 in human rRNA thus reflecting the trend towards increased complexity (Sharma, S. and Lafontaine, D. L. J. (2015) *Trends in Biochem. Sci.*).

This complexity of synthesis is augmented by a suite of surveillance molecules that degrade a defective ribosome either pre or post assembly and also in response to starvation or an excess of ribosomes. What may have started as endonucleolytic (cleavage within the molecule) or exonuclease enzymes progressed in the distant future to assemblies of nucleolytic enzymes, the exosome bodies in eukaryotes and the degradosome in prokaryotes. Entrance points in these structures resemble helicase as the proteins are unravelled.

Today these processes are estimated to consume 60% of a cells energy supply but in the Archaean era the catabolism was not ATP consuming, occurred randomly and released energy that could be used in anabolic biosynthesis. In eukaryotes, the surveillance and quality control system involves different groups of molecules for the large and small subunits (Lafontaine, D. L. J. (2010) *Trends Biochem Sci*), thereby lending weight to the hypothesis that the two subunits of the ribosome are very ancient and could have functioned separately once.

From this early stage, some of the proteinoid products of the protogene could have facilitated the formation of polysaccharide or polyphenol molecules such as hyaluronic acid (disaccharide of D-glucuronic acid and N-acetyl-D-glucosamine), chitin (N-acetyl-beta-D-glucosamine), lignin (polyphenol coniferyl alcohol based polymer) and cellulose (beta-D-glucose polymer) in small amounts with their obvious benefits to cell strength and stability.

The catalytic domains of rice and bacterial (Rhodobacter) cellulose synthase are very similar (Olek, A. T. et al. (2014) *The Plant Cell*, vol 26) and it is widely accepted that plants acquired this enzyme following the two endosymbiosis events, mitochondrion (proteobacterium) and chloroplast (cyanobacteria) that led to the algae and the chloroplast ~1.1 Gya. How far back does the original cellulose synthase go?

The biosynthesis of lignin, a polyphenyl compound, is based on phenylpropanes such as coniferyl alcohol which could have been readily available to the protocell to employ as a strengthening agent (Vanholme, R. et al. 2010) in small quantities.

It is unlikely for a protoribosome era-Non-Ribosomal Peptide Synthetase era to have occurred without a foundation in the stereochemical era. This foundation is now evidenced in Origin of Replication Initiation sequences on DNA that are recognised by stereochemical means by protein complexes that initiate binding of helicase and DNA polymerase.

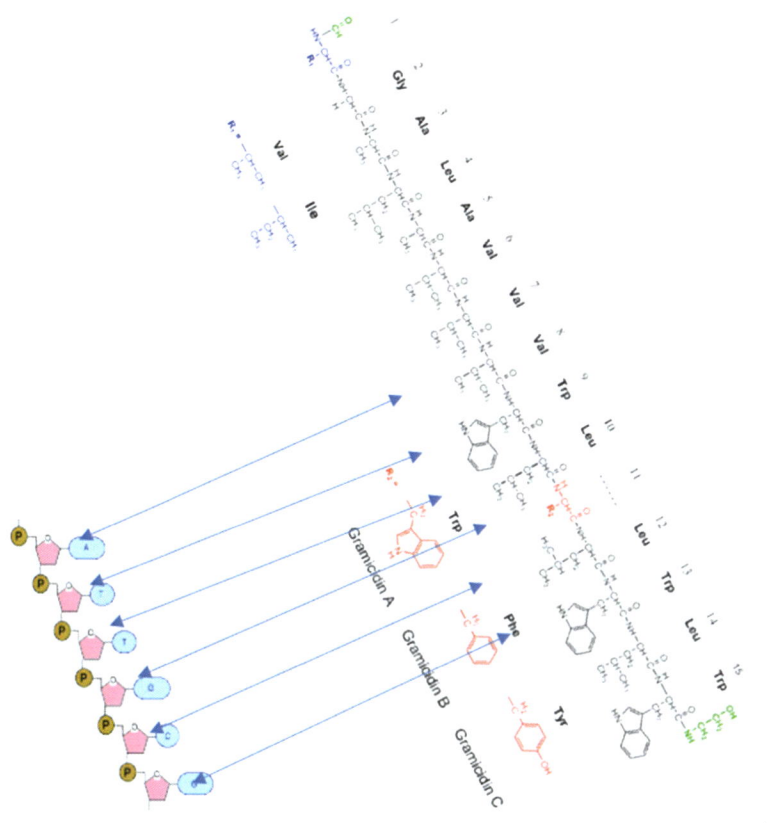

ABOVE - DNA (Left) Distantly opposed to a Gramicidin Non-Ribosomal Peptide segment that suggests the Hydrogen Bonding that could potentially occur between closer Proteinoids and Polynucleotides

BELOW - Protein Alpha Helix depicting side chains on the periphery, accessible for H bonding with Ribonucleotides in spiral Polymers.

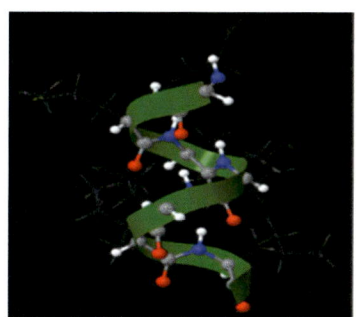
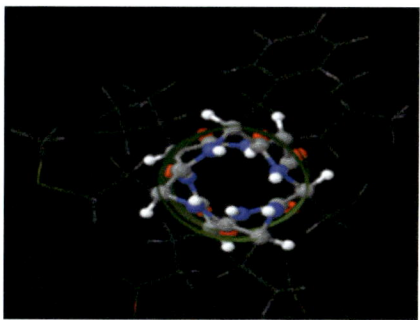

Crucial Phosphoryl Transferase

Prebiotic phosphorylation reactions commonly involved soluble polyphosphates and pyrophosphate which when boiled in salt solution yield cyclic Sodium Trimetaphosphate. In turn, cTMP, in the presence of a condensing agent like cyanogen or cyanamide, in hot conditions is a competent phosphorylase of sugars and nucleosides, often producing a 15% nucleotide yield. (Gull, M. (2014) *Challenges*, 5, 193–212).

More recent investigations have identified Diamidophosphate, derived from cTMP, to be a competent phosphorylase of nucleosides, amino acids, fatty acids and glycerol without the need for a condensing agent. Furthermore, DAP was found to promote oligomerisation and self-assembly (Gibard, C. et al. (2018) *Nature Chemistry*).

The nucleosides themselves were potentially formed in aqueous micro sprays of nucleobase, ribofuranose and phosphonic acid mixtures exuding from meteorite dust and dissolved in water or from a proteinoid ribophosphorylase within the protocell.

Extant bacteria employ phosphoenolpyruvate as a source of phosphate in their phosphotransferase system and there is no reason to doubt that this simple molecule was available to phosphorylate sugars and nucleosides catalysed by a proteinoid phosphorylase formed on the protogene with phosphocreatine as a phosphate buffer, itself formed from amino acid N methyl glycine (sarcosine) + cyanamide. In the absence of PEP, cTMP or Diamidophosphate the protocell could potentially employ acetyl phosphate which favours ATP formation from ADP (Whicher, A. et al. (2018). Prebiotic Chemistry, 48).

A great advantage in having some protocell phospholipid was demonstrated by Budin, I. and Szostak, J. W. in *PNAS* (2011, 108(13)), who showed an enhanced uptake of lipids by protocells with some phospholipids thereby resulting in increased growth rates and hence a natural selection advantage that was possibly present before a reliable code.

If these chemicals could phosphorylate an abiotically formed creatine (formed itself from N-Methyl glycine-i.e. sarcosine-and cyanogen in salt and base) to form creatine phosphate or thioacetate (activated by photochemistry to form acetyl phosphate) or form phosphoenolpyruvate from 2-phosphoglycerate then the prebiotic protocell has reactive phosphate buffers for some fast phosphorylation reactions.

Sugars and nucleosides could also be phosphorylated by disodium phosphate (Na_2HPO_4) in the presence of cyanamide, cyanogen or clay soils and at higher temperatures (50–100C). Phosphorylation of sugars served to prevent their exit from the protocell. The presence of Mg^{2+} can facilitate phosphorylation reactions by interacting with the terminal phosphate and stabilising it by a chelating mechanism. Furthermore, some phosphorylations were enhanced in non-aqueous media, which were common on the prebiotic Earth as they are today in oil reserves in which colonies of bacteria are prevalent.

Hydrolysis of polyphosphates can be catalysed by Cu^{2+}-Adenine resin polymers in acidic conditions (Srivatsan et al. (2001) *Chem Eur J*) to offer energy for coupling with endergonic reactions such as polymer building. One must be mindful that ATP (and all the other NTPs) hydrolysis is "high energy" in its yield of energy but requires only a fraction as much to activate due to inorganic or organic catalysts.

Importantly, polyphosphates, together with poly-R-(3)-hydroxybutyrate, can form channels in extant living membranes (R.N Reusch, 1999) which has the two-fold effect of providing channels of molecular interactions with the environment (Ca^{2+} and even DNA can pass) and in the Eoarchean could have provided phosphate for possible phospholipid synthesis.

The small aperture of the polyphosphate channel may have also reduced the hydrolytic activity of water to such an extent that the formation of oligopeptides and short nucleotide polymers could have been favoured.

A 2011 review by Lilley DMJ PTRSL B Biol Sci 366(1580) pointed out that contemporary ribozymes mostly carry out phosphoryl transfer reactions involving site-specific cleavage by a nucleophilic attack with the reverse reaction also catalysed. Smaller ribozymes, 70–150 nt long, use acid-base catalysis whilst the larger ribozymes act as a metalloenzyme by creating pockets with coordinating O atoms. Lilley concluded that the x 1 million rate increase afforded by ribozymes only brought the overall phosphoryl Transferase rate up to

1 substrate molecule/min with lab redesign, raising this to 10/min. due to the very low uncatalysed reaction rate.

The basic condensation reaction rate of an amine with a carbonyl is faster but is still a nucleophilic attack mechanism with many contributing factors when occurring near the PTC, not least of them the dehydration effect of the confined space of the PTC and the engineered alignment of the amino acid molecules to bring the rate up to x ten million over the basic amine-carboxyl reaction rate of 1/10,000M per litre per minute.

Lilley states that the ancient peptides may have bound primordial ribozymes to enhance their limited catalysis methods and rates (as cofactors) and that protein phosphoryl transferase enzymes were selected for due to their side chains providing a wide range of possible catalytic chemistries. This has brought the maximum catalytic rate of the most efficient enzymes up to 10 to the power of 18 (orotidine 5 decarboxylase) but took billions of years to develop this efficiency.

A hexamer of similar biotically produced (i.e. formed on the protogene) polypeptide monomers bound to a Mn^{2+} or Mg^{2+} ion and the biotic cell membrane to form a phosphokinase. The self-assembling capabilities of polypeptide monomers are mostly due to the electrostatic properties of their individual amino acids (Ma, B. et al. (2010) *ACS Chem Biol*).

It used the energy of protons entering the cell via primordial ion channels to transfer phosphate from cytoplasm soluble polyphosphates, pyrophosphate or phosphoenolpyruvate to the fatty acid-glycerol or isoprenoid-glycerol molecules to produce phospholipids. The ionic flux created by H^+ influx induces a perpendicular magnetic flux within the cytoplasmic membrane and hence an electromagnetic force that increases the energy per charged molecule in the cytoplasm, including phosphate.

Previously, the proteinoid phosphodiesterases demonstrated by Fox and Harada in wet-dry cycles could also potentially catalyse the phosphatase, phosphokinase or even nucleotidyl transferase reaction when substrate levels were high and conditions (temperature and pressure) were right. This phenomenon is demonstrated in the E. Coli tRNA ACC adding enzyme that also repairs the tRNA ends with its phosphatase and phosphodiesterase actions (Yakunin, A. F. et al. (2004) *JBC*). These latter two enzymatic actions were markedly inhibited by low tRNA levels, thereby emphasising the importance of concentration in reaction equilibrium.

Acidic oceans and acid rain meant protons were almost always in excess in the extracellular environment. Cell membranes that had reacted with sterols or glycerol in their formation were also more stable in heating situations, including the ubiquitous hot acidic volcanic pools.

The ancestors of the archaea were always at a great advantage in these situations but were fewer in number due to the greater availability of fatty acids. The inaccuracy and hence the variability of the polypeptide monomer formation on the protogene meant the heteromultimer phosphokinase was sometimes more efficacious, other times inactive and could alternatively transfer phosphate to other molecules or possibly form an Adenylyl Cyclase to start off cyclic AMP production as a cell signalling agent.

The phosphokinase group of multimers achieved variety by errors in their translation more than by being "promiscuous" in their catalysis of substrates. Some could potentially catalyse transfer of phosphate to acetic acid to make acetyl phosphate (which had prebiotically been formed from thioacetate and phosphorus by photochemistry), 2-phosphoglycerate, ribose, nucleosides and abiotically formed creatine or thiamine in the protocell.

Being in the membrane matrix, the phosphokinase used energy from proton or other ionic influx to power the reactions. Ionic flux across the membrane induces a perpendicular magnetic force in the plane of the membrane that can enhance certain reactions.

This scenario has some support in a phylogenetic study of protein phosphokinase by Scheeff, E. C. and Bourne, P. E. (PLoS, 2005), which indicated that a hydrophobic regulatory spine and catalytic spine at the core is highly conserved even though the substrate range is huge. This conserved core was reliant on a cooperative merging of domains and therefore could not be elucidated by sequence analysis alone.

Furthermore, the phylogeny of phosphatidylinositol kinase is at the root of the tree along with bacterial typical protein kinase, which they estimate to be before the divergence of the three domains of life. This conclusion is supported by Kennelly, P. J. ((2003) *Biochem J*, 370(2)), who reports a "phylogenetic trespass" that indicates an early predivergence origin.

Alternative explanation could involve a combination of convergent evolution and lateral gene transfer occurring long after the divergence, since the large size of these molecules (often 83kDa) plausibly demands a simpler phosphorylase in the Eoarchean. Woesian dendrograms can refute LGT but not convergent evolution and the several gene regulation methods outlined below (Ch. 21). Primordial phosphoryl transferases were likely to have been ribonucleoproteins, simpler proteinoids bound to metal ions or ribozymes.

Extant Phosphocreatine is absent in prokaryotes but in muscle tissue acts as a phosphate buffer for sustained ATP actin-myosin contractile reactions. There is no reason to preclude creatine, a simple molecule, from the biochemistry of protocells since its spontaneous breakdown product creatinine is an imidazolidinone and lactam that could potentially have been supplied by kerogen breakdown. Alternatively, creatine was formed from glycine reacting with arginine as it is today or by a more direct synthesis from sarcosine (N methyl glycine) + cyanamide catalysed by mafic rock (containing SiO_2).

Evolution led to more specialised phosphokinases e.g. ribose, thiamine whilst the original phosphokinase may have evolved, in the far distant future, into ATP synthase being ideally situated in the cell membrane, potentially coupling with evolving ion pumps (such as a retinal, benzoquinone or heme c molecule bound to an ion channel).

A less speculative scenario is found in a 2017 phylogenetic analysis that outlines the F1 module of ATP synthase to have evolved from an ATP dependent helicase and the Fo membrane bound subunit to have evolved from passive ion channels with other subunits accreting more variably across the three domains of life (Niu, Y. et al. (2017) *J Mol Evol*).

This would have occurred late in the evolution of bacteria and archaea but before the eukaryotes with the two types of ATP synthase, supporting the hypothesis of primordial divergence of the two prokaryote domains. Both ATP synthase have evolved from earlier Na^+ pumping ATPases. This occurred despite the inevitable horizontal gene transfer, which is ubiquitous and often described as rampant.

As the energy supply of the biotic cell became more secure and the environment became less acidic, the membrane bound ATPase and pyrophosphatase enzymes could alternatively pump protons out of the cell when intracellular ATP or PP levels were high.

ATPase and GTPase became so crucial in breaking the high energy phosphate bond that in the distant future conserved domains of these enzymes would actually be incorporated into enzymes that required active conformational changes (for example ATP dependant helicase or GTP dependent Ftsz) or translocation of macromolecules as performed by the ABC Transporters, a group of translocase. Molecular evolution appears to have favoured ATP for metabolic processes and motor proteins (such as kinesin or myosin) probably due to its 10-fold concentration compared to the other canonical NTP's and GTP for control and feedback proteins, with some exceptions such as the GTP dependent Ftsz (a tubulin analogue) or the ribosomal translocases.

The mechanism of discrimination involves stereochemical compatibility and hydrogen bonding between the NH2 or the O on the purine ring of ATP or GTP respectively and the appropriate amino acid residues in the enzyme. Having specialised out of steric necessity the cell cannot afford a depletion of GTP during an energetic phase hence natural selection favoured ATP for metabolic and adenylate kinase functions (Rogne, P. et al. *PNAS,* Feb 2008) with a backup of lactic acid fermentation in an energetic phase.

A major consequence of the "coded" formation of a phosphokinase was that it provided a second, more efficient system to the formation of ribose-1-phosphate in microdroplets, nucleotide breakdown or ribose 5 phosphate in the pentose phosphate pathway by serving as a ribokinase.

Together with a promiscuous purine and pyrimidine phosphoribosyl transferase (one that catalysed several transferase reactions) the early phosphoryl transferase group of catalysts whether ribozyme, proteinoid enzyme or ribonucleoproteinoid whose monomers were all read off the RNA protogene templates or the protoribosomes (see protoribosomes chapter 12) provided the cell with more efficient salvage pathways for degraded nucleotides.

De novo nucleotide synthesis was undeveloped at this stage and ingestion of molecules through pores or cell membranes diminished gradually on a per cell basis after the end of the Late Heavy Bombardment to be replaced by absorption of molecules from the lysed contents of colony members or other exogenous sources. The acquired loss of de novo nucleotide synthesis in the eukaryotic microsporidia like Cryptosporidium Parvum, an obligate parasite, is strong evidence that a cell can survive in a nutrient rich environment without de novo nucleotide synthesis (Striepen, B. et al. (2004) *PNAS*, USA), (Dean, P. et al. 2016).

The loss of oxidative phosphorylation and TCA cycle enzymes in these microsporidia as well as in bacterial intracellular parasites such as Rickettsia, Chlamydia and the proteobacterium Tremblaya princeps, an obligate endosymbiont of the mealybug that harbours its own proteobacterial endosymbiont, Moranella, demonstrates that a minimal organism (Tremblaya has 110 protein-coding genes) in a nutrient rich environment can survive and even thrive without all of the possible metabolic pathways (Lopez-Madrigal, S. et al. 2014).

The biotic cells could plausibly import their NTPs from the matrix in which they lived from the lysed contents of their neighbours through polyphosphate-hydroxybutyrate pores reported in extant E Coli. They can definitely cross C2 ceramide pores. Future depletion of environmental nucleobases and other nutrients provided a selective pressure for de novo nucleotide and amino acid synthesis, for predation innovations and for photosynthesis.

With inaccuracies in the code and the lack of start and stop codons, some multimers may have been useless whilst others had different substrates or enhanced catalytic activity.

This fake promiscuity based on uncontrollable variations in transcription and translation have now been replaced in the phosphoryl transferase group of enzymes (especially the alkaline phosphatases) with genuine promiscuity based on large active sites that can accommodate and coordinate substrates of varying shape and charge by "electrostatic cooperativity of the key catalytic residues" (Pabis, A. et al. (2018) *CISB*, 48, 83–92). These amazing enzymes are active at 80 degrees C and denature at 90C only to revert to their normal form upon lowering of the temperature.

In light of the Kennelly and the Pabis articles, it would not be a stretch of the probabilities to suggest that the cyclic AMP dependent protein kinases evolved at this time and randomly phosphorylated or dephosphorylated serine, threonine and tyrosine residues on proteinoids initially to unknown ends until Darwinian selection favoured those biotic cells that could use them for favourable enzyme activation and inactivation cycles, that is, control and feedback.

Classic Phosphoryl Transferase (PT) reaction

$$R_1OH + {}^{\ominus}O-\underset{\underset{O^{\ominus}}{\overset{O^{\ominus}}{|}}}{\overset{O}{\overset{\|}{P}}}-OR_2 \xrightarrow{P.T.} R_1O-\underset{\underset{O^{\ominus}}{\overset{O^{\ominus}}{|}}}{\overset{O}{\overset{\|}{P}}}\cdots O^{\ominus} + {}^{\ominus}OR_2 + H^{\oplus}$$

Membrane Evolution

The biotic cell membranes were composed of terpenoids (including the tocopherols, tocotrienols and quinones) fatty acids (including palmitate, oleic acid), sphingosine and other amino alcohols, ketoacids, glycerol, alkyl sulfonates, N-Acylamides and proteinoids but they could not be long-lived unless they evolved even more stable features. The hydrophobic nature of the fatty acids, ketoacids and terpenoids together with the mixing effect of waves and rain impact shaped the vesicles into small spheres with aqueous contents and trapped a host of other chemicals in the membrane, whether unilamellar or multilamellar.

Trapped proteinoids of neutral charge could act as ionophores responding to pH, UV light, electrolyte concentration gradients or pressure changes to alter their conformation to allow $H+$, $Na+$, $K+$, $Ca2+$ or $H2O$ to enter or leave the protocell without energy input whilst remaining closed at other times. Moving charges across the membrane comprise a current that induces a perpendicular electromotive (magnetic) force that can be employed as an energy source by the cell membrane for achieving the energy of activation of many reaction types.

These would be subject to molecular natural selection. After 4 G years of evolution, there are over 300 extant membrane ion channels or aquaporins most of them five subunit complexes composed of 6 alpha helices each that open in an ATP independent way in response to environmental triggers such as a change in $Ca2+$ levels.

The protocell ion channels had to be smaller and with less elegant, evolved shapes. They were most likely proteinoids of neutral charge with some ionophore function exerted by a fortuitous channel in the structure of the molecule. Evolution of complexity would eventually lead to some ion channels merging with a primordial retinal based proton pump so that signals to open (pH, pressure, light, ion concentrations) would result in an influx of protons to provide the energy to produce ATP from ADP.

This proton pump opportunistically used ATP to energise a conformational change when adequate light was unavailable. Hydrolysis of the ATP or pyrophosphate could occur by Cu(OH)2, Cu2+ ion bound to Adenine polymer resin (Srivatsan, S. G. et al.) and ribozyme or proteinoid monoesterases. This was necessary since at equilibrium with ADP the ATP molecule does not easily give up its phosphate and hence the energy release of the H-and-OH bond formation of hydrolysis.

One of the earliest proton pumps may have been a proteinoid based rhodopsin (with retinal in its structure) that responded to light with a conformational change of its retinal molecule to pump a proton or sodium cation out of the cell. In the early Earth conditions, ATP molecules released approximately double the (in vitro standard conditions) energy upon hydrolysis of ADP as they do now in vivo of eukaryotic cells (~54 kJ/mol). "ATP" in this scenario refers to any nucleotide triphosphate so the scope of their action is greatly enhanced.

As membranes dealt with extracellular perturbations, those with some shielding in the form of short mucopolysaccharides, a double membrane or other barrier had a survival advantage but also a problem to solve regarding diffusion of nutrients into the cytosol and waste products out. This also applied to those protocells that had trapped smaller protocells within them from the time of their initial formation.

The discovery that polyphosphates together with poly beta-(R)-3isobutyrate (Reusch 1999) can form channels in membranes suggests the possibility that a. they helped to phosphorylate and hence trap incoming molecules e.g. sugars or nucleosides and b. provided a region where the hydrolytic activity of water is so low (near zero) that polymer formation is favoured.

In the distant future, gamma aminobutyric acid (GABA) would be a neurotransmitter in complex animals again intimately associated with the cell membrane. The current complex microbial biosynthesis of hydroxybutyrate polymers from acetoacetylCoA is precluded in protocells which had access to abiotic glucose but not AcetylCoA so acetate, Cysteine, O-acetyl serine or phosphoenolpyruvate could substitute.

Pores analogous to gramicidin beta spiral dimers plausibly acted as a narrow backup pore system and several teams have reported ceramide channel formation (e.g. from N Acetylsphingosine) in planar membranes, liposomes and the outer membrane of mitochondria (Perera, M. N. et al. (2012) *BBA-Biomembranes*) that results in an increased permeability to proteins with upper mass limit of 60kD (Siskind, L. J. et al. (2002) *The J of Biol. Chem.*).

Any combination of the above channel types in the Eoarchean would have boosted the exchange of nutrients with the extracellular environment, which included the contents of lysed members of the colony.

The presence of urea as a condensing agent results in efficient phosphorylation of glycerol and nucleosides (up to 15%) by cyclic Sodium Trimetaphosphate. Failing de novo glycerol synthesis, some glycerol bisphosphate was produced by glycolysis, which is weakly catalysed by ancient ocean conditions. The formation of phospholipids then becomes plausible and, separately, nucleotides are formed from nucleosides. (Gull, M. (2014) *Challenges*, 5).

The amazing group of transmembrane enzymes the flippases, floppases and scramblases that catalyse the transport of phospholipids within the membranes (mitochondrial, nuclear and cytoplasmic) are too evolved and complex for our biotic cell but as the scramblases are energy independent (respond to intracellular Ca^{2+} concentration changes), are comprised of only eleven beta sheets arranged in a barrel around a single alpha helix and transport phospholipid in either direction within the membrane one is encouraged to believe a smaller version of this enzyme (possibly 6 beta sheets surrounding a beta helix) could have helped the biotic cell arrange its scarce membrane lipid amphiphiles advantageously.

This advanced structure could only form after the advent of the protoribosome but prior to that neutral proteinoid products of the protogene could potentially achieve the same function after diffusing into the membrane. The uncatalysed addition rate of one phospholipid molecule per several hours would be catastrophically low by this stage of evolution when some synthesis of fatty acids (bacteria) or isoprene based monoterpenes (archaea) supplemented the uptake from the environment (micelles, lysed colony members, dissolved carbonaceous chondrites).

This synthesis was most plausibly a result of a catalysed reversal of the catabolism process by established equilibrium laws of first, second or third order reaction rates. Supporting evidence is found in a 2012 chapter in Lipid Metabolism by WW Christie and Han Xianlin, which indicated that Acetyl chloride in pyridine at room temperature could acetylate lipids. Examination of Arrhenius Law suggests that not only is reaction rate increased by heat but when solved for energy of activation, that energy reduces with increasing temperature.

A 2018 phylogenetic analysis based on bioinformatics indicated a close relationship between scramblases and Ca 2+ gated ion channels (Medrano-Soto, A. 2018) *PLoS ONE*). The first scramblase could have been a membrane bound proteinoid ion channel that was replaced by canonical polypeptides of beta barrel tertiary morphology following the advent of the translation machinery. A consequence of having some phospholipid is increased membrane stability and lipid uptake rates (Budin, I. and Szostak, J. 2013).

Simulations (by Kathryn Scott et al. Science Direct 2008) have demonstrated a self-assembly of phospholipid molecules around membrane proteins of a known structure. There is no reason to doubt that fatty acids, ketoacids and terpenoids could do the same around primordial polypeptides.

Furthermore, polypeptides with neutral amino acid sequences have been shown to penetrate into plasma membranes, at least partially. One of these is FtsA, a prokaryotic actin homolog (as is ParM) that acts as a focal tether for FtsZ, a prokaryotic tubulin homolog, to bind and polymerise to help form the Z ring (with several other proteins) during binary fission. The demonstration by H Yanagawa et al. in 1988 of proteinoid-lipid membrane formation from amphiphilic amino acids and fatty acids in ancient ocean conditions is supportive of this scenario (*OLEB* 18).

The polypeptide products of the protogene ultimately could self-assemble into multimers that were primordial fatty acid or isoprenoid synthase enzymes which, like the non-ribosomal peptide synthetases, used their several domains to achieve one reaction and pass the molecule onto the next domain or monomeric enzyme until a phospholipid molecule was formed from acetyl phosphate (Acetyl-CoA not available yet), phosphate, glycerol and molecules generated by the pentose phosphate pathway or the citric acid (Krebs) cycle.

The same occurred with ketoacids until they evolved in another direction, metabolism, for reasons summarised in the formula availability x stereochemical affinity x functional efficiency. The polyketides evolved into secondary metabolites that affect self-defence and procreation whilst their enzymes, the polyketide synthases could become multidomain enzymes analogous to the fatty acid synthase.

The terpenoid synthases were hindered in forming large molecular machines by the cyclic nature of their products, the extensive use of their products in metabolic and other synthetic processes such as the phycobilins and their propensity to produce errant products with a single point mutation. Extant eukaryotic FASs are enormous (540 kD to 2.6 MD) molecules with as many as 48 domains that share homology with individual bacterial enzymes involved in fatty acid synthesis pathways (Bukhari HTS et al. (2014) *Structure* 22 (12)).

These multi domain molecular machines were once single enzyme units that catalysed both synthesis and degradation of fatty acids until the CoA complex evolved to add control to the anabolism and catabolism of fatty acids by monopolising many steps in the process.

The holin superfamily of pore forming proteins contain some with as few as 50 amino acids. They are dsDNA phage virus encoded proteins that congregate on cell membranes and acquire a hydrated centre that eventually lyses the cell. These could only have evolved in living cells that have the processes that allow the evolution of genes and controlled synthesis of their products. Together with porins which in the Archaean could have been single beta barrels of 8 strands, the choice of pores for the biotic cell was significant.

The fact that humans with 22,000 or more genes cannot synthesise a-linolenic acid, an omega-3 fatty acid or linoleic acid, an omega-6 fatty acid as well as the vitamin range of chemicals and nine essential amino acids highlights the importance of nutrition in biosynthesis but pertinently highlights the gradual loss of biosynthesis of certain nutrients that are plentiful in the diet by complex gene expression which did not exist at life's origin and exaptation processes that did exist.

Simplified diagram of the composition of a modern Cell Membrane with about 50% Protein content. A potential difference across the Membrane causes a significant ionic flux when pores open and an induced perpendicular magnetic moment that facilitates biochemical activity.

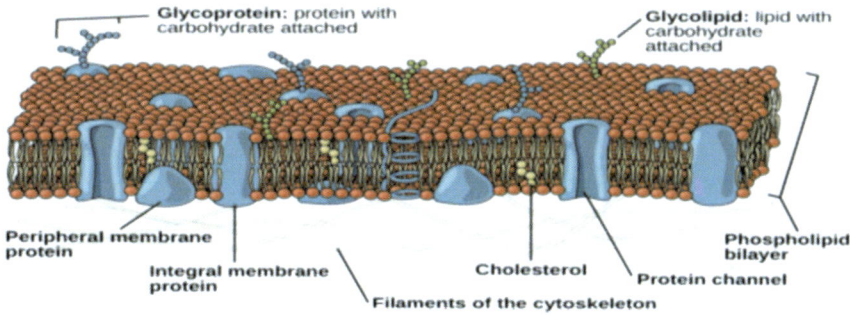

Protoribosomes and Polymerases

Similar proteinoid monomers with negatively charged regions that made up the phosphokinase could alternatively electrostatically bind Mg2+. At this stage of evolution, all the useful monomers were formed on single strand RNA-DNA protogenes as a 10 fold increased difficulty of polymerising DNA compared with RNA is not enough to preclude dNTPs from the polymer. Some ribozymes had nucleotidyl transferase activity from being transcribed off the appropriate protogene and forming ribonucleoproteins with other proteinoids.

Being positively charged at the Mg2+ bound end one variety of proteinoid multimer, possibly one of the first ATP independent helicases that unfolded ribozymes, had a net positive surface charge and hence bound a folded polynucleotide polyanion with some ribozyme activity as a peptidyl transferase (i.e. a protogene-peptidyl transferase ribozyme).

The peptidyl transferase had previously been free floating and was slow but could work on almost any amine-carboxyl pair it came into contact with, that is it was promiscuous. This may seem highly speculative but is supported by phylogenetic work (Petrov et al. (2015) *PNAS*) which describes an "essential core" peptidyl transferase rRNA of only 22 nucleotides in length to begin with expanding to over 80 nt by the time of the complete cell. In the cytoplasm, its function would be to produce oligopeptides and polypeptides on protogenes.

More likely is that the first peptidyl transferase ribozymes of reliable functionality were >100 nt in length and of variable sequence with some of the catalysis effected by the dehydrating effect of the proteinoid channel together with the side chains of some of the amino acids in that channel as well as the effect of the Mg2+ ion.

The peptidyl transferase catalysed a templated condensation reaction as the polynucleotide exited the decoding channel that resulted in a H2O molecule produced and a peptide bond between two amino acids already hydrogen bonded to the polynucleotide. No natural peptidyl transferase ribozymes other than the 23s rRNA of the prokaryotic ribosome and the 28S rRNA of eukaryotes are known in nature but in the laboratory several have been synthesised by using SELEX or other rapid evolution methods.

This scenario is also supported by the S1 proteins' ability to bind and also help release RNA in E Coli Qbeta phage RNA polymerase of which it is a part (Vasilyev, N. N. et al. (2013) *Nature Communications*). S1 proteins are found in the small ribosomal subunit. Unlike the standard RNA pol. shape of a "cupped hand" that of the Qbeta phage replicase, which recruits host bacterial EF-Tu and EF-Ts to form a holoenzyme has the shape of a helicase with a large central aperture exceeding 15 A. Phylogenetic studies suggest that ancient helicases have been seconded to the ribosome, the ATP synthase, the Dynein motor protein and the spliceosome.

Additionally, I Agmon in 2017 (*FEBS Letters* 591(20)) reported a 120 nucleotide peptidyl transferase RNA catalytic core that was conserved in sequence and presumably phylogeny across the three domains of life with several bases conserved over 90%. In the protoribosome Agmon envisioned this core to have been composed of two complementary tRNA like helices forming the core of a protoribosome and catalysing each other's replication.

In my hypothesis, the proteinoid protoribosome of helicase morphology has the p transferase ribozyme bound to the exterior and tRNA had not evolved yet. It was stable in convection currents due to the strength of the multiple ion-dipole bonds between the molecules and had a single channel that served as a decoding channel of helicase function that exceeded 15 Angstroms in width. There was most likely a family of similar multimers, some bound to ribozymes, others to replicase proteinoids, of approximately 60 kDaltons mass that could:

a. translate polynucleotides into polypeptides, the protoribosome that comprised a helicase bound to a slow but promiscuous peptidyl transferase ribozyme and Mg2+.

b. reverse translate polypeptides to produce polynucleotides, those multimers that bound a replicase ribozyme or replicase proteinoid enzyme and whose decoding channel was too small to accept polynucleotides: the translatase.

c. replicate polynucleotides from polynucleotides, those replicase multimers with a large enough decoding channel to accept a single strand polynucleotide (i.e. >15 Angstroms).

These molecular machines had only one channel, which could have been open, as in extant replicases or closed, as in a peptidyl transferase channel. Its main role was to passively guide the molecule to be decoded close to the catalytic site. The polymer being formed extended from the catalytic site outwards into the cytosol (just like the extant HIV reverse transcriptase and eukaryotic telomerase). This suite of polymer dependent polymerases evolved from the free floating nucleotidyl transferases, peptidyl transferase and proteinoid helicases.

Apart from catalysing the nucleophilic attack of the condensation reaction, it afforded the reaction a confined space where some dehydration could occur concurrent with some coordination of the substrates as well as the catalytic influence of the Mg^{2+} ion which includes a chelating effect on phosphates.

In this stereochemical era, before the evolution of specialised tRNA, the complex rotational functions of the ribosome were undeveloped other than their passive helicase rotational function.

Artificial helicases of some function in significantly lowering melting temperatures of polynucleotide double polymers (by 50 degrees C) have been achieved in laboratories (Gasiorek, H. and Schneider, H. J. (2015) *Chemistry-A European Journal*, 21(50)) and others have genetically engineered conserved ATPase and DNA helicase sequences and omitted linker sequences thereby demonstrating that a smaller active version of a helicase could accrete and be functional (Ansari, A. et al. (2014) *PLoS ONE*, 9(3): e90951).

Furthermore, the Yonath lab in 2022 reported some limited promiscuous peptidyl transferase activity, including the fragment reaction of several varieties of minimal prokaryote derived 23S RNA-protein accretions they had named protoribosomes from 2009. These were devoid of any translocation function by lacking a helicase but the experiments were admirably conducted at many varied temperatures (Bose T et al. (2022) Nucleic Acids Research 50(4), 1815–28).

Without a scenario of what came before or since this stage, the Yonath construct is a circular argument that demonstrates smaller segments of the PTC to have Peptidyl Transferase function.

The enzymes began at about 300 amino acids, which is 1/3 the size of the smallest extant polymer dependent polymerases but had less speed and could not discriminate dNTPs from NTPs so there was no reverse transcriptase. The short length of the decoding channel allowed for a molecular passage powered by Brownian diffusion alone, with NTPs only an occasional random contributor of energy at this stage.

There are many extant protein domains with potential decoding channels, including the helicases, haemoglobin, human syncytial virus RNA replicase and the orotidine 5 phosphate decarboxylase enzyme which has two channels in close proximity. Their channels are not used for decoding but for guiding smaller molecules through their interior for transport or catalytic functions.

Biotic cells with phosphokinase but no polymerase slowly evolved into biotic cells with one, two or all three polymerases, by which time the advantage over a protocell becomes obvious.

Once the protoribosomes formed then the direction of reading became selective in the 5'–3' direction for mRNA for complex stereochemical reasons and involving the selection of l-amino acids for polypeptide polymer formation making the 3'–5' mRNA entry through the channel a fruitless passage.

Paradoxically, for RNA strands, the replicase read the single strand template in the 3'–5' direction so that it could synthesise in the thermodynamically favoured 5'–3' direction. This marked a separation in the location of the replication or translation, replicase or protoribosome and meant that for a double stranded RNA the polymerase and the translatase used its passive helicase properties to separate the strands simultaneously to the polymer synthesis.

A stereochemical selection for l-amino acids in the protoribosome caused a gradual transition from proteinoids to polypeptides with trans configuration, as degraded proteinoid polymerases and protoribosomes were replaced by polypeptide polymers. The d-amino acids went into non-ribosomal proteins and metabolism where they persist to this day. Degraded rRNAs and ribozymes were replaced by the products of the replicases and reverse translatase.

At this point, a hot aqueous environment would favour the formation of beta sheets over the alpha spirals which have a much lower melting temperature (~100 C for beta barrels compared with 50 C for alpha spirals (Zhang, X. C. and Han, L. (2016) *Protein Cell*, 7(7)) but the cooling effect of a weaker sun, frequent blackouts by volcanic emissions and rainfall made temperature variation vis-à-vis all the other kinetic considerations of a reaction less significant to such a point as to make a concentration of reactants and catalysts the most pertinent.

Beta strand formation would favour the creation of more tiny holin-like pores. Either Beta strands or alpha spirals would be ideal molecules for passing through the decoding channel of the translatase due to their spiral structure forcing their side chains onto the exterior of the molecule. Cells lacking molecular machines were at a great disadvantage.

A strong extant clue to the predisposition of RNA and proteins to bind by electrostatic forces is the existence of over 2000 ribonucleoproteins in the Protein

Data Bank, including telomerase and the eukaryotic spliceosome in the nucleus that excises introns from mRNA.

The eukaryotic spliceosome is similar to a ribosome in that it is a large organelle (~1.5 MDaltons) composed of ribonucleoproteins which come together by complex signals and whose catalytic centre is thought to be a ribozyme. Its catalytic centre, a junctional triplex of RNAs, is almost identical to the group two introns catalytic centre (Yan, C. et al. 2015). Group 11 introns are only found in bacteria, some archaea and the chloroplasts and mitochondria of lower eukaryotes (Robart, A. R. (2014) *Nature*).

Their catalytic region is almost identical to the spliceosomal RNA catalytic region both structurally and in their reliance on Mg2+ and K+ binding motifs (Fica, S. M. et al. (2013) *Nature*). This points more to a convergent structural evolution with ribosomes but for a different, complementary function. The maturase enzyme of the group 11 intron is an intron encoded protein with a reverse transcriptase, endonuclease and splicing enzymatic function.

The r. transcriptase is phylogenetically related to RNA polymerases like the replicase described here. It is likely that spliceosome ribonucleoproteins were developed in prokaryotes before the great convergence into modern life but later evolved into group 11 introns and maturase for reasons of parsimony with regard to energy. Further evidence for this hypothesis is the parallel evolution of the major and minor spliceosome, which J Vosseberg and B Snel (2017) assessed by review to have been in LECA along with the major spliceosome in an advanced form.

The chance that the spliceosomes evolved from introns is less likely and the close sequence homology between most proteins of the major and minor spliceosome and a sharing of the U5 protein indicates a common evolutionary pathway. It also mirrors the protoribosome-metaribosome parallel evolution until they merged in their function (Ch.15). The loss of the minor spliceosome in protists and closely related phyla after mutation of their U12 type introns into U2 introns is strong evidence that a large molecular machine can be superseded.

Some clear evidence of homohexamer self-aggregation is observed in eicosahedral bacterial microcompartments (Carboxysomes and metabolosomes) that can partly assemble and disassemble based purely on fluctuations in temperature or pH (Kim, E. Y. et al. 2014). The only reason they didn't completely assemble and disassemble was they had up to nine different proteins in their structure. The evolution of these organelles provided an encapsulating mechanism for genetic material that preserved it during cell lysis and exposure to the environment until it could be taken up into viable cells and evolve into the viruses.

Intracellular delivery of polymers, nucleotides and amino acids was by Brownian diffusion but with time some amino acid delivery could occur by small tRNA precursor molecules (no anticodon yet) that had bound an amino acid on an overlapping section by hydrogen bonding or non-enzymatic or non-ribozyme induced 5' adenylation.

This latter method of aminoacylation has been demonstrated (e.g. Tamura, K. and Schimmel, P. 2004) by several teams. PB Moore and Steitz TA in RNA journal 2003 state that N formyl methionine bound to CCA trinucleotide alone can "serve in place of peptidyl tRNA" in the fragment reaction with puromycin in the aminoacyl tRNA position. This fact is common knowledge to workers in the field and is supportive of the scenario.

Double stranded polymers did not fit in the decoding channel but the hexameric shape of the polymerases often afforded a passive helicase activity that disrupted the polynucleotide double helix before entry (Takyar, S. et al. (2005) *Cell*). This helicase activity has been demonstrated in modern cytosolic ribosomes effected by the 30S subunit proteins S3 and S4 (Amunts S et al. Science 2015) as well as mitochondrial ribosomes which are 2/3 the mass of cytoplasmic ribosomes and have different RNA to protein ratios as well as specialising in translating proteins involved in oxidative phosphorylation.

A major consequence of the advent of molecular machines was that the increased efficiency of catalysis put an additional strain on the supply of amino acids and nucleotides and therefore the varieties used in this form of polynucleotide genesis or proteinogenesis plunged dramatically since they were relying on ingestion and salvage at this point. Availability (% optimal concentration) x stereochemical compatibility (% optimal) x functional advantage (% optimal) was probably the relevant equation for this molecular natural selection which was affected by the replicases and peptidyl transferase.

A tentative explanation for the absence of caffeine, theobromine and theophylline of the methylxanthine group of purine chemicals is that they could not be provided at the rate required and conferred no functional or stereochemical advantage.

The second component of this equation has been examined closely by researchers interested in the effects of structural substrate variations on DNA polymerase fidelity and a wealth of influences on this component has already been discovered including 1. Hydrogen bond formation which is important but not essential to polymerisation 2. Steric shape and fit 3. Hydrophobicity and solvation effects of water 4. Base stacking with Pi bonds and 5. negative selection on a molecular level (Lee, I. and Berdis, A. J. (2010) *Biochim Biophys Acta*).

An article by Oertell, K. et al. (2016) attributed 80% of the thermodynamic advantage, ~5kcal/Mol, to the kinetic effects involving the polymerase in DNA replication whilst h-bonding + base stacking contributed much less. The authors also found a x1000 fold discrimination of Watson-Crick base pairing over mismatches before proofreading. This figure provides a numerical guide to the second part of the equation but is dependent on the modern polymerases to deliver that x1000 advantage so it is unintentionally misleading in that the magnitude of the advantage is not inherent in the Watson-Crick bases themselves.

These findings by Oertell are supportive of the above loose equation with "available concentration" referring to the main contributor to these kinetic effects and a standardisation of the other kinetic variables(temperature, pressure, etc). Furthermore, solvation and water exclusion considerations affect the steric fit and also the kinetic effects of the catalyst and are included under both headings.

Catalytic activity is dependent on these various factors and is therefore left as a component of the first two parts of the equation, as is catalyst concentration. The uncatalysed reaction rate of the substrates in those temp-press-pH conditions would be a variable at the front of the equation, as would the inherent reactivity.

In its aim, the equation attempts to encompass and simplify the important aspects of a biochemical reaction, both instantaneous (variable, first and second part) and long term (survival value).

Point 5. above is better covered by the third component of the equation "functional value" since selection is not exclusively negative. The equation is a product rather than a sum due to the variety of the units of measurement involved and by using the "% optimal" potentially relates one process to another in a way that allows for natural selection on a molecular level to be taken into account and for the catalytic rate of the polymerase to reach any high figure.

Experimental evidence exists of a great tolerance by polynucleotides and the polymerases for inclusion of alternative molecules to the canonical choices, including radical alternatives like difluorotoluene, pyrene and nitropyrrole or nucleotides with methylated ribose sugars (Kool ET 2002 Annu Rev Biochem). This does not mean they can be used in the formation of RNA. What researchers now see as a fidelity issue was one of the selective processes that led to Earth's brand of life.

The protoribosome, translatase and primordial replicase were all subject to the same "errors" that DNA polymerases have but to a greater extent due to their infancy. The main reason for the sharp drop in amino acid choices was that the advent of the protoribosome blocked the use of beta amino acids and most d-amino acids but was able to use many non-canonical amino acids of l-alpha configuration.

Some evidence that this was possible is afforded by Josephson, K. et al. in 2005 *J Am Ch Soc.* and later Hartman, M. C. T. et al. in 2007 PLos, who were able to use "over 90 unnatural amino acids to produce individual polypeptides containing up to 13 different unnatural amino acids" each. In the biotic cell, this wide availability of substrates and promiscuity of peptidyl transferase enzyme was impossible in each cell but was plausible across colonies of cells in a wide aqueous region.

As in the case of the protogene, the change did not happen in all cells at the same time so the new system provided evolution with a variety from which to select. The difficulties of nucleotide synthesis made their variety drop proportionally greater to the amino acids. Selection of amino acid racemase that favoured production of l-amino acids from d-amino acids could have occurred in protocells as well as a strong selection for alpha amino acids driven by the greater fitness of cells with polypeptide products.

Some evidence for this is the work of SW Fox and Harada who appear to have unwittingly produced a racemase proteinoid by heating and wet-dry cycling of l amino acid solutions (Fox, S. W. (1973) *Pure Appl Chem*) followed by lysing them back down to an amino acid mixture which appeared to contain some d-amino acids. D-amino acids exist in biology in non-ribosomal peptides and peptidoglycans in some bacterial cell walls.

The polypeptides thus produced by the protoribosomes could adopt cis or trans peptide configuration and configure each of their psi and phi bonds according to the Ramachandran plot restrictions in the trans peptide configuration. The cis peptide bond configuration was far more problematic in that the side chains could interfere with the carbonyl or amino groups.

The helical shape of some polypeptides allowed the side chains to be positioned on the outside of the helix and to come close enough to the translatases catalytic core to allow polynucleotide polymerisation. Those that were in open strand form simply passed through the rtranslatase decoding channel and were decoded on a 1:1 (or 1:2) basis like the helical polypeptides. The fact that not all side chains would be on the correct side and position meant that the code was so "wobbly" as to be unimportant at this stage compared to the catalytic (anabolic) function of the polymerases.

This event potentially continues the 1:1+1 relation between amino acid and nucleotide that had begun on the protogene as some nucleotides were not in the appropriate 3 dimensional position on the protogene to hydrogen bond or base stack with an amino acid so that two amino acids may straddle 2 or 3 nucleotides. Neither of the alpha or beta helices nor the open strand peptides would always have the side chains in the position needed to cause a perfect stereochemical match.

Those polymerases that bound a ribozyme polyanion that was not a peptidyl transferase or could not bind an RNA molecule were better named polymer dependent polymerases.

The significance of the protoribosomes and replicases was that 1. a catalytic site was constantly at the site of the decoding channel thereby taking some aspects of randomness out of the older process of catalytic polymer formation on protogenes as well as 2. making directionality of decoding important. It is possible that 3. an RNA-polypeptide macromolecule is more stable and resistant to mutation or hydrolysis than its individual parts, thereby conferring an additional selective advantage to those cells that had them.

The protoribosomes could have 4. Produced enzymes with useful domains for continuing the non-ribosomal peptide synthetase, fatty acid synthase, terpenoid synthase and polyketide synthetase line of enzymes 5. The molecular machines, specifically the molecular architecture of the decoding channel of the reverse translatase and peptidyl transferase channel (when it acquired more domains to form an open channel) of the protoribosomes were responsible for the selection of trans polypeptides and l-amino acids respectively in biology and 6. This new system of proteinogenesis traded increased speed for some reduced variety of the substrates.

Significant evidence exists that the extant peptidyl transferase centre discriminates L-amino acids from D-amino acids (Englander, M. T. et al. (2015)

PNAS, USA) and that a second system of chiral selectivity for l-amino acids occurs in the aa-tRNA transferases (Tamura, K. (2011) *Int. J. Mol. Sci.*, 12, 4745–57). As l-amino acids are incorporated into proteins, the cytosolic reduction in their concentration drives a catalysed biosynthesis of those amino acids and drives the isomerase catalysed conversion of l-amino acids from d-amino acids via Le Chateliere's principle.

Furthermore, strong evidence exists that extant ribosomes can translocate tRNAs and read out a message in the absence of elongation factors and GTP because the process is "inherent in the ribosome and is thermodynamically spontaneous" (Spirin, A. S. (2002) *FEBS Lett.*). Brownian diffusion was the more likely driver in the Eoarchean.

What may initially be a useless random product of the protoribosome could, by forming a multimer complex with others acquire useful catalytic function, thereby starting a molecular product line, Darwinian evolution obviously found useful. Any significant length l-amino acid-d-amino acid ligation sequence by the non-ribosomal peptide synthetases which were still functional could result in pore shaped beta spirals either left or right-handed. The neutrally charged of these beta spirals could potentially insinuate themselves into the membrane to potentially provide a more reliable pore structure than the abiotic channels.

Upon formation by a reverse translation in the thermodynamically favoured 5'-3' direction, polynucleotides could enter the protoribosome decoding channel with their 2 base codon from their 5' end and act as a template for the protoribosome to translate a similar protein. This process would mean that the archive for the cell was on both polypeptides and polynucleotides and they thereby preserved each other's identity.

This positive feedback loop rapidly depleted substrates and was thereby suppressed by simple laws of equilibrium but catapulted life forwards in the process by defeating degradation. The rapidly diminishing variety of nucleobases on a per cell basis after the end of the late heavy bombardment drove the need for a codon to cover the relatively larger number of proteinogenic amino acids used to synthesise proteins and probably drove the selection of biotic cells with enzymes that catalysed salvage and de novo nucleotide synthesis pathways.

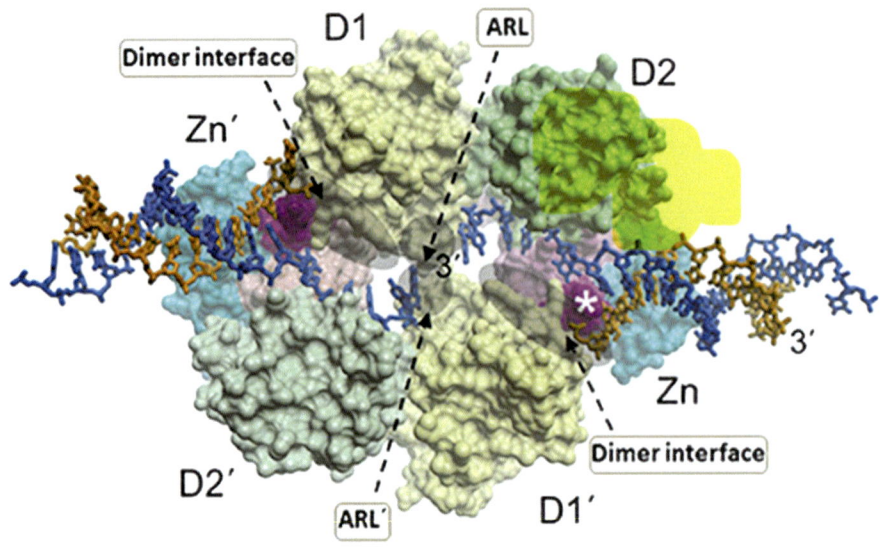

ABOVE - Modern Hexameric (6 Monomer) Helicase separating RNA into 2 strands. A Peptidyl Transferase At D2 Position (Yellow) along with Mg^{2+} could potentially constitute a Protoribosome with a Peptide formed directly on the RNA template. The H bond formation releases energy (21kj/Mol) for Peptide Bond formation
BELOW - Yeast DNA Helicase illustrates that the Full Ring structure shown above is not essential for efficient Helicase Function although A 2-Protein synergy has been found by experiment to be essential.

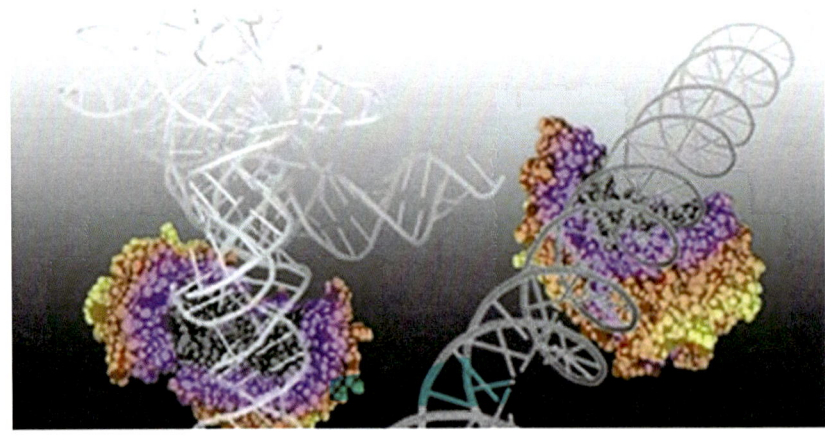

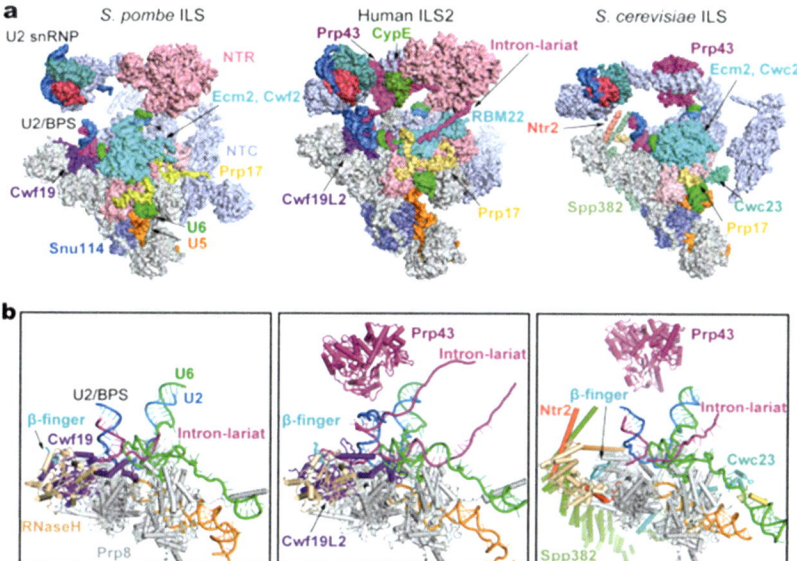

ABOVE - The human Spliceosome has 2x the number of Proteins (170 vs 80) of yeast S/Some (Eight of these are Helicase). Both rival the Mitochondrial Ribosome for Size and have a conserved Catalytic RNA Core Homologous to Type 2B Self Splicing Introns. Spliceosomes employ a great variety of Proteins (> 300 in Humans) Unlike Ribosomes with conserved Protein composition BELOW - Queuosine, Right, could H bond with 2 Amino Acids. Here Isovaline is shown distant and askew. Information was initially less important than bulk synthesis.

H bonds subject to Inverse Square Law for distance and can be weak, 1Kj/Mol, up to strong, 40 Kj/Mol depending on atom ID and Geometry and environment.

Reverse Translation? Really?

Reverse translation has the unfashionable stigma of an unsolved cold case whose victim was unloved and unimportant.

The great significance of reverse translation performed by a molecular machine is that polynucleotide protogenes are produced in the "image" of the analogous protein thereby creating a positive feedback loop that not only defeated the rates of degradation but also defeated a chaotic templating that might have led to useless protein products. Those biotic cells with useful catalysts had a backup means of templating similar catalysts.

This theory is not new but it opens up the possibility that the protogene and subsequently protoribosome products together with multimer formation could have led to the first replicase enzyme. All that was required was a decoding channel to be formed on the replicase by binding a multimeric helicase-like protein with a <15 Angstrom channel that could only accept polypeptides and a useful polypeptide directed nucleotide polymerase, the reverse translatase, could be formed.

The replicase can't discern the nature of the polymer it is interacting with, it is simply subject to the force of electromagnetism and Coulombs law that govern its magnitude, namely the inverse square of the distance between charges and proportional to the signed magnitude of the charges.

In the real world, the motion of the polymer and substrates means that the more complex Maxwell-Faraday equations and transient dipole forces are relevant but are inestimable at these speeds, varieties of molecules, magnitudes and cytoplasm permeability-permittivity.

If ribozymes were the first replicases, then reverse translation molecular machines could have been an additional polynucleotide polymerase thereby more easily overcoming the hydrolysis rates of the polynucleotides with a positive feedback loop that defeated degradation but eventually needed suppressing due to substrate depletions.

In this scenario, the protoribosome suite of molecular machines were a major cause of the l amino acid enantiomer selection in biology as well as being the major cause of the trans polypeptide dominance in biology as the beta spiral cis polypeptides, which had alternating d-and l-amino acids were starved of l-substrates by the l enantiomer selection by the protoribosome.

Therefore, trans polypeptides were the common form available to the reverse translatase decoding channel and when the resulting polynucleotides were translated by the protoribosomes they produced trans polypeptides. Cis polypeptides are now synthesised by non-ribosomal peptide synthetases in bacteria and rarely in some archaea.

As the protoribosomes grew in size and evolved into the 2 channel metaribosome-tRNA system (see below) then reverse translation may have been halted by the complexity of the new molecular architecture, the adapter molecules (tRNA and its aminoacylators) and the increasingly folded form of evolving proteins. With the increased efficiency of molecular machine formation the selective pressure for reverse translatase was lifted and they evolved in an unknown direction.

From that point on, Crick's dogma became true and correct in functional terms but not in the sense that the archive is the master command centre because it is often dictated to by translational recoding, nutritional limitations of the cell and the fidelity of splicing molecular machinery seen in all three domains of life which Walter Gilbert pointed out provides an added layer of variation of the mRNA sequence and hence the protein, the tRNA or the ribosomal RNA (Gilbert, W. (1978) *Nature*).

In this analysis, the redundancy of the code began very early in the evolution of the genetic code and was driven by the need for an unbroken transcript at a time when fewer nucleotide varieties were available compared to amino acids. It was also contributed to by the polypeptides traversing the reverse translatase decoding channel not always being within 4 Angstroms from the catalytic site.

The disparity in number between amino acids and nucleotides, the employment of the tRNA-like molecule, the increased folding of proteins with lower temperatures and as their length increased and the advent of protein-based feedback mechanisms on gene expression made reverse translation too difficult and unnecessary. The translatase probably evolved into the helicases including the AAA ATPase of the proteasome entrance and the hexameric export gate of the bacterial flagellum that threads the N-terminal end of the flagellin protein molecule through the 2nm pore of the growing flagellum for export to the growing end.

The HIN recombinase is another possible evolved progeny being as little as 21 kD in mass. If a translatase is ever discovered, then Cricks dogma would be breached; something which he himself always accepted as possible when he stated that "dogma" was a term he employed as a challenge for science to contradict. This happened when reverse transcriptase was discovered in 1970.

Limited steps in a reverse translation of dubious plausibility employing what the authors described as reverse tRNA (Arg.) have been demonstrated in experiments by M Nashimoto (2001, *J. Theor. Biol.*). The use of "reverse" tRNA, an adaptor molecule, is an optimistic possibility that was not pursued further and Nashimotos' theoretical scenario was different to that of this monologue.

The faithful deposition of pre procollagen and fibroin genes with glycine at every third or second codon respectively is achieved here when the code for nucleic acids: amino acids was 1:1 with no tRNA adaptor molecules to then morph into 2:1 after the mini tRNA evolved and 3:1 when tRNA evolved further.

These reallocations happened slowly for reasons of availability x stereochemical compatibility x survival value during the RNA archiving era and not in all molecular machines or all cells at the same time which cushioned the shock. Later following the transition to DNA archives (chapter 16), reverse transcriptase copied these codons down in the DNA archives.

The stereochemical affinity of polypeptides and polynucleotides has been demonstrated by several teams. The bases of nucleic acids are analogous to the aromatic side chains of Phenylalanine, tryptophan and Tyrosine as well as the aliphatic histidine as hydrogen bonding and base stacking partners as well as being compatible with other aliphatic peptide side chains (Brudno, Y. et al. (2010) *J. Am. Ch. Soc.*).

The fact that they Pi stack with each other in proteins was demonstrated by Wilson, K. A. et al. (2014), Kondo, J. et al. (2011), Chang, A. C. et al. (2003) and Seeman, N. C. et al. (1976) which supports the likelihood of the stereochemical era despite being conducted in standard conditions of temperature and pressure (25 deg. C, 1 ATM.) which were not representative of the Eoarchean.

The major implication of the possible existence of a translatase is that there were potentially two types of coding polymer, the polynucleotide and the polypeptide but the uniform, zip-like structure of the polynucleotides was selected for on the basis of the "easy read" involved in having the bases next to each other and facing away from the backbone of the molecule (the phosphates). The positive feedback of one coding for the other was unsustainable and unnecessary.

Nature would need to suppress a positive feedback loop involving the translatase which is exactly what it has done just as it has diminished the role and concentrations of reverse transcriptase enzymes to the point that it took until 1970 for their discovery. This suppression occurred at first by substrate limitations but were complemented later by natural selection against cells with a positive feedback loop that soaks up substrates needed for other vital reactions.

A second driver for translatase extinction was the adequacy of replicases to maintain the RNA archives once base mismatch repair enzymes and polymerase proofreading evolved.

The existence of extinct enzymes, including the translatase molecular machine of the stereochemical era, affords the only possible explanation for the extant coded formation of procollagen and fibroin (silk protein) which have glycine at every third and second residue respectively with pre procollagen also having a preponderance of proline or hydroxyproline every third amino acid. This is outlined in chapter 22 and reveals that fibroin and pre procollagen are truly ancient molecules, the latter of which permitted directed motion in multicellular animals.

The most elusive clue is the use of the -ve sense template DNA strand to produce the +ve sense strand of mRNA in order to translate proteins. These +ve sense mRNA codons represent the best stereochemical match to the proteinogenic amino acids, as was partly demonstrated by Michael Yarus.

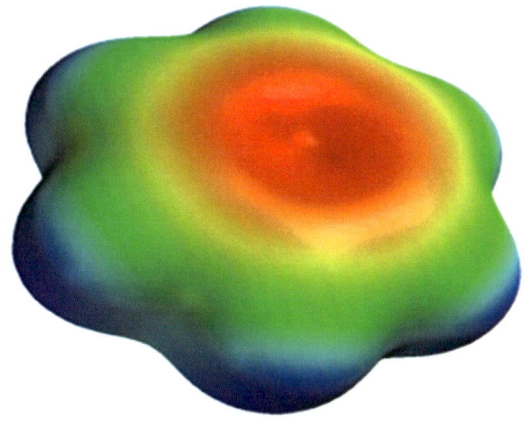

Benzene Ring Charge
BLUE +ve GREEN to RED -vwe
Hence aromatic rings can STACK by attractions between ring regions.

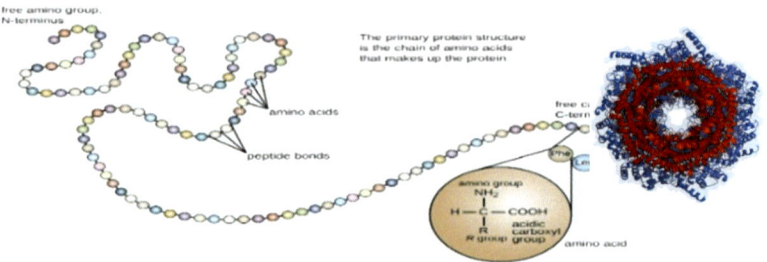

RIGHT - Entrance to Proteasome acts as Protein Helicase to unfold Proteins as does the entrance to bacterial Flagella which unwinds Flagellin Protein. LEFT - Unfolded Polypeptide

BELOW - Diagram of modified Cricks' Dogma (with Reverse Transcriptase discovered in 1970). Crick always said Dogma was a term he used as a challenge for science to modify.

Hypothetical Translatase now extinct.

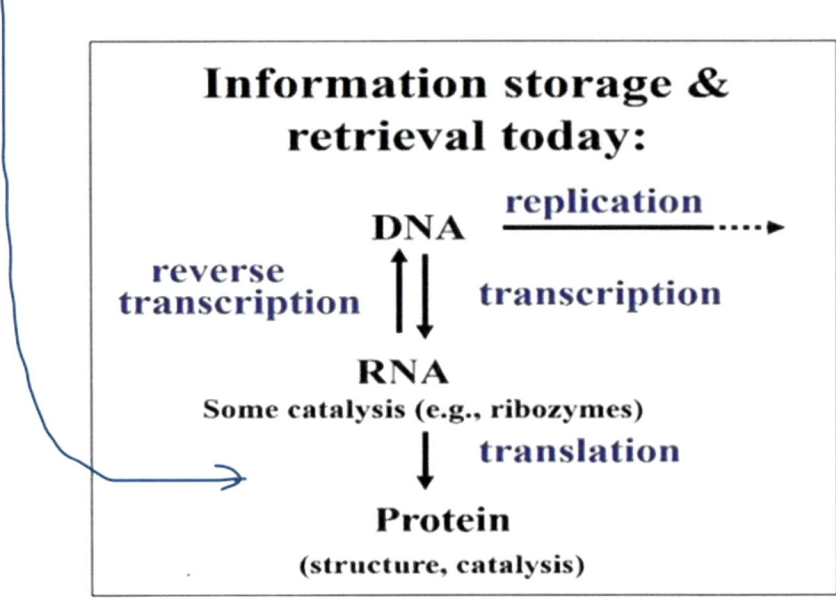

tRNAs and Their Aminoacylators

Some of the products of the protoribosome and replicases could reassemble into new protoribosomes with variations due to inaccuracy of the "wobbly" code and other multimers were better termed polynucleotide dependent polymerases since they lacked RNA.

The "code" for transcription was on a 1:1 basis for polynucleotide replication and 1:1 and/or 1:2 for translation and reverse translation regarding amino acid and nucleotide respectively so it was variable and probably much slower than today's reactions.

There were by this time, fewer proteinogenic amino acids (say 35 and reducing) and fewer nucleotides (say 10) used by biotic cells than in the protocell era so the thermodynamics and kinetics of the biochemistry had moved the situation far from chaos but nevertheless maintained it far from thermodynamic equilibrium (mechanical, thermal, chemical and radiative) as outlined by the Ilya Prigogine theory of molecular evolution. This disequilibrium is achieved by constant ingestion from and excretion into the environment.

Molecular evolution favoured cells with control mechanisms to prevent inaccuracy, oversupply and energy waste. The simplest feedback mechanism was the products of a reaction, in high concentration causing an increasing reversal of that reaction, a simple equilibrium law of chemistry that is part of Le Chateliere's principle which includes temperature, pressure and volume.

Delivery of appropriate amino acids to the catalytic site was mainly by Brownian diffusion. The replicases kept producing short chain polynucleotides if bioenergetics and substrate supplies allowed so in this scenario tRNA-like molecules would be produced. The proportion that were functional were short protogenes (kept in the open strand form by convection currents) or ribozymes.

Most often amino acids were delivered by Brownian diffusion but occasionally the tRNA-like molecules would deliver an amino acid (bound by Hydrogen bonds with the primordial overlapping tRNA section or uncatalysed covalent bonds to the 3' of the ribose phosphate [Tamura, K. and Schimmel, P.

(2004)]) to the peptidyl transferase site and peptide elongation would occur. Tamura and Schimmel demonstrated an efficient uncatalysed RNA minihelix aminoacylation and Turk and Yarus demonstrated aminoacylation with a SELEX derived 5 nucleotide C3 ribozyme derivative.

These two research accomplishments reflect a possible progression in the aminoacylation of tRNA minihelices from uncatalysed to catalysed by ribozymes and has been supported with theoretical work by Jean Lehmann et al. in 2009 (*PLoS ONE*) with simulation of self-catalysed aminoacylating RNA segments (25 nt long) producing short peptide sequences from AMP activated amino acids by aligning along a known RNA sequence.

The complex 3' acceptor stem ACC adding enzyme had not evolved yet but the 3' end could potentially be processed by RNAase ribozymes so aminoacylation was opportunistic and competed with diffusion powered amino acid delivery for polypeptide synthesis. The fragment reaction in which CCA-methionine alone can occupy the P site of the extant ribosome is evidence that this scenario is possible, effected today by the base pairing of C74 and C75 of the tRNA CCA sequence with G2252 and G2251 of the 23S ribosomal RNA. The sophistication of the extant bacterial ribosome makes this hypothesis even more plausible.

A progression from the minimal CCA is afforded in a review by Tamura K in 2015, who found that a minihelix composed of acceptor stem with ACC and T arm can be aminoacylated by aaRSs and take part in peptide bond formation by the ribosome.

Modern theories of tRNA evolution (Tamura, K., *Life (Basel)*, Dec. 2015) focus on developing a scenario that begins with the full 3 base anticodon and also point out that the great nucleobase variety on tRNA is designed by evolution to fine tune its tertiary morphology. This scenario accepts the second hypothesis but proposes the alternative possibility of a 1:1 +1 code for amino acid and nucleobase respectively, even when tRNA began to increase in length and complexity.

The second, third and even fourth base were there to be sensed but the variety of choices made the longer code impractical. Having said that, the physical presence of the anticodon loop, when it finally evolved and could consistently appose the mRNA forced a 3 base spacing of the code over a long period of time.

This means that these early mRNAs had either single amino acid-nucleotide H bonded or Pi stacked on a 1:1 or 1:2 basis or an RNA minihelix with attached amino acid delivered the amino acid with eventually only those mini helices that could hydrogen bond with the "mRNA" being able to get close enough to the PTC for their amino acid to be delivered. The PTC accepted both amino acid delivery methods for polypeptide elongation for aeons.

tRNA molecules began much smaller than the current 75 Angstrom length between the 3' amino acid end and the anticodon loop; little more than an acceptor stem. This claim is supported by phylogenetic studies that indicate that the acceptor stem of the tRNA molecule is the most ancient and conserved (Caetano-Anolles and Sun FJ. Frontiers in Genetics 9 May 2014).

Further evidence that this could work is the already mentioned observation that a CCA sequence aminoacylated with N formyl methionine can take the place of a peptidyl tRNA (Moore, P. B. and Steitz (2004) *RNA, 9(2)*). Until the aminoacylated RNAs that could adopt this role, the code was still secondary to the bulk production of catalysts and building blocks but continued to increase in importance.

Transfer RNA grew under the force of natural selection to this length as the distance between the decoding channel and the catalytic site on the protoribosome grew over many aeons. The crucial problem of maintaining a cognate relationship between the nucleobases on the anticodon loop and the amino acid at the 3' overlapping end of the tRNA molecule can only be solved by an adaptor molecule once the distance between them exceeds 4–5 Angstroms.

The first aminoacylator could have been a ribozyme that competed with a small aminoacylating enzyme for this role until the more flexible and bulky enzyme took over. The great age of such a control molecule-enzyme combination means it could evolve along with the anticodon whilst the protoribosomes competed and coevolved with the two channel metaribosomes (see below).

Class 1 aminoacyl tRNA transferase is mainly monomeric with a Rossmanoid fold and Class 2 is mainly dimeric or multimeric whilst class 1 aminoacylate the 3' hydroxyl of the Adenosines' ribose whilst class 2 aminoacylate the 2' hydroxyl. The universal transesterification reaction that places the amino acids on the 3' hydroxyl of the ribose may not have existed initially leaving the possibility open that the two systems evolved separately to accommodate two different ribosome types, the protoribosome and the metaribosome.

The different sequence homology, structures and phylogeny of bacterial aaRSs compared with archaeal-eukaryote aaRSs pointed out by Woese, C. R. et al. (*Microb and Mol Biol Rev*, 2000), can only be explained by a primordial divergence between the two prokaryote domains before the first modern cell. It is incumbent upon those who insist on a post LUCA divergence to propose the evolutionary forces that drove this late divergence. The more pertinent classification of aaRSs should be into bacterial and archaeal-eukaryote classes.

The aaRSs probably evolved from protein domains that were meant for the non-ribosomal peptide synthetases or the ribosome itself and inadvertently bound and aminoacylated small tRNAs that resembled Acetyl CoA. This poverty of substrate recognition has been improved over billions of years. The current error rate of aminoacylation before proofreading of 1 in several hundred was closer to 1:2 in the first biotic cells.

Both groups of aminoacyl transferase would have had a natural selection pressure against those that bound d-amino acids once the peptidyl transferase channel began to select for l-amino acids by virtue of a steric gate in the protoribosomes. The backup translation system, the protogene, together with variability between molecular machines would mean that errors and incompetence (e.g. "incorrect" amino acid added or aa-tRNA synthetase not long enough to span the distance between the anticodon and the amino acid end of the tRNA molecule) were not fatal to the cell.

The RNA-proteinoid world thus gradually became the RNA-protein world with the molecular machines enhancing the rate of polymer synthesis way beyond the rate of degradation provided nutrition was maintained. This rate increase put a selection pressure for enzymes that repaired RNA back to a functional state by base excision and nucleotide excision to restore functionality since it is far more parsimonious than degrading and resynthesing the whole dysfunctional molecular machine.

Together with the stereochemical preference for Watson-Crick base pairing over mismatches the code was tuned in an exclusive way to eventually have only five canonical bases A, C, G, T (ribosylthymine on RNA) and U with the subsequent evolution of mismatch repair enzymes. Today, these mismatch repair enzymes are almost exclusively focused on DNA with a couple of rRNA exceptions.

Even today, after 4 billion years of evolution, there is an error rate of approximately 1 in several hundred before proofreading in some aa-tRNA synthetases and 1:10,000 after proofreading due to the synthetase adding an incorrect amino acid to that tRNA. It is most unlikely that there was proofreading by polymerases in the Eoarchean but their products, the enzymes and ribozymes could take part in simple endonuclease and ligase functions that could be selected for.

This inaccuracy can cause disruption of translation or incorporation of the "wrong" amino acid into the peptide but can often occur without dire consequence. The extant methods of proofreading by aaRSs have been found to be 1. acylation exclusion of amino acids that are too large 2. hydrolysis of amino acids that are too small in an editing suite 20 Angstroms away by bending of the CCA-amino acid arm and 3. adenylation denial of amino acids without methyl groups by the Zn^{2+} ion (Berg, J.M. *Biochemistry*, 5th Edition).

The original cognate relationship when the molecules were small was electrostatic, just like those of polynucleotides in relation to polypeptides. The aminoacylator could also conceivably have been a ribozyme as demonstrated by M Yarus and R Turk at this early stage and was replaced later by natural selection with the protein enzyme, which had a greater variety of side chains.

The "wobbly" nature of translation today was more of a chaos in the Eoarchean and was secondary to the production of catalysts and potential control molecules on which natural selection could work.

The high error rate of translation compared to transcription at this stage could have been an added evolutionary driver for differentiation of RNA and DNA for reasons of archival stability.

Overproduction of protogenes (some of which were inactive, harmful or redundant), wasted energy thereby putting a selective pressure on the biotic cell to follow a more efficient path by the molecular evolution of more control and feedback molecules, whether RNA or polypeptide.

No sooner had a polar affinity been established between amino acids and nucleotides, it became remote with a need for tRNA to act as an adaptor to deal with the tyranny of distance (4 Angstroms) over which the hydrogen bond forces work effectively.

Any ribozymes on the replicases were eventually replaced by polypeptides with similar catalytic activity due to the greater variety of their side chains providing greater variety of catalytic possibilities but this never happened to the ribosomes due to their ability to aminoacylate a broad range of alpha l-amino acids, more than 90 (Hartman, M. C. T. et al. (2007) *PLoS ONE*), a feat neither demonstrated in an enzyme nor is it desirable in an aminoacylator or NRPS since it would define inaccuracy.

The catalytic peptidyl rate benefit of the PTC over the base amine-carboxyl ester—> peptide rate of 1/10,000 M per litre per second is x 1–10 million (Beringer, M. and Rodnina, M. V. *Molecular Cell*, 26(3), 311–21). This cannot be explained by molecule coordination and water exclusion alone and several other complex catalytic mechanisms working together are outlined by the authors, including stabilisation of the transition state and the coordination of the substrates by the molecular machines.

Yonath A and Agmon I in 2005 even mentioned the 2' hydroxyl on the terminal adenosine nucleotide of the 16s rRNA and an S1 protein in the SSU decoding channel of the ribosome. This would support the hypothesis that the small ribosomal subunit had its own PTC once. The assistance of EIF5A (and its archaeal homolog) in initiating peptidyl Transferase attests to the multifaceted nature of this catalysis and supports the hypothesis that initiation and elongation factors were once accretions on the ribosomal subunits.

The absence of a ribosomal protein within a 15 Angstrom radius of the PTC points to its strong ribozymal activity in situ, which may be enhanced by the PTC having nucleobase side chains protruding into the channel as discovered by the distinguished laboratory of GE Fox. This peptidyl Transferase activity is naturally lost when stripped of proteins in vitro or produced as a transcript for experiments, since this would affect its tertiary and quaternary structure.

Whatever length the tRNA was in the Eoarchean the use of an anticodon loop forced the length of the codon to 3 bases even if the second was a wobble base and the third a readable but unusable base. This would mean that the tRNA is one of the determinants of the length of the codon, the others being the ribosome and the aaRSs whilst the mRNA and DNA are a 1:1 template mechanism for each other and for the anticodon.

The work of Neumann, H. et al. (2010, *Nature*, (464)) in evolving a four base codon, aaRSs and tethered riboQ1 that could encode numerous "unnatural" amino acids is supportive of this hypothesis and scenario in general as is the fact that transcription or replication polymerases do not recognise Stop codons but rely on proteins, loops and single nucleotide repeat sequences to weaken and separate the double strand.

BELOW LEFT - A modern tRNA (PURPLE) bound by a modern Aminoacyl tRNA Synthetase (Blue) in contact with Anticodon Loop and Acceptor (Acc) stem.

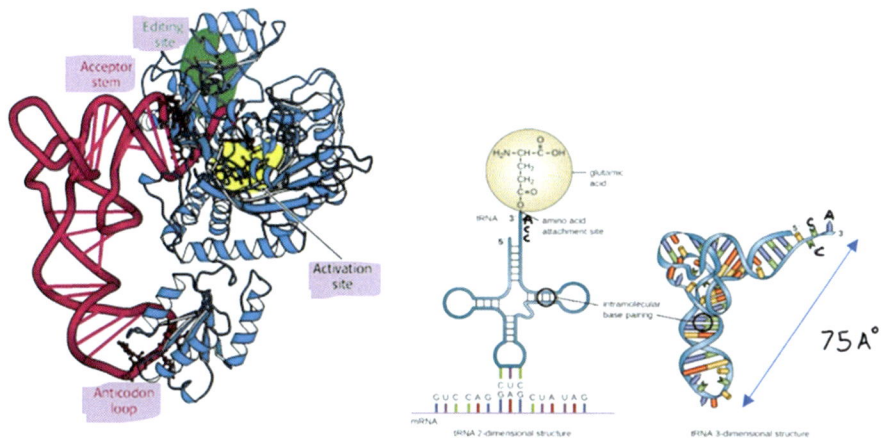

RIGHT - Micro RNA strands could resemble primordial tRNA.

BELOW - tRNA, mRNA and Ribosome depicting the mRNA start CODON AUG, the initiator tRNA-met, in the P (Peptidyl Transferase) decoding channel site. subsequent tRNAS all bind the A (Aminoacyl) site. E - exiting tRNA site.

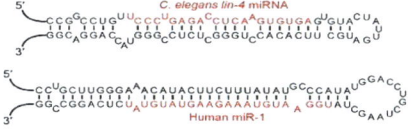

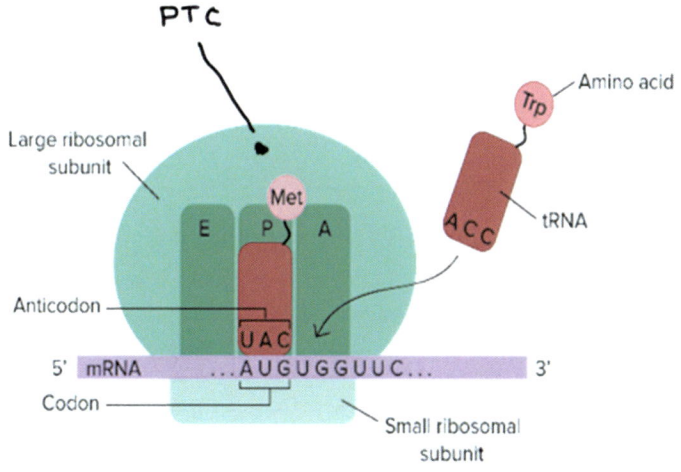

Metaribosomes and tRNA Evolution

Biotic cell life was slow until the advent of the ATP synthase and the modern cell quite late in the scenario. Even if environmental amino acids and nucleobases could be equal in variety and quantities, the problematic synthesis of nucleotides would again cause an imbalance in favour of amino acids. From life's origin, amino acids were in greater varieties, >400 amino acids compared to <300 nucleobases. In quantities by mass, at least 14:1, in favour of amino acids going by the Murchison meteorite.

Transfer RNA molecules were produced by the replicases which used primordial short RNA segments, including early tRNAs themselves as templates. Most nucleotides in cytoplasmic solution were available from the breakdown of existing polynucleotides in the biotic cell and from ingested nucleobases from the breakdown products of lysed colony members.

These were ribophosphorylated by the cells ribophosphorylase from ribose that had been produced by the pentose phosphate pathway or primitive Calvin cycles (unrelated to photosynthesis yet and which lacked the RuBisCo enzyme) to produce nucleotides.

As the protoribosomes grew in size through electrostatic bonding of more useful domains, the tRNA molecules accordingly increased in length to bridge the gap between the polynucleotide to be read and the catalytic site where the cognate polypeptide is polymerising. This "growth" took the form of selection of tRNA molecules that were the correct length and flexibility to do the job. This physical selection could transpose to a genetic selection for cells that could produce longer tRNAs that could do the job.

The structure, however, of any short RNA with a loop at one end and an overlapping section at the other end provides an ideal chemistry based platform for molecular evolution to proceed towards tRNA molecules. At the looped end of RNA strands, the bases may evert outwards to some degree in confined spaces where the hydrophobia is reduced to produce an ideal platform for chemical interaction and evolution of an anticodon, whether one or two bases long at this stage.

The D arm and anticodon loop of the tRNA in apposition to the aa-tRNA syn. and its subsequent passage through the ribosome after the aaRS detaches are confined spaces where the D loop and bases 34, 35 and 36 of the anticodon loop do evert appreciably, thereby making them "readable".

As the protoribosomes increased in size, some may have inadvertently created a second channel purely for reasons of chance molecular interaction and architecture (e.g. the open peptidyl transferase catalytic site acquired domains that covered it but allowed it to remain patent).

This phenomenon would open the way for tRNA like molecules to continue bridging the gap between the polymer in the decoding channel, mRNA and the polymer being formed in the peptidyl transferase channel (which was too small to accept mRNA), the polypeptide. This alternative system of translation, the metaribosome, competed and coevolved with the protoribosomes over millions of years and formed a platform for the continued evolution of the anticodon and codon.

The selective pressure for a two channel ribosome was the control aspect of a closed channel compared to an open one. No two-channel single bodied ribosomes exist in Nature but in the laboratory (Oreille, C. et al. (2015) *Nature*) an organelle called riboT, a tethered ribosome, has been synthesised by altering ribosomal RNA and was found to be adequately functional to maintain E Coli that were devoid of normal ribosomes alive.

This tethered ribosome would have more than a MegaDalton of mass, whereas metaribosomes may have been smaller than a viral reverse transcriptase at this stage, maybe 400 amino acids and 70 kDaltons including the polynucleotides. The small size meant that it could not achieve the "cupped hand" grip on RNA but rather allowed it to pass through the decoding channel.

Without the sophisticated coordination and rotation by the modern ribosome on inverted L.L. shaped tRNA-amino acid pairs (amino acid represented by the dots) the protoribosome and metaribosome could only work with relatively straight tRNAs (inverted I.).

What was the selective advantage of the protoribosomes increasing in size? One plausible answer is that the effects of mutation or coding error are minimised in a microorganelle compared to a smaller multimer. Lethal mutations or inaccuracies were counteracted by the control and feedback suite of modification molecules that began in the era of the protogene or else only affected the individual organelle, since the others were similar but different.

Natural selection of a Darwinian nature works at a cellular level between cells and a molecular level within cells. A second plausible answer is that the metaribosome continued to acquire and retain useful ribosomal RNA accretions and protein domains that assisted translation and prevented the two exiting strands from electrostatically bonding.

Strong evidence that this was possible is the increasing size of both large and small ribosomal subunits from mitochondrial ribosomes to the simplest prokaryotes (~2.6 MD) to single-celled eukaryotes to simple metazoans culminating in the complexity of the human ribosome of over 4 megaDaltons (Petrov, A. S. et al. 2015). This incredible variety of size has been correlated to increasing complexity; however despite this observation, K Watanabe in 2010 (*Proc Jpn Phys Biol*) found a highly conserved distance between tRNA anticodon loop and the ACC end, 75A.

This was despite a size variation of 40–50 nucleotides minimum in some mitochondrial tRNAs up to over 300 nt in the tRNA portion of tmRNA, a hybrid that serves to unblock stalled translation in bacteria. This conserved size must reflect a conserved distance in all extant ribosomes between the decoding channel and the PTC. It also reflects the physical flexibility of tRNA.

The creation of Ribo-T demonstrates the possibility of a functional two channel, single unit ribosome and has been replicated (Neumann, H. et al. (2010) *Nature*, 464) with Ribo-Q1 which was also engineered to decode 4 base codons as well as the Amber stop codon with some evolved aa-tRNA synthetases that could bind numerous "unnatural" amino acids.

This work demonstrates the ability of the ribosome to retain function following significant mutation as well as a flexibility in codon length and hints at the direction of codon evolution from shorter to longer with the aa-tRNA synthetases being capable of sensing ahead of the 2+1 anticodon. The ample size of the anticodon loop allows this flexibility but what size and shape was it in the Eoarchean.

A further example of a multi-subunit ribonucleoprotein organelle similar to a metaribosome is the eukaryotic specialised organelle, the spliceosome whose phylogeny is estimated to go back at least as far as the last eukaryotic common ancestor LECA (Collins, L. and Penny, D. 2005). The five discrete small nuclear ribonucleoproteins of the spliceosome could have once been destined for the metaribosome and have since been seconded to this new role.

Some evidence for this scenario is the similarity of sequences on the spliceosomal PRP22 protein with ATP dependent helicases and RNA binding motifs on the S1 protein of the small ribosomal subunit (Company, M. et al. (1991) *Nature*, 349).

Additionally, the biogenesis of extant ribosomes also involves the assembly of five sections, three for the large and two for the small subunit. Homology cannot plausibly be sought between these two organelles since the spliceosome has gone down a path of flexibility and variability in protein content, up to 300 different types, compared with ribosome proteins that are highly conserved within the bacteria domain or within the archaea-eukaryote domains and even more so around the PTC and decoding channel.

The possible loss of spliceosomes in prokaryotes reflects their parsimony with regards to energy, their continual deletion of selfish genetic elements by other means and their use of splicing endonucleases (archaea), self-splicing introns, group 1 (bacteria) and maturase assisted splicing introns, group 11 (bacteria, some archaea and organelles of eukaryotes) to achieve the roles of the absent spliceosome (Belfort, M. et al. 1995).

Has the prokaryotic spliceosome become extinct? Its subunits could have gone into ribosome and intron formation. How else could prokaryotes in the Archaean have improved the little fidelity their mRNAs had if not for a splicing organelle?

The inter-domain variability in the transcription termination methods and proteins suggests that the spliceosome undertook this role initially and that rho factors, poly A tails and mRNA palindromic loops with A-T rich regions that all help to cleave transcribed mRNA from the DNA template are a more recent evolution.

Logic would suggest that a control-adaptor-enzyme molecule (whether ribozyme or polypeptide) was necessary to ensure an appropriate amino acid for that anticodon loop (whether 1+1 or 2+1 bases long) was attached to the overhanging end of the tRNA-like molecule once the separation exceeded 4 Angstroms. This requirement came at a time when possible control and feedback molecules were being produced by molecular machines and were being selected for.

The CCA sequence was not a permanent feature of t-RNA at this stage and ribozyme exonucleases (primordial RNAase P) prepared the tRNA for aminoacylation. Primordial tRNA precursor molecules of the correct length that did not have the appropriate amino acid on the overlapping end and the appropriate cognate nucleobase and a "wobble" base on the anticodon at the appropriate looped end could less frequently achieve adequate proximity to the messenger polynucleotide strand being read or the peptidyl transferase site to deliver an amino acid and continued on its path away from the metaribosome.

Free floating amino acids could no longer enter the peptidyl transferase site once the genetic code became crucial and their occasional diffusion into the PTC became a rare, irrelevant event, since the molecular machinery was necessary to coordinate the substrates.

From this point on, a drop in an amino acid concentration for whatever reason would tend to cause a misacylation of that tRNA with another amino acid or a break in the translation. A prolonged diminution would therefore result in an instant archival change of that amino acids code or a Stop reassignment. This represents a second influence (the first being the replicase and nucleotide levels) on the archival code for life driven by nutrient levels and effector molecules influencing the archives.

A third influence on the code is the stress associated with not having enough tRNA isodecoders (tRNAs with the same anticodon but different body sequences) to cover the required coding task or a change in tRNA structure that inhibits aminoacylation and thereby mimics an amino acid starvation or inadequate tRNA numbers. This latter factor has been demonstrated by altering 4-thiouridine on tRNA which prevents an essential covalent bond with aaRSs and thereby prevents aminoacylation.

In modern cells, the complex feedback circuits cause a slowdown of growth and division and mRNA transcription for proteins that help deal with the stress are translated but in the primitive biotic cell these feedback controls were undeveloped and a reassignment occurred or a Stop codon was created until the negative selection pressure of having a Stop codon in the middle of a gene drives an appropriate molecular evolution. This evolution involves a backup supply of tRNAs, the suppressor tRNAs that can override a Stop codon by carrying an amino acid and an anticodon sequence that binds to a Stop codon.

The great importance of tRNA as the adaptor molecule meant it should not also double as a ribozyme since this would put a great strain on tRNA supply.

Despite the vast variety and numbers of tRNA, there is very little evidence of it doubling as a ribozyme, thereby supporting this hypothesis. Some of the large number of post transcriptional modifications may therefore have more to do with preventing ribozyme function whilst others have been shown to impart certain functions to do with aminoacylation or translation. The majority of these modifications have no identified enzyme and are most likely catalysed by non-specific acylator or methylator enzymes, thereby providing an insight into the primordial situation.

For replication and transcription fidelity, a suite of base excision repair, nucleotide excision repair and base mismatch repair enzymes almost certainly evolved from endonuclease, ligase and smaller polymerase enzymes at this time to fine tune the functionality of tRNA and archival RNA but have now transitioned to acting on DNA except for a couple that are active on nucleolar rRNA.

These RNA repair enzymes almost certainly gave rise to the inverted repeats seen today on DNA and used as phylogenetic markers or as sites of gene manipulation using Cre recombinase. RNA stem sections that had been repaired by base mismatch enzymes and polymerases to be complementary were unwound by helicase and then reverse transcribed into DNA archives following the advent of reverse transcriptase and DNA or else could be replicated to increase the RNA archive.

Inverted repeats in the era before the modern code simply consisted of any bases that would hydrogen bond with each other to avoid the looped motifs that are still evident today but were later replaced by canonical nucleobases. Gene duplications and transposition events would subsequently see these inverted repeats in more than one location.

The three factors 1. Replicase and nucleotide level effects 2. amino acid level effects and 3. Functional tRNA and aaRS levels all affect the "available concentration" part of the equation whilst the preference for Watson-Crick base pairs over non-canonical base pairs and catalytic activity of the replicase and aaRSs was the prime influence on the second part, "stereochemical compatibility".

It is reasonable to assume that the preference for Watson-Crick base pairs was initially less pronounced and needed a very long period of time to achieve the exclusivity (x1000 preference) we see today due to all the other kinetic and thermodynamic variables involved including the evolution of increasingly efficient polymerases.

In this analysis, the best explanation for the two sets of 10 aa-tRNA synthetases and two classes of ACC adding enzymes with different structure and amino acid sequence is the existence of two types of primordial ribosome, the metaribosome and the protoribosome that eventually acted synergistically when their decoding channel conveying the single-stranded polynucleotide was blocked by uncontrolled domain acquisition.

The rise of initiation factors could occur progressively over millennia due to the large number of molecular machines by this stage. Before the advent of initiation and elongation factors, the aaRS was attached to the amino acid-tRNA all the way to the protoribosome or metaribosome which then relieved it of the aaRS by a stronger complementarity of the codon-anticodon and the confined channels. The necessary implication of this possibility is that the aaRSs left the anticodon loop free to interact with the codon.

Indeed, this separation exists to this day as the EF-Tu that binds and guides tRNA to the A-site of the decoding channel do not get closer than 4 Angstroms to the anticodon. The widespread acceptance that the D loop and two D stems have highly conserved motifs within amino acid binding types (e.g. archaeal tRNA glycine) is probably a molecular fossil of this primordial era when the D loop and stems provided for the aaRSs a code initially comprising the anticodon (when tRNA was a minihelix) and later, in larger tRNAs, representing but not identical to the anticodon.

As the stereochemistry became impractical due to bulk and distance, the biotic cells with initiation and elongation factors derived from the ribosome or aaRS were selected for and the bulkier aaRSs detached after aminoacylating their tRNA. The initiation, elongation and release factors could all be domains previously accreting onto the aaRS or the ribosome. Supporting evidence comes in a review and phylogenetic analysis (by Kyrpides, N. C. and Woese, C. R. (1998) *PNAS*, USA) which found a much closer homology between the initiation factors of all three domains of life than was previously thought.

One archaeal initiation factor, IF1 and eIF2alpha had sequence homology with a bacterial ribosomal protein S1 which itself is a protein domain that is found in many RNA binding proteins. Furthermore, Sorensen H. P. et al. in IUBMB Life 2001 concluded that IF2/eIF5B are homologs whose G domain polynucleotide sequence (on the genes that encode them since the G domains are proteins) is "more credible" than SSU 16s rRNA for distinguishing strains and phylogenies of closely related species.

The original initiation factors bound to the ribosomal subunits to cause a dynamic merging with the Start tRNA and the mRNA to be translated.

It is conceivable that at some stage, in some biotic cells, protogenes coexisted with protoribosomes, metaribosomes and the modern ribosome until they all merged in a display of convergent evolution.

The scenario does not mean the three types of ribosome, proto, meta and 2-subunit used ten amino acids and ten tRNAs each. The numbers were closer to 20 each with some overlap (effected by isodecoders that were specific to each molecular machine) and diminishing with time, possibly 35 different amino acids in total. The current neat division of aaRSs into two groups of ten is inaccurate and misleading due to the presence of special aminoacylators for selenocysteine and pyrrolysine.

Phylogenetic studies of ribosomal RNA molecular evolution are consistent with these scenarios for functional ribosome evolution (Fox, G. E. (2010) *CSHPB* and Petrov, A. S. et al. (2015) *PNAS*) although the authors offer a sequential structural scenario of little explanatory value with regards to function. Petrov, A., Fox, G. E. et al. (2015) make the amazing discovery that PTC channel nucleobases extend into the channel almost certainly to contribute to the peptidyl Transferase function or folding function.

A major implication of this possible scenario is that life plodded along with two translation systems until the advent of the two subunit ribosome. Whilst protein domains produced by the two types of ribosome could aggregate by electrostatic and covalent bonds the subsequent convergence in the scenario described above would have been both a crisis and subsequently, a boon as the range of amino acids used per protein would increase, presumably with a boost in catalytic rates and varieties.

The non-ribosomal peptide synthetases continued to assemble and compete with the translating machinery for amino acid substrates, eventually acting as a supplementary system that was not limited by use of canonical amino acids or l-amino acids and was not under as much selective pressure for speed. These attributes led to the eventual extinction of NRPSs from higher eukaryotes and most archaea.

Strong evidence for repair innovations replacing lysis and resynthesis comes in the form of extant tmRNA. This tRNA-mRNA hybrid molecule is found in different forms in bacteria as well as in some protist mitochondria, some plastids including chloroplasts and bacteriophage viruses.

In E. Coli, it is 363nt long and serves to release stalled, defective mRNA by entering the A-site whilst bound to a dedicated protein SmpB and to elongation factor Tu. Its tRNA motif which is aminoacylated with alanine thence causes a resumption of translation with a GCA "resume" codon, a short 11 codon open reading frame that codes for a proteolysis marker and ends with a UAA stop codon (Janssen BD and Hayes CS 2012 APCSB 86:151–91).

This complexity has developed in bacteria before the LECA endosymbiosis event that led to the eukaryotes. Evidence for this is the finding of tmRNA genes and SmpB genes in all bacterial genomes (Keiler, K. C. and Ramadoss, N. S. (2012) *Biochimie,* 93(11)) as well as plastids and mitochondria whilst the archaea evolved a protein, the archaeal Pelota protein which is homologous to the eukaryotic Pelota protein and also to archaeal Release Factor-1.

The Pelota proteins bound to initiation factor 1A mimic a charged tRNA bound to EF-Tu in bacteria and thereby overcome a stalled translation (Kobayashi, K. et al. (2010) *PNAS*, USA) in an alternative manner. Both systems prevent the need to degrade and recycle the whole stalled ribosome.

The eukaryote forming endosymbiosis event led to the confinement of tmRNA to mitochondria and plastids, suggesting that eukaryotes and archaea retained the Pelota protein alternative method of unblocking a stalled translation. When this functional divergence occurred is a mystery other than that it was before the eukaryote domain arose.

Other similar proteins such as Dom34 in eukaryotes, bacterial RRF (ribosomal recycling factor) and a variation of aIF2 in archaea separate large and small ribosomal subunits post translation as well as during a stall thereby backing up the other stall mechanisms (Burroughs, M. A. and Aravind, L. (2019) *Int J Mol Sci*, 20(8)). The RRF of bacteria shares a domain with some aaRSs thereby supporting the hypothesis that the initiation, elongation, release and recycling factors were seconded from proteins previously accreting onto aaRSs or the ribosome.

A less explanatory alternative to the above ribosomal evolution would be a progression from the proto to the metaribosome which eventually became too large and complex to assemble fully before functional translation, resulting in subunit separation until the periodic translation event mimicked the assembly process.

The great desirability of having ample backup molecules of tRNA is reflected in the large number of isodecoders, isoacceptors and suppressor tRNAs (ones that can potentially bind Stop codons to regulate gene expression) that back each other up. This is reflected in the ten-fold number of tRNA genes compared to the minimum number of tRNAs required in eukaryotes and also in the extensive post transcriptional modifications possible (85 in total).

These facts do not mean tRNA gene sequence is unimportant. Despite the large number of post transcriptional modifications identified, the tRNAs are very conserved in their gene sequence with many crucial structure-function correlations identified. The most spectacular example of this paradox is the entirely conserved initiator tRNA (methionine) sequence in all vertebrates tested so far (Kolitz, S. E. and Lorsch, J. R. (2011) *FEBBS Lett.*, 584(2)).

This amazing fact can only be explained by a high fidelity DNA polymerase in the Cambrian in the common ancestor of all vertebrates (Picaia or Haikouicthys) ~535 Mya reflecting the need for methionine as a Start signal and that particular tRNA gene sequence for its efficient coding and aminoacylation. High fidelity proofreading backed up by mismatch repair enzymes and efficient splicing in the form of a spliceosome was also required to arrive at this amazing outcome.

It also means DNA base excision, nucleotide excision and mismatch repair mechanisms, including repair DNA pols. were present at this stage, having evolved from those acting on RNA. A less likely scenario is that reverse transcriptase was still prominent at this stage and reverse transcribed a "perfect" initiator tRNA which was retained by the processes outlined above, driven by molecular natural selection pressures.

This finding emphasises the central role of tRNA as the adaptor molecule but the fact remains that variability and hence flexibility is restored by nature providing several different tRNA isodecoders and isoacceptors for most amino acids as well as the suite of suppressor tRNAs and the post transcriptional modifications (85 in total are available). The tRNA genes for serine in humans numbers 28 and produces 21 different tRNA sequences (Geslain R and Pan T J Mol Biol 2010) so each of its 6 isoacceptors (with anticodons AGU AGC UCC UCA UCG UCU) has 3 or 4 isodecoders (with different body nucleotide sequence).

Mitochondria that have only one gene per tRNA, 22 in number, are subject to pathology when mutations occur in these genes since there is no backup. They already employ extreme wobble at the wobble base, almost invariably U, to cope with the minimal tRNA number.

Diagram of a MODERN 2 SUBUNIT RIBOSOME with mRNA, 3 tRNA and a growing Polypeptide exiting the Peptidyl Transferase Channel (PTC). In this state it resembles the 2 channel Metaribosome which did not separate into 2 when translation ended. E- Exiting P- Peptidyl Transferase. A- Aminoacyl.

The current decoding channel took over this role when the Proto and Metaribosome decoding channels became blocked by accretions. Initiator tRNA-methionine (with ANTICODON UAC) binding an AUG mRNA start CODON then took over translation initiation along with initiation factor(s). This is the best explanation for the 2 sets of 10 Aminoacyl tRNAsynth.

The PTC entrance is at least 75 a^0 (7500 picometres) from the decoding channel entrance. release factors have similar shapes and dimensions to tRNA and compete with them for the a site where they terminate translation by hydrolysing the last tRNA-Peptide bond.

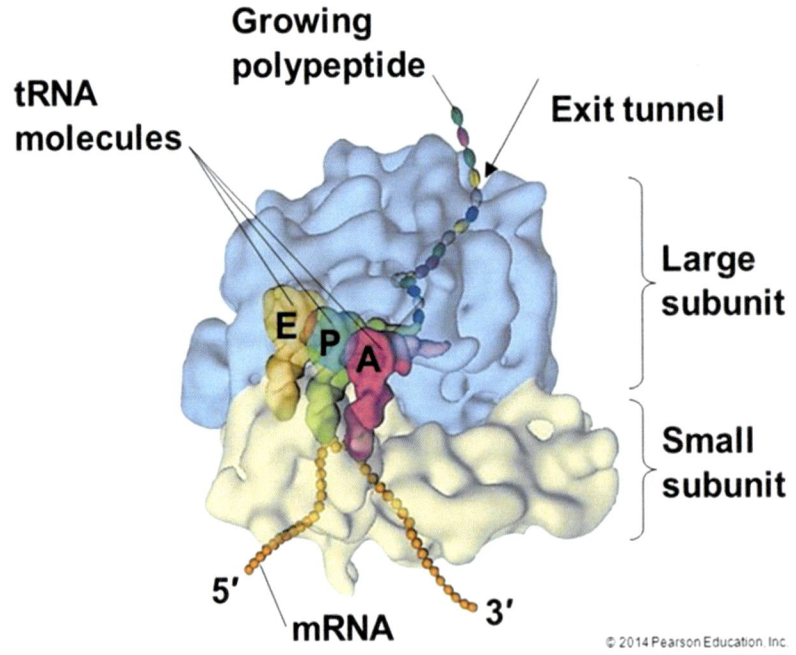

Specialising into DNA and RNA

Protocells always had some ribose reduction activity available from the action of the Sun (UV light component) and Hydrogen Sulfide in the presence of Copper(1)Cyanate (Ritson and Sutherland (2014) *J. Mol. Evol.*, 78, 245–50). An even simpler pathway to deoxyribose was by a sugar dehydration caused by transient high sulfuric acid concentrations which is most plausible in the Eoarchean. The H_2SO_4 would dehydrate ribose to Furfural with the reverse reaction sometimes incomplete in restoring both hydroxyl groups on C2 and C3.

Additionally, hydroborides, Formic acid, hydrogen and glucose are all powerful reducing agents. By the time of modern cells that could potentially contain some DNA then some molecules like NADH and NADPH would be available from salvage and inter conversion pathways to act as powerful reducing agents.

Previously, this could have been occurring on ribose molecules in the cytosol. A few deoxyribonucleotides, however, do not make DNA as we know it. A promiscuous, non-specific reductase in protocells could eventually evolve into a more specialised reductase of ferritin, ferredoxin, thioredoxin or glutaredoxin origin and were themselves reduced by the photochemical reductase effect of H_2S or, more recently, NADPH as larger genomes became an advantage.

Some small evidence for this origin is the Fe^{2+} ions in the catalytic domain of the ribonucleotide reductase and the importance of cobalamin cofactor in thymidylate synthase (dUMP to dTMP) as well as Cysteine and Tyrosine residues to its thiyl (S.) free radical generating function.

Following reduction of NTP's ribonucleotide reductase is now reduced by thioredoxin which itself is reduced by NADPH. Extant thioredoxin is a small oxidoreductase that has a close association with DNA as it acts as a sliding clamp loader in some Megavirus DNA polymerases to increase their processivity-i.e. rate of catalytic step execution (Bedford, E. et al. (1997) *PNAS*, 94(2), 479–84).

A review into the phylogenetics of the 3 classes of ribonucleotide reductase suggested an "unspecific H atom abstraction method" for the earliest reductase that later formed a dimer with "independent radical generation". This radical is almost universally a thiyl group formed on the cysteine. The dimer then evolved into the 4 modern classes of RNR (Lundin, D et al. Life 2015) that require cobalamin and/or Fe^{2+}-Fe^{3+}, Mn-Mn or Fe^{2+}-Mn^{2+} double ions as cofactors.

Logically, the extant ferritin phylogeny of ribonucleotide reductase is apparent in the use of iron ions. It is doubtful that a phylogenetic study based on the modern code could go back in time far enough to be accurate for a biotic cell whose code was still evolving. The group of reductase that require adenosylcobalamin must have arisen latest due to the sophisticated synthesis of this cofactor. Parallel with a function in metabolism, the reduced nucleotides could be incorporated into polynucleotides.

An alternative possible molecular origin of the RNRs is the superoxide dismutase group of oxidoreductases that may have evolved early in evolution to protect the biotic cells from free radicals generated during minor oxygenation events triggered by reaction of large quantities of K_2MnO_4 with boiling water or TiO_2 in UV light with water.

A phylogenetic study of dismutase enzymes concludes an age measured in billions of years – "some of the original enzymes found in primitive life" – but probably starting in the great oxygenation event more than 2 Gya (Case, A. J. (2017) *Antioxidants*), if the billions of years cannot be specified then 3.60Gya is as likely a figure as 2.40 Gya.

A recent research article has elucidated a RNR of Class 1e in some pathogens (Aerococcus uriosis expressed in E. Coli) derived from tyrosine to form an ion independent dihydroxyphenylalanine free radical generating mechanism that still required a flavoprotein activase to provide the superoxide from O_2 (Blaesi, E. J. et al. *PNAS*, USA, 115(40), 10022–27). This would tend to support the superoxide dismutase origin hypothesis or it could be a modern evolution.

Common sense would suggest the NTP reductase preceded the DNA polymerase or reverse transcriptase in order for there to be reduced NTPs in adequate concentration for the polymerase to select. Necessity dictates that it is now a highly conserved enzyme across all three domains of life and it is the rate limiting catalytic step in dNTP de novo synthesis.

Despite this conservation across the three domains, the levels of rNTPs exceed the dNTPs by approximately 36-190 fold, leading to extant rNTP misincorporation surpassing all other DNA lesions in frequency (Ganai, R. A. and Johansson, E. (2016) *Molecular Cell*). Conversely, high dNTP levels due to a shift in equilibrium by the use of non-canonical NTP's would result in misincorporations in both DNA and RNA.

It could be inferred that the three classes of ribonucleotide reductase are an example of convergent functional evolution from diverse ancient oxidoreductases that have continued to diverge in their morphology, oxygen sensitivity and mode of thiyl free radical generation past the era of reverse transcriptase into the era of DNA polymerases. This is consistent with a primordial divergence of archaea and bacteria.

Proofreading of rNTPs by the DNA pol. 3'-5' exonuclease is inefficient but nature has had time to evolve extra repair mechanisms such as RNAaseH2 and topoisomerase 1 from the era preceding DNA, the RNA-Protein world. The use of topo.1 in this fashion hints that this enzyme group may have been an ancient RNA endonuclease-ligase only to have evolved into the topoisomerase with an untangling function or repair as the DNA strands got longer and tangled.

Some evidence for the great age of DNA polymerase comes in a 2014 phylogenetic study that places the origin of mammalian and yeast DNA polymerase X in a common ancestor of two bacillus species, including B subtilus (Bienstock, R. J. et al. 2014). The Bienstock article is specific for one class of DNA pol. and does not illuminate the evolutionary path far enough into the past for one to infer an origin.

Reverse transcriptase and RNA pols. are homologous to flaviviral reverse transcriptase and ancient RNA pols. Being a type of selfish genetic element, these viruses got their RNA pol. genes from primordial biotic cells. This reflects the more recent advent of DNA dependent DNA polymerase and that reverse transcriptase was likely the first DNA polymerase.

Concurrent to the evolution of the reductase was the evolution of folate, a cofactor necessary for thymidylate synthase to catalyse the synthesis of dTMP from dUMP. The use of Thymidine in DNA was a backup to the use of reduced ribose nucleotides and evolved gradually. The para amino benzoic acid portion of folate (vitamin B9) came from the Shikimate pathway, the Pterin from GTP reactions and the polyglutamate from glutamate amino acid.

If cyanocobalamin (vit B12) was evolved by this stage as an offshoot of chlorophyll or heme-biosynthesis (both being Tetrapyrroles) then the synchronous cofactor facilitation of methionine biosynthesis from homocysteine would round out the cyanocobalamin (B12) cofactor facilitation of tetrahydrofolate (vit. B9) synthesis from folate. This interdependent series of reactions occurred late in the evolution of the biotic cell, reinforcing the likelihood of RNA dominated coding previously.

Those cells with the polynucleotide reductase could store more genetic information by concentrating their polymers in stable double helices composed of an increasing proportion of deoxynucleotides whose hydrolysis rates were much lower than RNA. This teleological argument outlines the evolutionary driver for DNA being selected but one needs to ask how it came about.

In this scenario, the advent of polynucleotides with either DNA or RNA content only arose at the very end of the primordial biotic cells' evolution, after the advent of the 2+1 base codon, the start and stop codons, dedicated nucleotide reductase enzymes and finally came about by the action of more sophisticated polymerases that could distinguish between reduced NTPs and NTPs in the cytoplasm and dTMP from dUMP.

The enormous size of a viral T7 phage reverse transcriptase, 882 amino acids is testament to this complexity with the smallest efficient DNA polymerase of bacteriophage PRD1 being 553 amino acid residues long (G. Jung PNAS Vol. 84 Biochem. 1987) whilst the smallest nucleotide polymerase known is a base excision repair DNA pol. X of the African Swine Fever Virus at 20 kiloDaltons or about 182 amino acids are long and have extremely low fidelity (Maciejewski M W et al. (2001) *Nature Structural Biology*, 8, 936–41).

Baogen Duan et al. (2012) induced an acquisition of DNA polymerase activity with a single mutation of Tyr639 (to Phenylalanine) of a phage T7 RNA polymerase. Investigation of the mechanism of this change revealed Phen639 destabilised the active site, thereby allowing non-cognant NTPs to bind and for translocation to occur.

Another extant example of a reverse transcriptase that can produce a DNA strand from either RNA or DNA template is afforded by the HIV reverse transcriptase that reverse transcribes the HIV RNA strand and then polymerises a template on that DNA strand after using its nuclease to break down the HIV RNA strand.

Biotic cells that coded for these specialised nucleotide polymerases were selected for due to the benefit of task segregation and specialisation. With the evolution of protein polymerases that could discriminate between the two types of nucleotide triphosphate, some RNA polymers were now reverse transcribed to ssDNA with a consequent separation of the two types of nucleotide polymer over millions of years by molecular evolution favouring DNA as an archive of what the cell needed due to its stability and RNA as a messenger and control molecule due to its flexibility.

The 10 fold rate advantage of non-enzymatic RNA polymerisation was inconsequential before polymerase enzymes evolved, balanced by the far greater stability of the DNA backbone.

In this analysis, it took millions of years for the biotic cell to evolve the specialised polymer with an affinity for reduced ribose NTP's and exclusive use of dTMP as one of its archiving molecules. It is plausible that as the two polymers, RNA and DNA were coevolving natural selection favoured those cells whose polymerases could distinguish dNTPs from NTPs and UTP from dTTP until by the time of the modern cell with binary fission and 1000 genes DNA polymerases evolved from the many types of evolved reverse transcriptase.

Nobody can infer exactly when this occurred, most likely following the end of the Late Heavy Bombardment and sporadic giant meteorite strikes up to 3Gya.

During the segregation aeons base excision repair enzymes, nucleotide excision repair enzymes and mismatch repair enzymes including polymerases initially acted on RNA and later transitioned to DNA when that archiving became entrenched. Even today, a couple of mismatch repair enzymes work on ribosomal RNA.

Some replicases could act on DNA to start the DNA dependent RNA polymerases, which eventually superseded the replicases in mRNA production. RNA Replicases themselves are diminished to the point that they are only found today in viruses and eukaryotic organelles.

It is highly likely that ancient reverse transcriptase produced a hybrid molecule that conferred increasing backbone stability over millennia until the steric gate was eventually tuned almost to perfection to produce DNA. The ssDNA would pass through the RTase a second time to produce the second strand and thus dsDNA. This phenomenon is observed now in HIV replication.

Without advanced control and feedback mechanisms, gene polyploidy was the norm so that upon budding the biotic cells had enough genes and molecular machines to survive. The uncertainty of this outcome drove increased controls, including the ligation of DNA genes to produce long chromatin strands and the ParM actin homolog that attaches to plasmids and elongates to push them to opposite sides of a dividing or budding cell.

The fact that some extant helicases act as passive ratchets powered by Brownian diffusion upon finding a partly separated double polynucleotide helix encourages one to think that a multimer of polypeptides could have achieved this function from early in the evolution of double stranded polynucleotides and probably preceded the helicases that were powered by ATP.

The archives were consolidated before the specialisation of DNA from RNA but the reassignments could continue into the DNA-RNA-Protein world since the new codons do not always need to be reverse transcribed anyway-half of the reassignment was happening at the aa-tRNAs-tRNA interface in what is now known as "translational recoding", an error which can become a permanent reassignment if cognant amino acid levels fall too low or rise too high for too long.

These reassignments were in addition to any reassignment by the replicases and DNA polymerases due to depletion of their usual substrates resulting in what would today seem like a mistake, a fidelity issue whereas in its early evolution these "non-natural" incorporations into the code were variations that molecular selection could work on to take a certain pathway towards the universal code.

In this period, however, the "RNA" was a polynucleotide with more than four bases (as it is today due to post transcriptional modifications) and some nucleotides in it were reduced (as in a primer) and the reverse transcriptase had to match the RNA bases it read with a canonical reduced base (A, C, G, T) or whatever else was available, stereochemical and functional. The polymerases did not all achieve specificity for NTPs or dNTPs at once so the possibility that reverse transcriptase was the first to acquire this "steric gate" is plausible but, nevertheless, a convenient teleological argument.

Some circumstantial evidence for this possibility is the existence of the retroviruses that use reverse transcriptase and integrase to insinuate their RNA strands into the DNA archives of cells where they are then expressed as if they were host genes and the work of Gerald F Joyce and B Samanta who evolved a ribozyme reverse transcriptase that can catalyse DNA synthesis by adding up to 32 dNTPs to an RNA template-primer complex at a rate of 2 per minute (Samanta, B. and Joyce, G. F. (2017) *eLige*, 6:e31153.2017). This RNA reverse transcriptase required a primer and laboratory evolution of RNA segments all seemingly designed to prove the existence of the RNA world.

Additionally, the presence of minuscule amounts of reverse transcriptase in the telomerase and retrotransposon enzymes of most eukaryotic cells and in type

11 intron maturase of bacteria may suggest they are a molecular fossil from a time when reverse transcriptase was an even more significant part of a biotic cell, acting upon short RNA fragments to produce short DNA fragments.

A review into the phylogenetics of reverse transcriptase found a dual origin with intron type11 RT (part of the maturase enzyme), telomerase and flavivirus RNA dep. DNA pol being homologous whilst retroviral RT was of a different sequence and structural phylogeny (Zhao, C. and Pyle, A. M. 2017). This hints at a possible primordial evolution of reverse transcriptase from simple RNA replicases that acted on short polynucleotides.

Indeed, the structural similarity of HIV reverse transcriptase and poliovirus RNA dependent RNA polymerase is striking. Both have the "cupped hand" shape with the replicase being 461 residues long and 53 kDa (Hansen JL et al. (1977) Structure 5(8) while the RT is more than twice as large, 117 kDa attributable to the additional nuclease domain of the RT and the self-evident progression from smaller to larger enzymes with time and increased sophistication.

This progression could only have happened in the host cells that had the nutrition and anabolic chemical pathways with feedback controls that permitted this evolution to occur.

Until the DNA archive was laid down the archival polynucleotide and the transcribed polynucleotide that was to then be translated were one and the same, RNA and they were short. Following significant segregation of RNA and DNA Cricks dogma was reinforced but nature had to deal with the mRNA being both translatable to produce protein enzymes or building blocks and also reverse transcribable to produce a potential positive feedback loop and an excess of DNA.

The need to suppress this outcome hints at the reason why reverse transcriptase is ubiquitous but in minuscule amounts and in limited roles and has been superseded by DNA polymerases which are controlled in their function partly by histones coiling the DNA into nucleosomes. The acquisition of mitochondria that now facilitate energy buffering via ATP in eukaryotes made the production and maintenance of their huge archives possible. The consequences of high telomerase and reverse transcriptase levels are evidenced in the immortal and fast growing HeLa tumour cell line.

Having touched on the similarity of action between retroviruses and retrotransposons there is debate amongst scientists which came first and how they were derived. Both require the integrase enzymes to incorporate themselves into the target DNA so it is plausible that they have a common ancestor molecule before DNA-RNA differentiation.

Retroviruses are also an example of molecular evolution in another way; even though they comprise a few per cent of the human DNA (2–4x more than protein-coding genes) only a couple are still active by being essential for the host.

Amazingly in humans, this gene HERV-1 codes for syncytin 1, a retrovirus capsid protein, which is crucial in maintaining an immunological barrier in the placenta between the foetus and the mother by inducing a merging of cell membranes of the cytotrophoblast cells to form a syncytium, the syncytiotrophoblast, an enormous fused polynucleate structure (like a cling wrap filter between the placenta, which is part of the foetus and the uterine endometrium, which is part of the mother) that cannot be penetrated by the mothers' killer T cells since they only travel in spaces between cells.

The known exchange of some cells between mother and foetus does not negate this finding since quantities and replication rates are most important and the significance of the exchange has not been elucidated.

Even though the amount of reverse transcriptase in somatic cells is small, the telomerase enzyme itself in humans is composed of 1182 amino acids which reflects the complexity required to perform this task.

The ss DNA would pass through the reverse transcriptase a second time to produce dsDNA (as does the extant HIV virus rev. transcriptase) to form an archive of biotic cell genotype that was more stable than RNA.

Being lost by altering a single catalytic residue the sophistication of an enzyme or ribozyme that can discriminate between NTPs and dNTPs means that DNA was present very late in the biotic cells' evolutionary scenario, by which time passive helicases could allow access to the codes in the double helix strands and metabolic cycles-nutrient acquisition systems, especially a folate analogue and a competent one carbon metabolism that provides dTMP, glycine and methionine to the point that adequate methionine levels reflect the health of the cells' one carbon metabolism. Proofreading and DNA repair had become more established by this stage.

The supremacy of specific nucleotide sequence-protein control and feedback molecule pairings is highlighted in the replication of Cadang Cadang coconut viroid RNA by DNA dependent RNA pol11 in coconut plant eukaryotes. How is a specialised, complex transcribing polymerase exapted into this replicase role by such a minimal (246–7 rNTP) polynucleotide entity? The rod like secondary shape of the viroid contributes to this phenomenon. (Steiger, G. and Riesner, D. (2018) *Nucleic Acids Research*).

Primers and primase may be relics of this early RNA polymerase world before the reductase enzyme could adequately raise dNTP levels and reverse transcriptase became entrenched as the DNA pol. of that era so that an occasional dNTP would be in the primer but not many. The whole need for a primer may have arisen from the progressive reduction in nucleotide varieties following the advent of the protogene and subsequently the polymerases.

This may have driven the need for a primer as a guide to the ancient reverse transcriptases which would have taken the form of natural selection against those cells with DNA polymerases that did not have a recognition sequence for that primer. There has not been any selective advantage to replace something complicated that is working well other than to have a more evolved DNA polymerase take over after a few (11–30) NTPs and dNTPs have been laid down as a primer.

The plausibility of this scenario is supported by human mitochondrial RNA polymerase, a single subunit enzyme that is encoded in nuclear DNA, that acts as a helicase and primase during mitochondrial DNA replication whereas its usual role is in transcribing mitochondrial DNA genes into mRNA (Arnold JJ et al (2012). Biochimie Biophys Acta. 1819 (9-10): 930-938).

This non-specific use of dNTPs and rNTPs by primase may reflect that it is an ancient polymerase probably derived from ancient RNA replicases. This has been supported by phylogenetic studies which relate the primases to repair polymerases and plasmid replicases (Guilliam, T. A. et al. (2015) *Nucleic Acids Res.*, 43(14)).

The authors attribute the poor selectivity of the primases for dNTPs or rNTPs as the price to be paid for their extreme physical flexibility. This scenario is supported by the molecular weight of the bacterial primase DnaG, 60 kDa, that is larger than poliovirus replicase but smaller than HIV reverse transcriptase with the RNA polymerase domain of this 3-domain primase monomer not only smaller than the poliovirus RNA pol. but lacking the "cupped hand" shape in favour of a helicase morphology.

The phylogeny of archaean-eukaryote primases is distinct from that of bacteria (Guilliam, T. A. et al. 2015) thereby supporting a primordial divergence hypothesis.

The sharing of classes of DNA pol. between bacteria and archaea points to a shared origin from reverse transcriptase at approximately the time of the fully functional modern cell which in this scenario had to have occurred by 3.0–3.5G years ago in order to defeat dilution and degradation and to compete for limited resources with other biotic cells with variant chemical systems.

RNA replicases originated from the primordial replicase described in Chapter 12 as they acquired second channels with Mg2+ metal cations and became unable to maintain the helicase form, evolving into the iconic "cupped hand" shape, all of which whether single subunit or multi subunit have a large and small aperture in their structure.

This scenario is hinted at in the morphological progression from human respiratory syncytial virus RNA replicase which is of this helicase form with a central channel exceeding 15 Angstroms to the Hepatitis C RNA polymerase that appears closer to a cupped hand (Sesmero, E. and Thorpe, I. F. (2015) *Viruses*, 7(7)) to the poliovirus RNA replicase that has the distinctive "cupped hand" shape. The binding of Qbeta phage replicase with the bacterial host EF-Tu and EF-Ts before functionality to form a helicase shaped molecule supports this hypothesis (Kidmose, R. T. et al. (2010) *PNAS*, USA, 107(24)).

Between the time of our biotic cell and the modern cell of 1000 or more genes, the DNA dep. RNA polymerases acquired the twin double psi beta barrel motifs and the sandwich barrel hybrid motif that all three domains of life possess with the highly conserved catalytic core comprising two Mg2+ ions and a conserved amino acid sequence (aspartic acid-bulky amino acid e.g. phenylalanine-aspartic acid-glycine-aspartic acid) between the two DPBB. This hypothesis is supported by the absence of these motifs in the T7 (E Coli) phage DNA dependent RNA polymerase and human mitochondrial single subunit replicases.

This points more towards convergent evolution and accurate splicing events driven by the catalytic efficacy of this sequence over time rather than an indication that it was evolved in a common ancestor of the three domains of life.

Despite the cupped hand shape when viewed in the PDB archives in complex with the double-stranded polynucleotide they are replicating or transcribing the polynucleotide is not "gripped" by the cupped hand of these ancient replicases but passes from the "thumb" to the "fingers" across the "palm", thereby entering and leaving the polymerase from available molecular pores.

The DNA dependent DNA polymerases are a large group of enzymes across the three domains of life. They evolved from around the time of the modern cell (despite DNA being already present from the advent of reverse transcriptase) from reverse transcriptase and maintain their own double psi beta barrel and conserved catalytic sequence motifs dependent on aspartate.

The large number of DNA dependent DNA polymerase classes and specialities defies a simplistic origins statement but with reverse transcriptase having a nuclease domain and a cupped hand polymerase domain, it defies credulity that DNA dependent DNA pol. did not evolve by an imperceptibly small mutation from reverse transcriptase (which themselves had evolved from replicase) to be followed by variable evolutionary associations with other proteins of various origins in the multi-subunit holoenzyme.

This origin from reverse transcriptase affords a second reason for the decline in RT prominence to that of the need to suppress the positive feedback loop RNA—>DNA—> RNA, namely that its role was superseded by DNA polymerase when there was enough of a DNA archive with some diploidy or polyploidy.

The RNA Pol11 has both a cupped hand shape as well as two large channels, the smaller of which allows NTPs to enter for RNA polymerisation. Could these channels be the ancient decoding and catalytic channels of the translatase or replicase?

The idea that DNA polymerase can only add to a primer strand is a justifiable observation of the vast majority of situations but a generalisation that is falsified by a recent article which has reported that an ancient family of primer independent Family B DNA polymerases of good efficiency that are coded for on mobile genetic elements (such as mitochondrial plasmids) exist in some bacteria and mitochondria. Their current role is mainly in DNA repair (Redrejo-Rodriguez, M. et al. (2017) *Cell Rep.*), but they are capable of proofreading, strand dissociation and template dependent DNA polymerase activity.

Furthermore, some of these polymerases of phage virus origin use a protein primer. The proteobacterial lineage in which they were found is estimated to be more than 2 billion years old. This is good evidence that primers were not needed in the protocell or early biotic cells but arose later.

Alternatively, it could signify an evolved loss of the need for primers in these specific bacterial replication processes due to the shortness of the transcript. A further case of a primer independent DNA polymerase is a mutant T7 RNA polymerase, Phe639 in place of Tyr639, that can use RNA or DNA templates and NTPs or dNTPs depending on what is available (Sousa R and Padilla R 1995 EMBO J).

In either case, this evidence points to the polymerase as being the determinant of whether a primer is needed, not the DNA itself and the absence of primer use by many RNA polymerases points to the advent of primase long after the advent of templated polymerisation possibly for reasons of speed (efficacy). Even tRNA can be used as a primer that binds the primer binding site (PBS) of retro-viral RNA to prime the reverse transcription of an RNA gene into a DNA gene.

This observation has led to a nomenclature of endogenous retroviruses based on tRNA amino acid binding type and hints at a time in the Eoarchean when a variety of molecules could have bound a PBS to initiate reverse transcription.

The production of useless mRNA or DNA fragments was a feature that would constitute a negative selection pressure due to the waste of energy and the consequent need to recycle the substrates. Fully evolved Topoisomerase did not exist yet meaning the DNA could only unwind enough to make short mRNA, ssDNA or tRNA molecules and in any case DNA was rather short and less compact since the histones were yet to evolve.

A phylogenetic study by Forterre, P. et al. in 2007 Biochimie found topoisomerase to have appeared early in the formation of the DNA world with the several families and two types to have originated independently. As DNA lengthened and tangled, the biotic cell had endonucleases and ligases on hand to employ in "snip and ligate" function that topoisomerase represents. The sharing of homologous subunits or modules, according to the author, reflects an age when function was a more discrete entity of much smaller sized proteins.

Type 1B topoisomerase are "distant relatives of Tyrosine recombinases and telomere resolvases that share a fold and catalytic chemistry despite sequence divergence". (Escudero, J. A. et al. (2016) *Nature Communications*)

These extant enzymes were most likely all derived from ancient endonucleases and ligases that competed and coevolved with ribozymes of the same function until they cooperated in some cases as ribonucleoproteins. Nature favoured those cells in which these enzymes performed useful functions such as deletion of deleterious genes or duplication and retention of favourable genes.

Thus, what we now see as specialised DNA splicing endonucleases were almost certainly derived from ribozymes and enzymes that did the same to RNA before the advent of DNA and some of these enzymes evolved into topoisomerase and gyrase, which prevented entanglement of DNA. Molecular fossils of controlled RNA editing are represented by prokaryotic introns, type 1 and 11, with eukaryotes being represented by the spliceosome.

Okazaki fragments could not be formed reliably yet as it was difficult enough to replicate one strand at a time. Despite this, either of the two DNA strands could be transcribed or replicated resulting in eventual suppression of transcription of the coding strand (the complementary template strand is now transcribed) for reasons of parsimony but genes can exist on either strand of DNA upstream of a promoter region.

For replication, there was an evolution towards the synchronous Okazaki fragment replication system for reasons of efficiency and parsimony.

Double stranded DNA could not enter the 2 channel metaribosome because it lacked a helicase and was too wide but the non-specific polymerases could transcribe dsDNA (that had been unzipped by passive helicase) into a messenger RNA strand to be translated by the metaribosome or function as tRNA and other non-specific replicases simply copied tRNA-like molecules or feedback control type molecules directly.

This process began by Brownian diffusion powering helicase ratchets that used temperature or chemically induced openings in the double helix to continue separating the strands. The rate of polymerisation of polynucleotides or polypeptides would be slow, ATP independent and conceivably were prone to interruption or pause for a multitude of reasons, including inadequate substrates or energy.

A polymerase attached to the passive helicase would render ATP unnecessary since its motion would be powered by Brownian diffusion and one needs to be mindful that ATP is not needed in polymerase chain reactions in vitro. The mRNA forming Polymerases worked on both RNA and DNA until the stability of DNA and the negative selection pressures of maintaining two archiving systems caused a gradual transition to transcription by DNA dependent RNA polymerase.

During the differentiation aeons the primordial promoters and suppressor binding operator regions had to exist on both DNA and RNA but have transitioned by natural selection of modern cells that used reverse transcriptase to transfer these sequences to the archival DNA. The presence of riboswitches in prokaryotic mRNA reflects that an ancient system that works well can be retained indefinitely.

TOP - Simplified diagram of DNA depicted as a double helix with a major and minor groove and RNA depicted as a single strand containing Uracil instead of Thymine and which folds back on itself. William Thomas Astbury in a 1946 Cambridge Conference reported an identical distance between DNA Nucleotides in DNA and Amino Acids in unfolded Proteins and predicted "A stereochemical relation of deepest significance".

BOTTOM - Single strand Protein - Primary structure. Easy to imagine RNA-Protein H bonding-templating in this unfolded state.

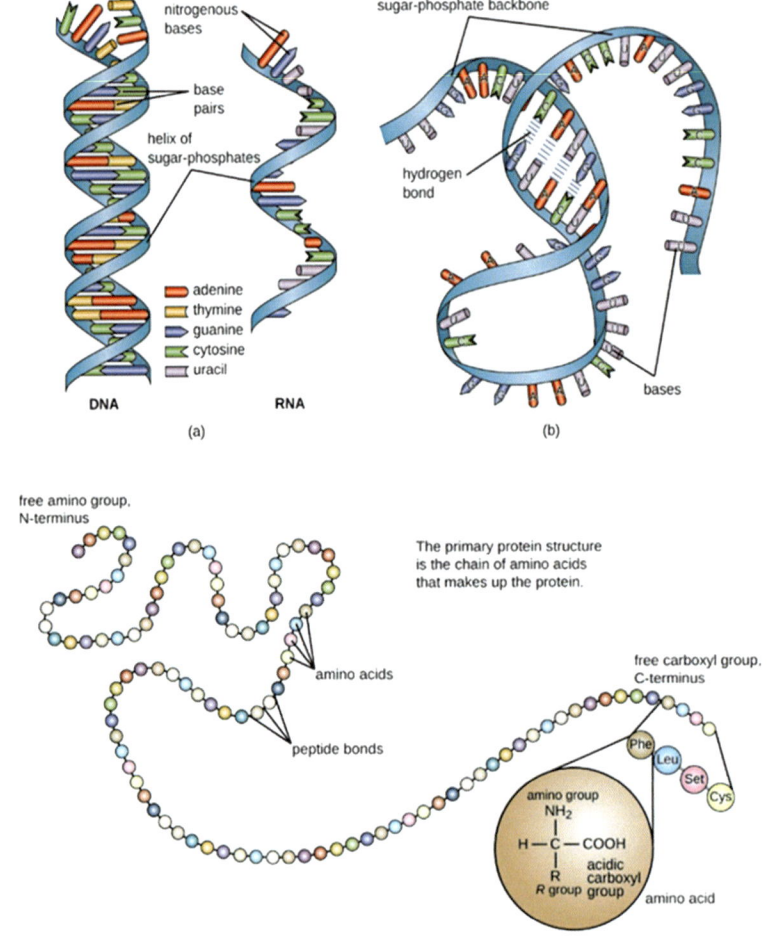

Need for Start and Stop Codons

The existence and effectiveness of the Shine-Dalgarno (UAAGGAGGU) sequence on prokaryotic mRNA and its complementary sequence (AUUCCUCCA) on the 16s rRNA of the small ribosomal subunit points to this type of recognition sequence being first recognised by the replicases even before a Start codon existed, driven by Coulomb's law embodied in H bonding. The extant variability in the Shine-Dalgarno sequence in prokaryotes and its absence in some prokaryotes and all eukaryotes suggests that a variation of it may have attracted the first polymerases on RNA.

Most likely, the primordial transcription initiation sequence was a variation of the SD sequence that improved fidelity of translation and hence survival and division rates long before molecular natural selection of the first Start codon and amino acid. Some evidence for this possibility is the Kozak sequence (5'-GCCACCAUGG-3') that has evolved in some eukaryotes to facilitate this function as well as the greatly enhanced binding affinity of polymerases to certain RNA or DNA sequences, for example, an origin of replication initiation (ORI) sequence.

The Kozak sequence actually has the AUG start codon in the sequence, unlike the SD sequence which is found in the 5' untranslated region of prokaryotic mRNA which comes before the Start codon. This would suggest the longer sequence is more essential to reliable polymer binding than the shorter Start codon.

When DNA was evolved the original recognition sequence was laid down in the archive by reverse transcriptase, eventually to mutate into the DNA sequences that codes for the S-D sequence, the Kozak sequence, TATAA box, the Pribnow box and origin of replication initiation sites.

Natural selection meant that those biotic cells that had polymerases and protoribosomes that could detect a reliable 3 base codon to complement the primordial Shine-Dalgarno sequence were favoured because evidence exists that methionine and N formyl methionine are presently the most effective first amino acids in a protein and confer a survival advantage (Drabkin and Raj Bhandary, 1998) even though it is generally rare in protein sequences.

This means that molecular machines that could detect the SD sequence analogue and the codon for Methionine were favoured and those that solely used a lengthy recognition sequence were more likely to have premature STOP codons by embarking on transcription before the cell was nutritionally ready to begin.

Reasons for this include steric fit with initiation factors and the ribosome as well as the fact that methionines' presence in adequate amounts indicates a healthy one carbon metabolism and a bioenergetic readiness of the cell to successfully engage in high fidelity translation (Bhattacharyya S et al. 2016).

Furthermore, the Start codon was a backup to the original Shine-Dalgarno sequence and vice versa, thereby affording more reliability. This complexity also served to exclude selenomethionine and s-adenosyl methionine from the translation system except in the case of high concentration when selenomethionine can be misincorporated into proteins in place of methionine resulting in misfolding problems (Plateau, P. et al. (2017) *Nature Scientific Reports*, 7).

Subsequent to the evolution of the reverse transcriptases, this Start codon, whatever three base codon it was in the Eoarchean, was copied into the archival DNA to be transcribed when nutritional requirements and feedback signals allowed. The original Start codon could have been different in the Eoarchean or may not have coded for any amino acid.

This discussion does not mean START codons came first. Counterintuitively the inevitable depletion of nucleotide and amino acid varieties meant STOP codons were instantly and variably formed in both archival and messenger RNA sequences, even when they were both RNA and even when the codon was two nucleotides long, thereby creating a stress that the biotic cell had to overcome. Modern cells of all three domains have complex feedback circuits that protect their archives by slowing growth and division rates during amino acid starvation, as well as promoting synthesis of proteins that deal with the stress.

These were not present in early biotic cells resulting in misacylations, reallocations and premature Stop codons, which slowed growth and replication in an uncontrolled way. The negative selection pressure of early STOP codons was counteracted by alternatively charged tRNAs weakly binding those codons, outcompeting release factors and thereby causing a translational recoding.

Alternatively, the biotic cell could evolve de novo synthesis pathways for the depleted nucleotides or amino acids that created them by molecular evolution acting on existing metabolic or synthesis pathways. In the archival polynucleotides, any mutation or misincorporation caused by depletions or oversupply could cause a stop or reassignment in the transcription, which either produced a novel mRNA or a useless transcript to be degraded.

The region before the primordial Shine-Dalgarno sequence and between it and the Start codon became a fertile region for protein or other control molecules to enhance or inhibit the expression of the gene. These promoter regions not only fine-tuned the gene function but later led to speciation that compounded the speciation caused by environmental pressures or errors in replication, transcription or translation long before multicellularity was possible.

This primordial ability of proteins to bind polynucleotides was simply driven by the force of electromagnetism displayed in hydrogen bonds, Pi bonds of base stacking and permanent or transient dipole attractions and gave Darwinian evolution something to work on. From this scenario, however, gene expression began in the RNA-protein world and DNA was later updated by reverse transcriptase.

DNA began short and possibly mixed, as in a primer strand but by the time of the modern cell (>1000 genes) could form into large circular chromosomes since polymerases had acquired polynucleotide recognition sites by this stage and dNTP levels had reached adequate levels to be favoured by DNA replicases.

Termination of translation was merely a physicochemical interruption or the end of the polynucleotide until certain domains meant for the aa-tRNA synthetases or early ribosomes evolved into release factors in the vicinity of the ribosome and translation ended by the absence of a charged tRNA binding thereby permitting the binding of a release factor to that codon. This accounts for the morphology of release factors resembling tRNA.

This seemingly random event constituted a major crisis for the biotic cell that was paid for with an increased death rate or reduced growth rates if termination of translation occurred too early. The codons that sterically attracted the release factors were codons that could not attract an aminoacylated tRNA. These codons were replicated (RNA archive) or reverse transcribed (DNA archive) and then incorporated into the as yet undifferentiated archives as STOP codons.

Hence, the STOP codons were plausibly created by a prolonged decrease in availability of individual amino acids or their tRNAs resulting in that codon on the mRNA being untranslated at the ribosome and bound by a release factor. Before the advent of release factors, proteins simply released into the cytoplasm by the kinetic energy of the mRNA and protein strands breaking the last amino acid-tRNA bond.

A subsequent return of that amino acid level would not necessarily result in its return to the translation system because the tRNA and aaRS may have evolved in such a way as to not bind it. Darwinian evolution on a cellular level then selected for those cells that had stop codons at useful locations in the genes. Early stop codons are a well-known negative natural selection pressure so every amino acid depletion that did not result in a reassignment to another amino acid inadvertently created a Stop codon and a break in the protein.

This tends to form a pseudogene or non-coding gene. This was selected against until these Stop codons were placed in advantageous locations and the tRNAs that could not be reassigned were degraded. Natural selection against cells that embarked on translation when energy and substrates were low led to the selection of methionine as the universal Start codon for reasons already mentioned.

Cells that could add an alternative amino acid-tRNA to an existing Stop anticodon simply created a reassignment, however temporary.

The extant three stop codons, UGA, UAG and UAA could reflect the recent reassignment of tyrosine and tryptophan codons to Stop function due to their depletion by relying on the Shikimate pathway along with phenylalanine more so than can be attributed to the redundancy of the code.

The three Stop codons now provide a backup codon supply if tRNA numbers fall too low as in the case of bovine mitochondrial tRNAs that number 22 and have assigned one of their stop codons, UGA, to an amino acid, tryptophan (usual codon UGG) whose ACC anticodon is a close match and its ACU wobble anticodon is a perfect match. The Start codon can also be reassigned in this situation of low tRNA numbers, in this case to AUA (one of Isoleucines codons) but is still translated as methionine (Suzuki, T. et al. 2014).

The hypothesis that reassignments of codons occur when tRNA numbers fall too low is strongly supported by a study of mammalian mitochondrial ribosomes where U is a universal first base as well as many other reassignments due to functioning with only 22 tRNAs.

BELOW - Diagram of release factors, proteins that compete with tRNA to bind stop CODONS UAA, UAG and UGA, resemble the shape of tRNA and also Hydrolyse the last tRNA-Amino Acid bond. **Figure a** helps to illustrate gene Introns-Exons with the Exons (depicted as colored boxes) expressed and Introns (Intervening lines) to be spliced out

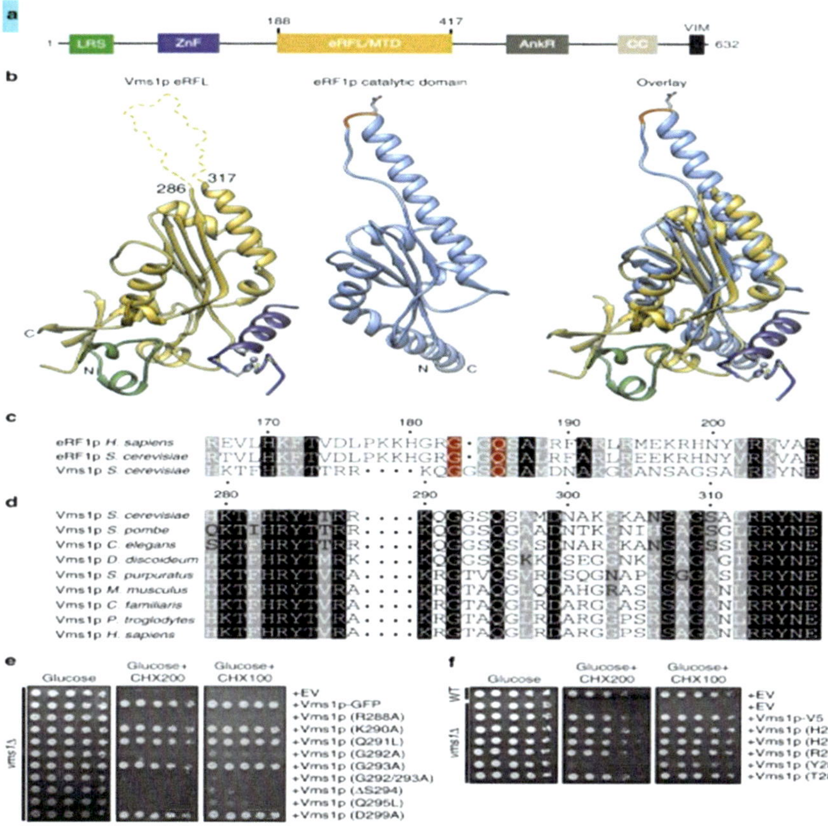

BELOW - mRNA showing the full Shine-Dalgarno sequence AGGAGGU upstream (5' side) of the start CODON AUG (GREEN) binding the 16S rRNA complementary sequence UCCUCCA of the prokaryotic small ribosomal subunit.

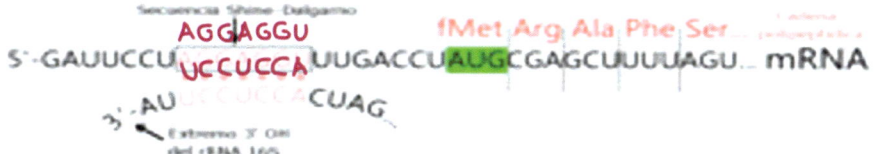

Viruses and Introns

The phenomena of lysis and passive expulsion or ingestion through polyphosphate-hydroxybutyrate or C2 ceramide pores could have given rise to the viruses in the form of polynucleotide exchanges as the encapsulated polymerase, polynucleotide and any molecules they were electrostatically bound to be expelled or ingested during these processes.

This passive means of transferring genetic information and replicases from one cell to another could plausibly evolve into the encapsulated viruses with cell membrane breaching proteoglycans as biotic cells evolved cell walls, s-layers or double membranes, thereby making them impervious to uncontrolled intrusion. This is evidenced today by two processes of genetic exchange called transduction and transformation.

Additionally, with time and evolution of secretion systems involving a pilus, conjugation, a direct injected exchange of genetic material could occur.

Viroids constitute the smallest and simplest life form, relying totally on physical forces around them, such as the aerosols or pollens in the wind and including the actions of living beings for their survival and propagation. At the higher end of the viral complexity, scale are the double stranded DNA viruses that must enter an eukaryotic nucleus to multiply and those viruses that encode all of their genes on one continuous operon together with those that carry their own polymerase and protease to cleave one protein from another.

These advanced mechanisms could only have evolved in cells that had the complex interrelated pathways and metabolism that could create them so they could be seen as a simple entity like the viroid, merely differing in the amount of complex molecular machinery they take with them upon lysis of the host.

The exocytosis may have been a mechanochemical merger of an internal compartment with the cell membrane and subsequent release of its enclosed contents. This apparently overly simple process is effected today by a highly energetic process involving clathrin molecules as well as porosomes that use a suite of complex proteins including SNARE proteins, a process that was impossible in the Eoarchean but can also be achieved by passive chemical means in simpler membranes.

HIV uses complex, large glycoproteins such as haemagglutinin and neuraminidase in the capsid component it coded for the previous host to build that bind receptors for glycoproteins (such as sialic acid) on the next host's cell membrane. These highly evolved proteins with longitudinal channels in their core were impossible in the pre protoribosome biotic cell but smaller, simpler versions could have evolved by the end of the Eoarchean due to the ribosome and polymerases.

The likelihood of a cell membrane that was a combination of phospholipids and fatty acids means viroid-like polynucleotides could potentially penetrate directly through the fatty acid sections or alternatively enter through polyphosphate-poly isobutyrate channels. Another possibility is that small polynucleotides encapsulated in moderately sized proteins (total mass less than 60 kD) directly penetrated N acetylsphingosine rich regions of the membrane, which form pores as has been demonstrated by Siskind et al. (*J Biol Chem*, 2002). If this scenario was true, then transduction and transformation have been occurring as a primitive form of sexual exchange since life began.

The evolution of the holin group of protein superfamilies is more likely to have occurred as part of the evolution of predation following the end of the late heavy bombardment. This evolution was a simple modification of pore proteins initially employed to facilitate ingestion of nutrients evolved into conduits of laterally propagating genomes which were already short and in pieces. These processes led to the viruses and viroids with evolved products from biotic cells penetrating prokaryotic membranes. Those that couldn't were dispersed and slowly degraded.

Even today the mode of breach by protein coated viruses not enveloped by cell membrane such as rotavirus is not well understood (other than to describe it as receptor mediated endocytosis that forms an endosome), even though high resolution electron microscopy of the capsid proteins involved has been achieved.

The mode of cell membrane breach in lipid membrane bound viruses is better understood and involves a merger of the viral and cell membranes by the action of hydrophobic proteins that penetrate the membranes and bring them together by conformational changes in the proteins. It is debatable whether this was possible in the Eoarchean.

The presence of fullerenes in meteorites and hence in protocells makes a slow, passive version of this process with fatty acids moulded around fullerenes plausible.

JA Fuerst and E Sagulenko in 2013 reported a suite of proteins in Planctomycetes, Verrucomicrobia and Chlamydiae superphylum that could be involved in endocytosis, a process which has been observed in the planctomycete Gemmata obscuriglobus.

Yet another conduit, much later in evolution, is the primordial secretory system that led to the varied pili, fimbria and "injectisome" or pilus that evolved in parallel with flagella and archaella probably by the time of the modern prokaryotic cell more than 3 Gya.

In the view of this analysis, the coconut cadang-cadang viroid at minimum 246–247 ribonucleotides long with no protein-coding genes is the smallest living thing on Earth by falling under the most simple definition of life. The viroid simply uses the hosts RNA polymerase 11 and substrate supply to propagate itself so if something of the same size existed in an Eoarchean environment its use of a passive vesicular secretion system mode of transfer, polyphosphate pores or C2 ceramide regions of cell membrane from one protocell to another is plausible.

In effect, the polynucleotide is a predator that uses the rest of the protocell as a substrate and energy source in order to replicate itself. The most minimal extant selfish genetic elements are MITEs, a non-autonomous Miniature Inverted repeats Transposable Element, discovered in the laboratory of Susan Wessler over 20 years ago, which are 50–500 base pairs long (Han, Y. and Wessler, S. R. (2010) *Nucleic Acids Research*). The smallest of these is the same size as polynucleotides formed on montmorillonite by James Ferris.

With such minimal selfish genetic elements including introns, type1 and 11, found in bacteria and with archaea having their own introns and intron encoded proteins, the debate is endless as to which came first. I am an "Introns early" advocate in line with Walter Gilbert who first coined the term in 1978, one year after their discovery, since indiscriminate transesterification and ligase function is a plausible capability of primordial ribozymes, progressing to targeted splicing over millions of years of natural selection.

Non-coding segments of the gene in the Eoarchean were a disruption of the gene that would have been deleterious initially but provided a variety of length and sequence on which evolution could work as well as driving the evolution of splicing and ligating ribozymes and enzymes culminating in the sophistication of the spliceosome, an entity probably created by an assembly of ancient ribosomal protein candidates with splicing ribozymes.

Non-coding DNA of any sort, including introns, is a phenomenon of Nature showing off its abundance, excess of energy, splicing and catalytic-control ability which is highlighted in the eukaryotes with their excess of energy derived from mitochondria. Pertinent to this trend, Cyanidioschyzon merolae, a single celled eukaryote that lives in high Sulfur, acidic hydrothermal pools, is not only the most minimal genome eukaryote at 5,331 genes but only 26 of those have introns.

One can infer that its solitary mitochondrion and chloroplast, together with scant nutrients, cannot provide the energy to sustain replication and splicing of much "junk" DNA, many genes (it has as few as E Coli) or many introns. None of C. merolae tRNA genes have introns, a situation which is borne from parsimony.

Between the viroid and the virus is the satellite virus of intermediate size with minimal coating and coding as well as gene transfer agents, which are a specific evolution of prokaryotes. The satellite viruses rely on viruses and the host to replicate and then compound the pathogenicity of the infection.

In the long run, host cells, when viewed as a group, survive and incorporate those viruses into their genome, occasionally to mutually beneficial ends. More often, they are slowly turned into pseudo genes and then into non-coding DNA by the transposons and retrotransposons that are inserted into them together with other unrectified mutations and unrepaired replication errors.

Simplified diagram of a modern virus with lipid membrane and RNA or DNA as well as a Protein Capsid.

Advent of De Novo Nucleotide Synthesis

As the biotic cells multiplied by active budding and, in the variety and complexity of their chemical systems, ingestion of nucleobases and the salvage pathways for nucleotide synthesis became insufficient. This inadequacy was compounded by a diminution of meteoritic organic chemicals in the environment following the end of the late heavy bombardment. Cells that had enzymes that could transform glutamine, aspartate, glycine, formate, bicarbonate and ammonia (some extant bacteria use NH3 instead of NH2 from glutamine) into nucleotides via multi step catalysed reactions were selected for.

These de novo synthesis pathways had been developing as offshoots of the existing metabolic pathways such as the Wolfe cycle or amino acid interconversions and were in addition to ingested nucleosides from lysed cells in the colony, internal salvage pathways which involve only two steps (phosphokinase + phosphoribosyl transferase) and interconversion pathways that evolved in synchrony with the salvage pathways (Caetano-Anollés, G. et al. 2013).

These interconversion enzymes (e.g. Adenosine Deaminase that produces Inosine) subsequently developed variants that could alter nucleotides in situ on RNA (the post transcription modification enzymes) to add to its already flexible nature, thereby restoring the variety that availability limitations had reduced. Extant post transcriptional modifications on tRNA alone number 85 across the three domains and at least half of those have identifiable effects on cell biology.

The other half could well be altering tRNA molecules in order to suppress any potential unwanted ribozyme activity, which would diminish their effectiveness as an adaptor molecule by being exapted into this catalytic role. Paradoxically, many post transcriptional modifications have no known enzymes for their catalysis, thereby lending weight to the hypothesis proffered in this manuscript. The catalysis is most likely to be affected by non-specific methylating or formylating enzymes, since an uncatalysed synthesis would be catastrophically slow.

The sum of these processes was the maintenance of a certain balance of cytosolic nucleotide concentrations that varied from one era to another but were crucial to the efficient functioning of the various polymerase enzymes.

Previously some de novo nucleotide synthesis could occur by the Sutherland-Powner method or variations of it but they were uncontrolled, sometimes uncatalysed and quantitatively inadequate compared to ingestion through pores and salvage pathways catalysed by primordial phosphokinase enzymes. The substrates required also became cytotoxic (e.g. NH_3, HCN, benzene) and had to be bypassed.

Some significant evidence for this claim comes in the work of Caetano-Anolles K with proteomics phylogenetic studies indicating a >300 million year progression from an abiotic synthesis of nucleotides to enzymes that could salvage or synthesise nucleotides de novo (Caetano-Anolles, K. (2013) *PloS*, 8(3)).

Phylogenetic analyses are marred by not having alterations to the code by reason of availability of polymerases, nucleobases and translational recoding factored into the algorithms and the lumping of salvage and de novo synthesis into one group by the authors is a bit naïve. From 3.8Gya to 3.5Gya is adequate time for a steady molecular evolution from ingestion alone to salvage and interconversion plus ingestion to de novo synthesis plus salvage, interconversion and ingestion.

Further evidence that salvage pathways could exist alone in an environment where the nucleobases, ribose sugar and phosphate are plentiful is the case of microsporidia such as Cryptosporidium Parvum, an eukaryotic gastrointestinal parasite that has lost the need for de novo nucleotide synthesis by relying solely on salvaging purines and pyrimidines from the host (Striepen, B. et al. (2004) *PNAS*, USA).

The same is true for bacterial intracellular parasites such as Chlamydia and Rickettsia but these advanced (4 G years) organisms have nucleotide transporter proteins on their cell membrane (Heinz, E. et al. 2014). Our biotic cell relied on diffusion through pores such as polyphosphate-isobutyrate or ceramide pores.

The decline in availability from meteorite sources also made the salvage and interconversion pathways inadequate. This survival advantage did not require the previous great diversity of nucleobase structure because it was driven by function and substrate availability and "sense" could be made out of it by the emerging 2+1 base anticodon. Furthermore, the use of de novo nucleotide synthesis was not a crisis for the biotic cell because it was an additional process to salvage and absorption, as well as not occurring in all cells at the same time.

As competition for nutrients increased with cell division (budding) the codon identity increased in importance in its evolution from being an electrostatic proclivity secondary to the bulk production of enzymes and ribozymes to being a crucially important element in archiving, transcribing and translating the cells' genotype with accuracy.

Previous availability of great varieties of nucleobase in adequate concentration diminished on a per cell basis with biotic cell population increase and the advent of polymerases since they also became intermediates in other biosynthesis and metabolic pathways so the emerging 2+1 base codon made significant nucleobase variety unnecessary.

Developing adequately fast and precise synthesis pathways for 2 nucleotides, Uridine Monophosphate (a 6 step enzymatic process) and Inosine Monophosphate (an 11 step enzymatic process), from which the rest could be quickly formed by methylation etc was less challenging for the biotic cell than to evolve a dedicated pathway for each nucleotide.

The additional five steps required for the purine de novo synthesis reflect the challenge of assembling an extra imidazole ring over the single pyrimidine ring as well as the sophistication of assembling a phosphorylated ribose molecule in the process. The natural inclination is to suggest that pyrimidines dominated since they were easier to synthesise (6 steps vs 11 for purines) but the bulk of the substrates came from salvage and inter conversion pathways.

Polymerases favoured using A, C, G, T and U due to the x1000 thermodynamic and kinetic advantage over other bases and thereby caused an enhancement of synthesis of these five bases by the effect of Le Chateliere's principle of equilibrium.

It has been estimated that 50 ATPs are needed for each nucleotide triphosphate synthesised if one includes the substrate synthesis (Heinz, E. et al. 2014). This calculation does not take into account the ingestion and salvage pathways but nevertheless a higher energy requirement came at a time when evolved ATP synthesis pathways had advanced adequately so the purines and pyrimidines could be synthesised at adequate rates.

Having proposed this scenario, one must be open to the likelihood that the original de novo synthesis pathways were variations of the extant ones, possibly shorter. Even today there are variations between domains with bacteria using

NH3 instead of glutamine as a nitrogen source. Absence of oxygen meant alternative, less efficient electron transport chains powering proton pumps together with ATP from the ATP synthase, glycolysis and fermentation were used to power the de novo synthesis pathways.

In this scenario, ATP synthase evolved after the minimal 50 protein-coding gene cell and could be driven by proton gradients created by alternative electron acceptors. Before that period, the energy came from triggered openings of Na+/proton channels following electron transport chain powered proton pumps creating a significant proton gradient.

From an energy economy point of view, the synthesis pathways would preferably stop at UMP and IMP but ingestion of a greater variety was possible, the salvage pathways were producing more variety and the archival polynucleotides needed more than 4 (2x2) or 8 (2x2x2) combinations to cover the more than 20 proteinogenic amino acids in use.

These factors, along with limited rates of replication and transcription, the energy cost of a longer codon (2x2x2x2x2 = 32 combinations of U and I to cover 22 amino acids) and limited substrate supplies, stopped the evolution of a two base code.

As complexity grew over 4 billion years over 300 nucleotides exist in RNA but evolution has had time to select for enough enzymes to make those post transcriptional modifications and the cost in energy is much less to produce five for the archiving, transcribing and translating (A, C, T, U, G). It was no accident that de novo synthesis of nucleotides took this pathway because the selection pressure of the concentration x stereochemical affinity x functional value equation was always present.

Previously, A, C, T, U and G were the best stereochemical fit (currently x1000 over non-Watson-Crick pairings-not necessarily so high in the past) but not the most available (concentration). Now they were both available, possibly due to their equilibrium levels, as well as being the best stereochemical fit thereby having a positive effect on survival rates. They have therefore dominated replication and transcription ever since.

Some experimental evidence for the likelihood of this scenario is a review in 1982 by A Kunz that outlines significant genetic effects of a dNTP imbalance and a 2018 series of experiments that demonstrate a significant effect of base modifications on RNA polymerase and reverse transcriptase fidelity (Potapov, V. et al. (2018) *Nucl Acids Res*).

Furthermore, a review by Ganai R. A. and Johansson, E. in Molecular Cell 2016, 62, found that rNTPs were the most common misincorporation into DNA (36–190 x higher conc. of rNTPs in vivo than dNTPs) and that a rise in a particular dNTP level resulted in an increased chance of it being misincorporated thereby leading to a permanent mutation upon replication. DNA replication fidelity also fell with a balanced increase of concentration of the four main nucleotides.

Presumably, a high concentration forces an "induced fit" in the enzymes active centre, where coordination occurs with metal ions and catalytic side chains.

Hypothetically, with prolonged concentration variations, these nucleoside variations would result in a steric gate evolution of the RNA polymerases to bind alternative nucleotides, thereby creating a mechanism for the evolution of the code. Proofreading by the DNA pol. and repair by enzymes of mismatches caused by various means were undeveloped, resulting in a much faster evolution of the code.

Since the nucleotide choices diminished gradually over millions of years, the transcription of tRNA had to suffer limitations which affected its flexibility and efficiency. This consequence was actively detrimental to translation speeds and growth rates of cells and therefore drove the selection of post transcription modification enzymes and the provision of supernumerary tRNAs which have tended to not only restore the great variety that was originally available but make specific alterations (e.g. methylation) that influence tRNA function.

De novo synthesis of amino acids was also selected for as catalysis and larger proteins placed a great demand for them, but many are still "essential" (9 in humans) in that they must be ingested. The curious case of proline, one of the extant proteinogenic amino acids, involves the N of its pyrrolidine ring forming part of the peptide backbone.

When taking into account its negative value to alpha spiral stability and its slowing of the rate of translation when it arrives at the ribosome the suggestion of this scenario is that it insinuated its way into the group of proteinogenic aa's by being an alpha amino acid available in adequate concentration and a good stereochemical fit to its aaRSs and initiation factors at a time when beta sheets dominated protein structure.

The stability it confers to beta sheets and procollagen left handed spirals is pertinent to this hypothesis as is the fact that proline is an organocatalyst that facilitates the aldol reaction, amination and oxyamination amongst others, all in an asymmetric synthesis that favours one enantiomer product over others.

The lack of nucleotide variety in adequate concentrations resulted in the polymerases binding alternative nucleotides. The resulting instant mutations, when occurring at the first base of the codon would lead to reallocations at the mRNA-tRNA-aa-tRNA synthetase interface so that the first nucleobase in the codon could be used to code for 2 or more amino acids and the combination with the second nucleobase determined the correct amino acid, whilst the third was readable but less relevant. This reallocation led to each one of the four canonical nucleotides taking the first position of sixteen codons.

The point of transition to the 2+1 codon system on archival polynucleotides that were not differentiated regarding DNA or RNA and used the multiple reading frame-frame shifting system of archiving occurred when there were insufficient varieties of nucleotides to code for the proteinogenic amino acids being used (e.g. 5 nucleobases [5x5 = 25 combinations] for 35 amino acids). The control molecules, mainly aa-tRNA synthetases read ahead to the third base in the anticodon on the tRNA or its proxy on the D or T arm.

This "reading ahead" took the form of a simple electrostatic affinity that was previously sensed but was unusable in practice. The potentially catastrophic effects of a frame change to the archives was plausibly averted by the gradual and quantum nature of the change with amino acid levels, NTP levels, anticodons, aaRS, codons, polynucleotides, polymerases, ribosomes, biotic cells and colonies all acting as quantum units of variability that cushioned the shock of the change over a long period of time to be survivable. In any case, variability was a constant situation that surviving cells dealt with if it wasn't fatal.

Transfer RNAs are transcribed off the archiving polynucleotides so the first 5 prime base in the anticodon is base 34, the wobble base. Variation here is not a calamitous alteration as evidenced by bovine mitochondrial tRNA anticodons that number just 22 in variety and all have Uridine at position 34.

In a sense, the tRNA represents the archival code to the translation enzyme world together with the many post transcription modification enzymes and therefore it is the polynucleotide that adapts the length of the codon as required. Some evidence for this mutability of the code and aaRSs is the work of Neumann et al. in producing a tethered functional ribosome and evolved aaRSs that could read a four base codon and a set of non-canonical amino acids. This evolving of the aaRS hints at the lengthening of the codon with time.

The subsequent reallocations have been driven by continuing declines in nucleobase and amino acid availability (concentration) as polymers got longer, polymerases got faster and biomass increased. Some significant evidence for this scenario is afforded in a review by RA Ganai and E Johansson in 2016 (*Molecular Cell*, 62) who report a decreased DNA replication fidelity with either a balanced increase of dNTP levels or an unbalanced change in dNTP levels.

At the translation level, evidence is afforded by the observed 25 fold lower specificity for Tyrosine by its aa-tRNA synthetase when Tyrosine availability is limited. The consequence was an increased binding of phenylalanine, an amino acid of a similar structure (Raina, M. et al. 2014).

This experimental demonstration has had no effect on the mRNA codon for Tyrosine (UA-) or Phenylalanine(UU-) due to the brevity of the experiment but in this scenario, in an extended or total Tyrosine depletion in the prokaryotic environment there would be a pressure to reallocate the codon for Tyrosine (UA-) to Phenylalanine (UU-). Medha Raina may well have demonstrated the way Tyrosine lost two of its codons, UAA and UAG, to become Stop codons.

Therefore, misacylations became passive reallocations to give us the genetic code without even breaching Cricks dogma, which became true and correct after the advent of tRNA isodecoders, isoacceptors (tRNAs with the same amino acid but different anticodon) and their aminoacylators.

The complexity of enzymes and metabolic pathways by this stage meant that nutritional depletions were counteracted by the evolution of synthesis pathways rather than permanent translational recoding so a tyrosine depletion in the above example would result in increased mortality or reduced growth rates in the survivors until they increased the efficiency of the synthesis pathway for it, namely the Shikimate pathway which itself is an evolution of the primordial reaction of phosphoenolpyruvate with erythrose-4-phosphate.

The coded synthesis of several tRNA isoacceptors provides a backup in times of amino acid depletion, as some isoacceptors may be aminoacylated more efficiently than others. Such synthesis pathways that seem circuitous may have evolved to exclude toxic chemicals, such as benzene or phenol, from their substrates and Hess's law tells us the enthalpy of formation of the same product from the same starting reactants cannot be greater by following a circuitous pathway.

Thus with the development of a large archive of polynucleotide codons and enzymes the code for life on Earth became entrenched across the surviving species as those biotic cells that could respond to a depletion of a complex nutrient with an evolution of its synthesis pathways outcompeted the rest. This trend is highlighted in plant and fungal eukaryotes compared with animals that can more widely ingest nutrients.

The Animalia has lost the ability to biosynthesise adequate amounts of several amino acids, nine in humans. This trend towards loss of synthesis in the situation of plenty is occurring in a concurrent environment of reduction of amino acid varieties that are used in proteinogenesis as evidenced by the necessary post translational modification synthesis of amino acids hypusine (from lysine), dipthamide from histidine and the inventive use of Stop codons to synthesise pyrrolysine and selenocysteine.

Amino acid limitation has had a similar effect on misacylation of cysteine, glutamine and histidine tRNAs in the laboratory of J Parker reported in 1989 (*Microbiol Rev.*, 53(3)) in the range of a x10 up to x80 increase in misacylation rate.

Plateau, P. et al. in 2017 report a conversion of high doses of selenomethionine in Saccharomyces cerevisiae to selenocysteine with subsequent misincorporation into proteins in place of Cysteine resulting in protein misfolding and toxicity.

These misacylations would previously, in a primordial world, be permanent in a prolonged depletion or oversupply of these amino acids and the translational recoding would become an instantaneous archival recoding. This is merely a change in what the DNA code represents and totally different from reverse translation or a breach of Cricks dogma.

The dual influences of the equation conc. x stereochemical affinity x functional value at the replicase level and at the translation level (amino acid-tRNA-aaRS) morphed the genetic code into today's comprehensive but complicated guide. Further experiments by H Edward Wong et al. (2018, *Biochem,* 57, 49) involving individual amino acid starvation of cultured eukaryotic cells found they not only resulted in misacylations but also base mismatches at the wobble position (tRNA postn 34) or the first codon position (tRNA postn 36).

The alterations were too extensive and numerous to describe here in detail other than to say they support and broaden the hypothesis. The probability is that various suppressor tRNAs as well as non-cognant acylated tRNAs substituted for the unacylated tRNAs by simply out competing release factors for binding to those codons.

The "available concentration" part of the equation appears to be an oversimplification of chemical kinetics but it standardises the other variables (pressure, temperature, catalyst concentration and efficiency, nature of the substrates, etc.) in order to highlight the main factor amongst them in the natural selection of the code; concentration of like substrates at the catalytic site and their stereochemical affinity with reactants.

Experiments and review by Oertell, K. et al. in 2016 (*PNAS*, 113(16)) on DNA replication fidelity found that the free energy advantage of Watson-Crick base pairing (hydrogen bonding + base stacking) over mismatched pairs was only 1/10 of the required 5–7 kcal/mol and the remainder was achieved by the kinetic effects involving the polymerase.

This is supportive of the equation proffered here with an emphasis on concentration but the authors were, rightly, not interested in subjective evolutionary advantage of mutations in their experiments. This 1/10 thermodynamic contribution needs to be seen in perspective with the x1000 preference for canonical base pairs, which is mostly happening at the polymerase catalytic site.

In this analysis, pyrrolysine and selenocysteine once had their own codons but they became "stop" codons if their tRNAs could not bind another amino acid as their levels fell for whatever reason. Alternatively, if their tRNAs began binding other amino acids during a period of depletion of these two amino acids their codons were instantly reassigned to the bound amino acids. With a post transcriptional modification suite of enzymes by this stage, the tRNAs could evolve away very quickly.

That depletion has remained for many species but those that could evolve reliable de novo synthesis pathways for these two amino acids because they conferred a survival advantage have developed a novel use of the stop codon with a control molecule of RNA origin, the SECIS element, in the case of selenocysteine as well as a special aminoacylator and elongation factor.

In the case of pyrrolysine, a special class 11 aaRS that is encoded in a gene cluster for pyrrolysine synthesising enzymes charges a special tRNA with a CUA anticodon (normally one of aspartic acids' anticodons or methionines suppressor tRNA) to incorporate pyrrolysine into polypeptides. It could be inferred that when pyrrolysine returned to adequate concentrations due to natural selection favouring cells with the two enzymes that catalyse its synthesis in the cytoplasm from lysine (3-Methyl ornithine synthase and pyrrolysine synthase), an aminoacylator recruited the suppressor tRNA from methionine with its CUA anticodon and added pyrrolysine to it in order to suppress the Stop codon.

Presumably, it can appose the UAG stop codon because of the quantum nature of a codons transit through the ribosome and the fact that CUA anticodon, in reverse, matches UAG Stop codon. With the middle base pair A-U hydrogen bonding in a canonical Watson-Crick manner, the charged tRNA outcompetes the release factors for the UAG Stop codon. This scenario still allows for UAG codon time to have been reallocated from Tyrosine to Pyrrolysine during an earlier period of depletion.

Even with the recruitment of stop codons on mRNA and flexible aminoacylators that carry these two amino acids, they have to compete with release factors for these codons on the mRNA. The negative selection pressure of having Stop codons in various locations in the exon of a gene caused by depletions drove de novo synthesis pathways for these amino acids and for novel translational recoding techniques such as recruiting suppressor tRNA.

Pyrrolysine is only found in prokaryotes and is especially useful in methanogenesis in the transfer of the Methyl group (Srinivasan G et al. 2002). Selenocysteine is found in all three domains of life. When selenocysteine was depleted, its codons became Stop codons except for those tRNAs that could be aminoacylated with serine. This reassignment to serine was presumably taken advantage of when selenocysteine synthase and serine kinase was evolved by cells that needed the antioxidant effect of selenocysteine (Xu, X. M. et al. 2007).

These two enzymes most likely worked in solution in the cytoplasm long before they were seconded to modify serine in situ on tRNA. If selenocysteines concentration was inadequate or it could not sterically outcompete serine for the tRNA with the ACU anticodon (UGA Stop codon on mRNA), its synthase could create it in situ on the tRNA. Again, the quantum nature of the mRNAs transit through the ribosome and the complementary binding of UGA Stop codon with serines AGU codons' anticodon UCA (in reverse), the middle G-C hydrogen bond helps the process along with a dedicated elongation factor interacting with the SECIS element.

Selenocysteine probably had the four UG-codons and during a period of depletion these were reallocated to tryptophan and cysteine only for tryptophan to lose UGA to Stop during a period of depletion borne from relying on the Shikimate pathway.

Even though Selenium is highly reactive, there is no evidence for cytotoxicity of selenocysteine but rather that it was never able to return to previous levels due to the need for serine, from which it is made, in purine, pyrimidine, glycine, Cysteine and tryptophan synthesis.

The innovative synthesis, coding and translation of SeC were driven by its usefulness in proteins with antioxidant activity due to its lower reduction potential yet, paradoxically, high levels in cells would cause misincorporation into proteins during translation in place of Cysteine thereby resulting in protein misfolding and pathology (Plateau, P. et al. (2017) *Nature Scientific Reports*, 7). This is different to toxicity in the poisoning sense, which starts in small doses.

These two examples of Stop codons matching the reverse anticodon of an amino acids tRNA is another example of superwobble, normally caused by very low tRNA varieties. In this case, however, the middle nucleotides of the codon-anticodon match perfectly and the others can still hydrogen bond weakly. This flexible base pairing is also resorted to by the fact that initiation and elongation factors will not assist an unacylated tRNA through the ribosome but will assist a cognant (appropriate anticodon), acylated tRNA to complement a Stop codon with or without the assistance of control molecules (SECIS, initiation factors).

In effect, they outcompete the release factors for the Stop codon. The "strict rule" that position one and two of a mRNA codon can only hydrogen bond in canonical Watson-Crick pairs with anticodon bases at position 36 and 35 respectively is slowly being falsified by experiments and observation (such as those of H Edward Wong et al. 2018) as well as the significant number of suppressor tRNAs that can bind Stop codons when they have non-canonical base pairing at positions 1 or 2.

Even if the polynucleotides were differentiated into DNA and RNA the archives did not need changing, the codon simply coded for a different amino acid for practical reasons of availability, a phenomenon conventionally called "translational recoding". In a prolonged depletion, this actually becomes a permanent archival (DNA) recoding without refuting Cricks dogma, which became true and correct once the translatase became extinct.

More evidence for this phenomenon is the substitution of molybdenum by tungsten in ferredoxins, zinc by cadmium and iron by copper as an oxygen carrier in arthropods and some molluscs. Furthermore, some substitution of Phosphate by Arsenic in a Halobacters' Nucleic Acids and proteins in Mono lake California is further evidence that similar substrates can partially replace each other in important biochemistry (Wolf-Simon et al. 3 Jun 2011).

> BELOW - A complex roche biochemical pathways poster possibly hanging on a professors 'wall is still too simple to depict natures' variety, abundance and interrelatedness.

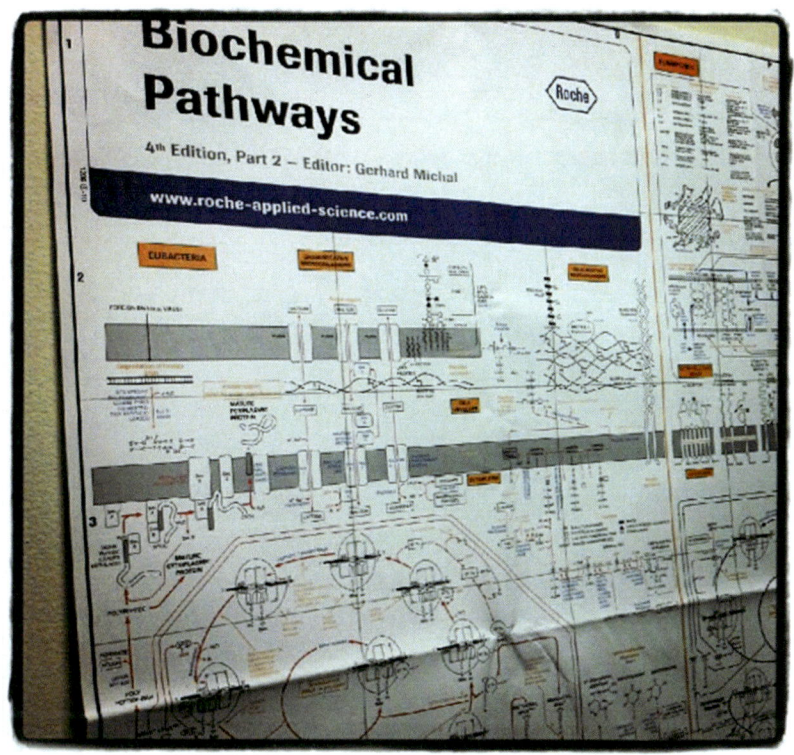

Continuing Evolution of the Codon

One would reason that a living cell could not survive a change in the codon length for its archiving function but this notion is falsified by the Neumann, H. et al. 2010 article that demonstrated ribo Q1 and a four base codon evolution that coded for "unnatural" amino acids.

By occurring gradually and not in all molecular adaptors (tRNA and aa-tRNA synthetases) or molecular machines (polymerases and ribosomes) at the same time, all cells or all colonies of cells at the same time and by occurring at a time when the multiple reading frame-frame shifting system of archiving was in use, the selection pressure was applied to morph from the 1+1+1 (1 fixed, 1 wobble, 1 unusable) into the 2+1 (2 fixed, 1 wobbly) base system as the de novo nucleotide synthesis pathways greatly diminished the nucleotide choices available for archiving and transcription at the higher rate that was required.

Concurrent to the altering of the code as nucleotide choices, diminished pressure was also applied from the translation apparatus-amino acid pool to change what the archive stood for. Even when the codon was 1+1 (one fixed and one wobble base) the other nucleobase, the unusable base was readable but the redundancy was so great as to make it unusable (e.g. 10x10 possible bases = 100 two-base combinations for say, 35 amino acids).

The transition (the "first reallocation period") happened at the replicase-RNA archive interface as well as the transfer polynucleotide-messenger polynucleotide interface without altering Cricks' polynucleotide-> protein dogma that produced catalysts because these molecules catapulted metabolic and synthesis pathways forward. Biotic cells that could produce aminoacylators that could read a three base codon were selected for because the two base codon was inadequate to code for 23 amino acids when only four ribonucleotides were available in adequate concentrations (4x4 = only 16).

These constraints caused the "second reallocation period" that produced the modern 2 firm + 1 wobbly base. The third extant base is termed "wobbly" in this hypothesis because it can often be represented by any of the four bases. During both of these periods, individual reallocations were increasingly constrained by the availability of nucleotides, that is, their cytosolic concentration, which affects their concentration at the polymerase catalytic site. A review article by Traut TW (Mol Cell Biochem 1994 Nov 9; 140 (1):1-22) reported average extant intracellular nucleotide levels as ATP at 3.15 mM, GTP at 0.5 mM, UTP at 0.56 mM and CTP at 0.3 mM with the deoxy NTP's at concentrations 100 times lower.

This accounts for the neat and even distribution of four nucleobases in sixteen of each first and second positions of 64 combinations. As the thermodynamics and kinetics of the replicases began to select the four main nucleotides, the rapid, transient reduction in their cytoplasmic concentration stimulated their synthesis by Le Chateliere's principle provided substrates and catalysts were available.

The potential even distribution of the third base is defeated by the low number of proteinogenic amino acids, 22, the Start codon and the three Stop codons, thereby causing great confusion in a simple reallocation process effected by the product-availability x stereochemical compatibility.

An inadequate number of aminoacylators or tRNA would mean some codons became STOP codons as this mimics the depletion of amino acids and is a known negative selection pressure if it occurs near the start or middle of a gene. Multiple reading frame genomes were phased out by the polymerases' recognition of Shine Dalgarno like sequence analogues and Start codon analogue on the polynucleotides and some endonuclease or post translational protease or phosphorylation activities could have regulated the proteins to be functional to a greater or lesser extent.

The archive continued to be laid down by polynucleotide replication at a time when RNA and DNA had not differentiated and the molecular machines could not differentiate between the two types of nucleotide (reduced or not reduced). By the time DNA was selected for due to its stability, the 3 base codon and the start codon had already been selected for due to their respective selective advantage.

Whatever the original "start" codon was and whatever amino acid it coded for could be analogous to the current situation of AUG representing methionine (AUA in mitochondria) because it reflects the health of the cells one carbon metabolism and by being rare its adequate levels reflect a readiness of the cell to initiate translation. This readiness was reinforced when the isodecoders (tRNA) of the START amino acid began to bind initiation factors.

The pressures of nucleotide availability, base pair compatibility, stereochemical affinity with the polymerase catalytic site and other kinetics brought down the use of nucleobases in DNA to only 4, Adenine, Thymine, Cytosine and Guanine. Extant examples of morphing of the genetic code give some insight into ancient processes:

1. The spontaneous deamination of cytosine to produce Uridine on a gene results in it being paired with adenosine upon replication and when that strand is replicated, the adenosine is paired by the DNA pol. with thymidine resulting in a net mutation of Cytidine to thymidine.

2. Free radical oxygenators can convert guanosine to 8-oxoguanosine which, when the strand is replicated is paired with adenosine and when that strand is replicated it is paired with thymidine resulting in a net mutation from guanosine to thymidine (Ganai, R. A. and Johansson, E. (2016) *Molecular Cell*, 62, 745–55).

3. Formation of 5-methyl-2'-deoxycytidine (m5dC) on DNA as a known heritable epigenetic mark (Huber SM et al. (2015) ChemBioChem 16(15). All these mutations are point mutations and do not have the same significance as an across the population starvation of a crucial substrate such as Adenine.

In example 3 above, the m5C would not be an epigenetic mutation or mark in the Archaean period but a legitimate pyrimidine available in solution to be incorporated into the archives to be paired with whatever was most kinetically and thermodynamically favourable.

The modern polymerases are promiscuous in capability (Kool ET 2002 Ann Rev Biochem (71) but not in practice due to the limitations in availability (concentration + access to the catalytic site) afforded by the salvage and biosynthesis cycles that help sustain the code via some homeostasis of the substrate concentrations. Their specificity is also a result of "active site tightness" (Kool, E. T. et al. 2002), another term for stereochemical affinity at the catalytic site.

The sixteen (4x4) codes of the 4 base system do not cover the 20 amino acid choices available if only 2 anticodon positions are involved in coding, thereby making the third position crucial to coding for amino acids. Being so close and "available", it was within the capabilities of the translation ribozymes and aminoacylators to read ahead to the third "wobbly" base to fine tune the code for life as it does now when it senses the base identities of tRNA position 37, 38 and 39.

In the RNA-protein world, replicases doubled as transcriptase enzymes and did not have to adapt drastically since they were template driven and the start codons coded for amino acids as well. This adaptation involved a selection against those cells with the inadequate tRNA aminoacylation and translation machinery that could not read the three base codon. Together with the knowledge that AUG on the mRNA that codes for methionine confers a survival advantage, the conclusion is that the coding infrastructure was laid down at a time when the archival and the messenger polynucleotides were one and the same, RNA.

Apart from the work of Neumann et al. 2010 who engineered a four base codon, evidence is found in the decoding system which has been shown to benefit from the base identity at position 37,38 and 39 on the tRNA. Parallel to and probably preceding this evolution, the D loop with both D stems is crucial for recognition by aa-tRNA synthetases to add the correct amino acid and, in certain cases, the discriminator base at position 73 on the acceptor stem is crucial.

This phenomenon is a form of the "reading ahead" already mentioned but also an experimental observation that impacts translation efficiency and growth rates. It indicates that the aa-tRNA synthetases can sense different parts of the tRNA, not just the anticodon. In their infancy, when they were both small, two bases on the D loop may have been the primordial anticodon.

With the advent of initiation and elongation factors from proteins previously accreting onto ribosomes or aaRSs the T arm (two T stems and one T loop) became increasingly important in ribosomal and initiation-elongation factor recognition of the correct tRNA for that mRNA codon, thereby providing a second backup.

In the case of bovine mitochondrial ribosomes, extreme wobble and non-canonical allocations have evolved by operating with only 22 tRNAs to cover 61 amino acid coding codons (Suzuki, T. et al. 2014).

This "superwobbling" most often takes the form of unmodified Uridine occupying the anticodon wobble position (the first position, U34) (Rogalski, M. et al. 2008).

Without the backup systems described above, single mutations lead to significant pathology. DNA could not possibly direct this system, it has evolved by feedback loops and increased morbidity and mortality or reduced growth and division rates in defective coding systems.

The translation apparatus, including tRNA, initiation and elongation factors and aaRSs was the interface that allowed a second type of reassignment of the codons and therefore a gentle falsification of Cricks dogma, in effect if not in fact, even beyond the age of reverse translation. It is impossible for DNA to drive Cricks' dogma if the molecules that execute it are incompetent. They had to evolve competence first in an era when the archival and the translated polynucleotide were one and the same, RNA.

Earlier in evolution, when there were 8 nucleobases in use, the metaribosome with two channels could achieve translation by employing 64 (8x8) existing tRNA-like molecules and their adaptor (Aminoacyl tRNA ancestor). With only 30 amino acids in use, the second codon-anticodon position had some wobble as a base pair at this stage. Hence, the degeneracy of the coding system for life is apparent.

Increasing complexity made the accuracy of transcription and translation increasingly important. The extant large ribosomal subunit serves to significantly initiate protein folding and hence to avert any possible electrostatic binding of the protein being formed to the mRNA thereby averting the serious problem of separating the strands.

It is possible that Nature was never able to acquire a helicase that could separate polynucleotide strands annealed to a polypeptide strand once ambient heat gradients became unreliable or, more likely, these polypeptide-polynucleotide helicases became redundant with efficient protein folding and thence evolved into one of the numerous (more than 95 in humans) extant DNA, RNA, RNA-DNA hybrid helicases or AAA ATPases (that unravel defective proteins at the entrance to the proteasome) or spliceosomal proteins as the cell selected for control molecules (chaperones, transcription factors etc) to keep the newly formed proteins and polynucleotides apart.

As accuracy and complexity increased, temperature gradients became unreliable as a means of separating polymer strands and cells with dedicated molecules like passive or ATP dependent helicase were selected for.

Archiving of the genome by DNA employs four bases A, G, T, C in a three base codon and mRNA transcription employs four bases A, C, G, U in a three base codon whilst tRNA can use A, C, G, U as well as a choice of Inosine Monophosphate or one of 8 Cytidine or Uridine (e.g. pseudouridine) variations in the third "wobble" base position, 13 base choices in total for the wobble position in the 3 base anticodon (Murphy, F. V. (2004) *Nature SMB*). The non-canonical wobble bases are all post transcription modifications which can also affect rRNA and other RNAs.

Since 2010 (Ikeuchi, Y. et al. *Nature CB*,. 6(4), 277–82) a newly discovered role of Agmatidine (Cytidine+agmatine) in some Archaea in the wobble position of tRNA-isoleucine parallels the use of lysidine in some bacteria and pseudouridine in eukaryotes in the wobble position of Isoleucines AUA anticodons and are a specific post transcriptional molecular evolution of these extant domains driven by the need to defeat the ambiguity caused by methionine (AUG) sharing an anticodon with isoleucine under the Crick wobble base rules, namely UAU that decodes AUA of isoleucine.

This phenomenon is a further clue that methionine was reallocated a codon from isoleucine when it returned to adequate levels. Those who read too much into individual base pairing are ignoring the role of aaRSs, elongation factors and the ribosome in this process which is apparent by the fact that several archaea use pseudouridine instead of Agmatidine.

In effect, the wobble base rules are falsified by the suite of suppressor tRNAs that can bind an early Stop codon to ensure a gene is expressed. These often have mismatches at any of the three codon-anticodon positions signifying that those who write "rules" in this regard are being overruled by the force of electromagnetism, the phenomenon of molecular evolution and the simpler laws of chemistry embodied in Le Chateliere's principle.

An illustrative example is the presence of queuosine in the wobble base position of eukaryotic and bacterial tRNA molecules that have a purported GUN (guanosine, uridine, N is any nucleobase) anticodon for histidine, aspartic acid, asparagine and tyrosine. Queuosine does not even appear in the updated wobble base rules nor is GUN an anticodon for aspartic acid or asparagine under these rules.

Queuosine has been demonstrated to improve translation speeds and fidelity thereby avoiding protein misfolding but by being in the anticodon almost certainly achieves this by suppressing premature stop codons UAA and UAG which have possible GUU and GUC anticodon complementarity under the updated wobble base rules. Both of these anticodons are on possible isoacceptors for glutamine under the updated wobble base rules as well as on suppressor tRNAs carrying any of the four amino acids mentioned above. These facts therefore highlight the ambiguity of the genetic code which Nature is constantly combating or employing to provide variety and flexibility.

In this scenario, the plausible beginnings of the modern code are at this time (3.78–3.6Gya) as the large suite of control and feedback molecules choose start and stop codons in open reading frames to begin the modern era of cell biology 20–200 million years after the end of the Late Heavy Bombardment.

The extant reduction of the minimum number of cytoplasmic tRNA varieties to 30 (Cyanidioschyzo merolae), when codon numbers are 64 is a demonstration by Nature of what 3.8 billion years of evolving control molecules can do but also demonstrates the reason for the "rule" that no codon can be allowed to be useless or blank, namely that it would cause a gene disruption, a STOP assignment if not bound by an alternative tRNA.

With aminoacyl-tRNA synthetases reduced to 20 per cell, the trend is apparent that evolution is using control molecules to add another order of accuracy to the translation of the code for life.

Indeed, a 2001 review of the aa-tRNA synth. database indicated some bacteria do not have a full complement of 20 aa-tRNA syn. enzymes but instead use enzymes and novel pathways to charge their tRNAs (Szymanski, M. et al. 2001). One of these simply involves an enzyme that converts aaRS-glutamic acid to aaRS-glutamine by acting on the glutamic acid charged tRNA (glutamine) alone.

This process is analogous to the selenocysteine synthase pathway and also one of the two 5-aminolevulinic acid C5 synthesis pathways in chlorophyll synthesis. Is 5-aminolevulinic acid one of the amino acids formerly used in translation?

These numbers below 20 (the number of aaRSs used by mammals) are even fewer than the 22 tRNAs of a mammalian mitochondrial tRNA suite which uses extreme wobble and some odd allocations (e.g. AGA or AGG for stop and AUA for Methionine) to cover the available codons (Suzuki, T. et al. 2014). This number in excess of 20 in mitochondria can be explained by the contribution by the host to codon choices.

If the redundant (alternative) codons coded for "any" amino acid the error rate in proteins would be catastrophic due to the modern selection pressure for accuracy. This feature of the code (being comprehensive) has, therefore, evolved into being as longer, more complex enzymes and stop codons were selected for and was not always present. The presence of introns and other non-coding DNA segments may hint at the supremacy of the splicing ribozymes and enzymes.

The fact that there may be several different tRNA molecules, isodecoders (same anticodon but sequence variations in the body) (Parisien, M. et al. (2013) *RNA Biol.*) for each isoacceptor (tRNAs with different anticodons but charged with the same amino acid) is good evidence that Nature had the ability to produce many more than the minimum tRNA molecules (30 in Cyanidioschyzon merolae eukaryote), to code for 61 combinations (4x4x4 minus 3 Stop codons) and indeed eukaryotes have hundreds of tRNA genes and functional tRNAs.

E Coli has 86 tRNA genes of which 47 are expressed (as tRNA molecules) possibly reflecting a parsimony borne from a lack of mitochondria. This excess from the minimum is necessary for a backup of supply and for possible involvement in gene regulation.

In the case of aaRS, however, it went down a different evolutionary pathway because it is less demanding in energy and error avoidance to evolve and operate 20 aminoacyl tRNA synthetases per cell, one for each amino acid, rather than 61, one for each amino acid coding codon.

In eukaryotes the hundreds of tRNA genes (>500 in humans but nearly half are silent-Torres AG Bioinformatics Biol Insights 2019 13) have other functions including gene regulation by providing many suppressors tRNAs (aminoacylated tRNAs that can bind a Stop codon) that cause a read through of premature Stop codons thereby nullifying a nonsense mutation or reviving a pseudogene.

This system is energy efficient and uses the wobble base system that was always present. This would suggest the reason for the degeneracy of the code, namely that the tRNAs and their synthetases bind the next best molecule with stereochemical fit during a period of depletion. Highly specialised molecules would become redundant and then be selected against if they did not follow this course.

Strong evidence for this control oriented solution to the code for life is the case of the aa-tRNA synthetase for alanine which can correctly aminoacylate the tRNA for alanine even though the anticodon loop has been removed by laboratory techniques. Together with other evidence the conclusion is that the base sequence at the "elbow" region of the tRNA molecule, the D stem-loop-stem, is recognised by the aa-tRNA syn. for alanine.

This does not mean it can be used in translation since initiation and elongation factors play a role too in addition to the anticodon-codon apposition. Other aa-tRNA synthetases are so specific they do not use a proofreading system

(Berg et al. (2002) *Biochemistry*) to charge the tRNA with the correct amino acid.

The de novo synthesis pathways for nucleotides did not evolve instantly. It is conceivable that they continued to evolve along with the ATP synthase and ATPase energy currency system until the DNA replication suite of control molecules (the cyclins and cyclin-dependent kinases and their inhibitors) evolved along with cytoskeleton molecules like prokaryotic actin and tubulin homologs (ancestral ParM and FtsZ respectively) to drive the spectacular phenomenon of binary fission.

The rate at which this process occurs is both energy and nutrient dependent and is driven by the selection pressure to produce daughter cells with an equal chance of survival.

The 64 codons code for 20 proteinogenic amino acids in humans, 9 of which are essential in the diet as their synthesis pathways have been lost or are inadequate.

Selenocysteine and pyrrolysine need control molecule (the SECIS element) and enzymes to employ stop codons for their coding and a 23rd amino acid N-formyl Methionine is the START codon in bacteria, chloroplasts and mitochondria but is not used by eukaryotes or archaea. The trial and error of natural selection that chose methionine and N Formylmethionine as the best start amino acids also had to deal with rises and falls in the availability of these two amino acids.

During a period of depletion of methionine and its formylated molecule, their tRNA isodecoders began to bond existing proteinogenic amino acids via their aa-tRNAs enzymes thereby producing the proteinogenic amino acids with one or two codons and possibly stop codons of that era.

The initiator tRNA for methionine is absent in organelles signifying that it is a "modern" evolution. It is phylogenetically closest to the tRNA for proline rather than the tRNA for meth. (Bhattacharyya, S. et al. 2016). The fact that methionine can be synthesised de novo by prokaryotes and plants signifies a need borne from depletion in these organisms compared to the Animalia which can more actively and widely ingest nutrients.

This possible depletion is a strong indication that methionine was supplied by a simpler synthesis pathway previously and the modern ones involving folate are a recent evolution. In mammalian bovine mitochondria methionine is coded for by AUA, one of Isoleucines' codons (Suzuki, T. et al. 2014) due to the odd allocations forced by having only 22 tRNAs.

Could this be a molecular fossil from the time when Methionine was allocated one of Isoleucines codons after returning to the translation system in archaea and eukaryotes? Bacteria went down the same path but the methionyl formyl transferase may have become a methionyl tRNA formyltransferase due to a reduction in cytoplasmic methionine levels and an acquired toxicity of N-formyl methionine as it interfered with burgeoning biosynthetic cycles involving methionine.

Hypusine is found only in eukaryotic initiation factor 5A and in some archaea IF 5A. Hypusine may have been used in the ancient protein domains that have evolved into EF-P (elongation factor P) or EIF5A (eukaryotic initiation factor 5A) since these molecules are homologs. EIF5A stimulates translation with a peptidyl transferase reaction. Hypusine may well be one of the amino acids that has become disused in aminoacylation due to not being available in the concentrations required.

Hypusine is currently formed by a two-step (deoxyhypusine synthase + deoxyhypusine hydroxylase) post translational catalysed process that alters lysine in situ on all eukaryotic EIF5A (strictly conserved) and some archaea IF5A but it may have been more readily available in the Eoarchean from various sources. Strong evidence for this hypothesis is the high level of hypusine found in the urine of people with hyperlysinaemia. This hypusine would be formed by lysine + spermidine —> deoxyhypusine + 1,3-diaminopropane —> hypusine.

With hypusine depletion, the surviving archaea were selected for their higher deoxyhypusine synthase and DH carboxylase activity until it finally became active in situ on the elongation factors. Thence its 4 codons would have been allocated to Stop function and/or existing proteinogenic amino acids, thereby adding great confusion to the search for an elegant explanation of the genetic code.

Hypusine depletion could have resulted from the increasing ribosomal activity and would have constituted a major crisis for the archaeal biotic cell which the survivors overcame by evolving the deoxyhypusine synthase and deoxyhypusine hydroxylase enzymes that catalyse the transformation of lysine in situ on the protein. Hypusine was replaced by the process of translational recoding and never returned to the tRNA aminoacylation level. It became a post translation modification.

The reasons for this is that 1. hypusine was not essential in great quantity and therefore its incorporation into polypeptides didn't require the great speed of ribosomal peptide synthesis and 2. lysine from which it is made was shunted into many other pathways. The unusually long structure of hypusine would also have been an evolutionary hindrance, although it can potentially fit into the PTC channel (50Angstroms), potentially slowing the ribosomal protein synthesis rate.

It is highly likely that deoxyhypusine synthase and DH hydroxylase initially functioned in solution before resuming that catalytic action on lysine in situ on the archaeal IF5A. In order to maintain hypusine levels, these enzymes would tend to deplete lysine, thereby forcing a molecular evolution towards post translational modification. Could the same be true for hydroxylysine and methyllysine?

A second such case is dipthamide, a post translation modification of histidine that is found in eukaryotic and archaeal elongation factor 2. Was dipthamide once an Archaean proteinogenic amino acid? Up to seven genes currently code for its three-step synthesis but in some species of archaea and Parabasalids (protist Eukaryotes) it has been lost without dire consequence by the presence of a paralogous EF-2 gene (Narrowe, A. B. et al. [2011]).

It was most likely selected against by being a target for bacterial toxins from which it gets its name (Diptheria), by simply not being essential for survival in these species or due to its depletion in the extracellular environment. Dipthamide levels returned in those species that needed it and could synthesise it post translationally, in situ, on the EF-2 GTPase from histidine by evolving the necessary 1. 3-amino-3-carboxypropyl backbone transfer from SAM 2. SAM Methyltransferase thrice and 3. dipthamide synthase enzymes. Analogous to the situation with hypusine its original codons were reassigned at the tRNA anticodon-aaRS level to other amino acids or Stop function.

In mammals, its absence leads to death at the embryo stage and, as with the case of hypusine, it is likely that the dipthamide synthase suite of enzymes originally acted in cytosol solution in archaea before acting on histidine in situ on EF2.

It is far more parsimonious to alter histidine in situ post translationally rather than maintaining cytosolic dipthamide levels and depleting the cytosol of histidine and imidazole from which it is biosynthesised. If this hypothesis regarding the evolution of hypusine and dipthamide use in archaea is accurate, then it is further strong evidence for the primordial divergence between bacteria and archaea, that is before the advent of the modern cell.

N formyl methionine as the bacterial initiator is another case that is formylated presently in situ on tRNA but was likely formylated in solution in the Archaean period until it became toxic to bacteria as well as archaea by interfering with other methionine metabolic cycles. After a period of relative depletion, methionine returned to usable levels in both domains by the evolution of its de novo synthesis pathways with bacteria evolving a methionine formylase that worked in situ on the initiator tRNA. This also maintained cytosolic methionine, which is vital for the cells one carbon metabolism.

The likely most recent reallocations to Stop function for reasons of depletion are the UAA, UAG from tyrosine and UGA from tryptophan due to the Shikimate pathway being responsible for the biosynthesis of all three aromatic amino acids being inconsistent in maintaining adequate levels for the aminoacylation of their corresponding tRNAs.

Over 400 different amino acids are employed by non-ribosomal peptide synthetases in prokaryotes and 140 amino acids are used in humans as secondary metabolites such as neurotransmitters and transport molecules.

The scenario that led to the two bodied ribosome was likely the uncontrolled growth through passive electrostatic acquisition of domains that may have inadvertently blocked the decoding channels which need to be quite wide (>14 Angstroms).

Following electrostatic bonding, some covalent bonds, such as isopeptide or thioester bonds, could have made the aggregation more permanent. Being gradual and not affecting all metaribosomes at once there was enough time for the cell to use a metaribosome with a blocked single stranded polynucleotide channel as well as a protoribosome with a blocked polynucleotide channel and the initiation-elongation (translocases) factors that bring the two subunits together along the mRNA strand.

These molecules were able to turn the potential disaster into the selective advantage of allowing several copies of the polypeptide to be produced almost simultaneously by the action of several ribosomes, the polysome, engaging and translocating one mRNA strand. Some evidence for this possibility is the phylogenetic study by C Woese and N Kyrpides in *PNAS* USA in 1998 that found a closer homology between initiation factors in all three domains of life than previously thought.

The authors postulated that the initiation factors were possibly present in the (mythical) LUCA in a simpler form and found one type of them, IF2 and eIF2 alpha were homologous to a bacterial ribosomal protein S1 which opens up the possibility that initiation and elongation factors evolved from molecules that were previously accretions onto the ribosome or aatRNA synthetase. This hypothesis is strongly supported by the close domain homology between bacterial ribosomal recycling factor (RRF) and several aminoacyl-tRNA synthetases (Burroughs, M. A. and Aravind, L. 2019).

A difference in age has been suggested between the large (younger) and small (older) ribosomal subunits, leaving the possibility open that they were once a metaribosome and a protoribosome, the former being an evolution of the latter. Furthermore, this is an example of convergent evolution, as the multiple ribosomes straddling mRNA (the polysome) to produce multiple protein strands is analogous to the multiple polymerase straddling of DNA to produce multiple mRNA copies.

A mRNA headed for the blocked protoribosome decoding channel would divert over the 16s rRNA (which in our scenario was the protoribosome peptidyl transferase), interact with the initiation factor and initiator tRNA (Meth) to bring the metaribosome (with a blocked decoding channel) close enough so that the amino acid on the CCA arm of the tRNA was in the region of the peptidyl transferase of the metaribosome. When the second tRNA arrived at the aminoacyl site, translation could proceed.

The extant Shine-Dalgarno sequence and Start codon may not necessarily be the original ones and upon blocking of the protoribosome (small subunit) channel the Start codon performed the task alone until the current SD sequence and its 16S complementary sequence was evolved (or engineered by the spliceosome).

The current 16S rRNA has not been found to have any peptidyl transferase activity when naked in vitro but this is also true of 23S rRNA (Mankin, A. S. et al. *RNA* 5(5), 605–8). In situ some minimal contributions to peptidyl transferase function by the 16S RNA terminal Adenine-OH as well as the S1 protein of the small subunit (SSU) were claimed by the Ada Yonath lab.

Table 3
Polynucleotide Codon Evolution

4.1 Gya LIPOSOMES, COACERVATES
>300 nucleotides. >400 amino acids
Short ribozymes short peptide enzymes
Polar affinity 1aa:1+1 base or 1:1

PROTOCELL PROTOGENE TEMPLATE 4Gya
80 nucleobases 140 amino acids
Multiple Reading Frame
Polar Affinity 1 aa:1+1 base or 1:1

PROTORIBOSOMES. 3.80Gya FIRST REALLOCATION EVENT

30 nucleobases 70 amino acids
Multiple Reading Frame ends by Shine-Dalgarno primodial analogue
Codon 1 aa:1 base or 1:1+1
A1 to A6, G1 to G6, C1 to C6, U1 to U6 and T1 to T6.

LARGER PROTORIBOSOMES-tRNA PRECURSOR 3.75Gya
20 bases 50 amino acids reduced in no. by concentration x% stereochemical fit x survival advantage
Codon still 1:1+1
e.g. 1-aa1 coded by A1 C3.
e.g. 2-aa2 coded by C2 G5.
second base position is wobbly.
METARIBOSOME-tRNA 3.70Gya
10 nucleobases 35 amino acids
bases A1, A5, G1, G5, C1, C5, U1, U5, T1, T5.
Codon still 1:1+1
e.g.1 alanine-G1 C5.
e.g.2 pyrrolysine-U1 A1.
e.g.3 selenocysteine-C4 G1.
e.g.4 hypusine-A1 G1.

SECOND REALLOCATION EVENT

DE NOVO NUCLEOTIDE SYNTHESIS, FAST POLYMERASES, START AND STOP CODONS 3.65Gya

translatase extinct

5 nucleotides-A, C, G, T, U. $\quad$ 5 x 5 = 25 so the third position needed for

26 amino acids $\quad$ coding whilst 2nd position became more fixed

Codon 1: 2+1

End of Multiple Reading Frame

e.g.1. Alanine-GCU, GCA, GCC, GCG, GCT.

e.g.2. Pyrrolysine-UAX.

e.g.3. Selenocysteine-UGX X = any of 5 bases.

e.g.4. Hypusine-AGX.

SECOND REALLOCATION EVENT

POLYMERASES SPECIALISED RE RNA/DNA

2-SUBUNIT RIBOSOME 3.50 Gya

4 bases-A, C, G, U for RNA-A, C, G, T for DNA

23 amino acids (20 + pyrrolysine + selenocysteine + N-formylmethionine)

Codon 1:2+1

e.g.1 alanine-GCU, GCA, GCG, GCC.

e.g.2 pyrrolysine-reallocated to stop (UAG+UAA+control molecule) and Tyrosine (UAC, UAU).

e.g.3 selenocysteine-reallocated to stop (UGA+SECIS), Tryptophan (UGG) and Cysteine (UGG, UGU).

e.g.4 hypusine-reallocated to arginine (AGA/AGG) and serine (AGU/AGC).

e.g.5 methionine and N-formylmethionine allocated AUG from Isoleucine.

Table 4.

mRNA CODON	Amino Acid	No. of Anticodons possible under revised Base rules
1. AAA	Lysine	11
2. AAG	Lysine	11
3. AAU	Asparagine	6
4. AAC	Asparagine	6
5. ACA	Threonine	12
6. ACC	Threonine	12

7. ACU	Threonine	12
8. ACG	Threonine	12
9. AGA	Arginine	28
10. AGG	Arginine	28
11. AGU	Serine	28
12. AGC	Serine	28
13. AUA	Isoleucine	11
14. AUU	Isoleucine	11
15. AUC	Isoleucine	11
16. AUG	Methionine	9
17. CCC	Proline	12
18. CCA	Proline	12
19. CCG	Proline	12
20. CCU	Proline	12
21. CAU	Histidine	6
22. CAC	Histidine	6
23. CAG	Glutamine	11
24. CAA	Glutamine	11
25. CGU	Arginine	28
26. CGG	Arginine	28
27. CGA	Arginine	28
28. CGC	Arginine	28
29. CUU	Leucine	28
30. CUA	Leucine	28
31. CUC	Leucine	28
32. CUG	Leucine	28
33. GGG	Glycine	12
34. GGU	Glycine	12
35. GGC	Glycine	12
36. GGA	Glycine	12
37. GAA	Glutamine Acid	11
38. GAG	Glutamine Acid	11
39. GAC	Aspartic Acid	6
40. GAU	Aspartic Acid	6
41. GCU	Alanine	12
42. GCC	Alanine	12
43. GCA	Alanine	12
44. GCG	Alanine	12
45. GUU	Valine	12
46. GUG	Valine	12

47. GUA	Valine	12
48. GUC	Valine	12
49. UUU	Phenylalanine	6
50. UUC	Phenylalanine	6
51. UUA	Leucine	28
52. UUG	Leucine	28
53. UAA	STOP	10
54. UAG	STOP	9
55. UAC	Tyrosine	6
56. UAU	Tyrosine	6
57. UGG	Tryptophan	9
58. UGA	Stop	10
59. UGC	Cysteine	6
60. UGU	Cysteine	6
61. UCC	Serine	28
62. UCA	Serine	28
63. UCG	Serine	28
64. UCU	Serine	28

MNS = k x e x C x S x F   Inapplicable to most inorganic molecules. Wholly ingested molecules, food, vitamins, toxins analysed at source cell too.

MNS – molecular natural selection (useful molecules/minute)

k – uncatalyzed product synthesis rate from specified substrates (moles/litre/min) where C=100

e – catalyst rate increase (eg. X 10^4) x catalyst conc. (% optimal). In place of k_{cat}/k_m

C – concentration of reactant substrates (% optimal)

S – stereochemical affinity of reactants (reactivity x stateW)

F – functional value of product (% optimal)

NOTE – MNS of a product is low if it is a. produced inefficiently b. is poisonous or c. useless. MNS is high if a product has many diverse functions or one crucial function.

EXAMPLE- ATP + AMP ←--→ 2ADP

Enzyme- Archaean adenylate kinase

MNS (ADP)= 10^{-6} x 10^4 x 10^{-2} x 10^{-2} x 10^2 x 10^2

= 1 x 10^{-2} moles/ litre/min.

= 6.02 x 10^{21} molecules ADP/ litre/min.

Cell volume=1x10^{-15} litres results in 6 x 10^6 useful molecules/min/cell. If F~ 0 (eg. HCN) then MNS approaches 0.

F is species or domain (ie DNA) relevant eg. NH$_3$ is a waste in eukaryotes but usable in prokaryotes in place of glutamine.

On Past the Eukaryotes

Many would find it hard to accept that the coding system was initially random and secondary in importance to bulk protein, polynucleotide and catalyst production. Nevertheless it is consistent with the phenomenon of similar enzyme and ribozyme activity being achieved by domains that are different from each other in their sequence and tertiary structure (and therefore in their phylogeny). It is also consistent with the observation that one protein can have several diverse functions in a cell, an interactome; for example, Elongation factor Tu in bacteria can 1.

Select, bind and energise (by GTPase) a tRNA-amino acid for the A-site of the ribosome 2. Co localise with cytoskeleton proteins (MreB) beneath the plasma membrane to assist in maintaining bacterial morphology, 3. Assist in refolding of denatured proteins in vitro, that is chaperone-like activity and 4. Act as a domain on the Qbeta phage RNA polymerase (along with EF-Ts which is the GDP release factor for EF-Tu) during proliferation in E Coli.

Additionally, the promiscuous ability of certain catalysts, such as the phosphorylases suggests that one sequence can catalyse several related reactions.

Furthermore, the ability of mature erythrocytes and platelets in humans to survive and function for many days without DNA illustrates that a narrow functional range can be achieved without a genetic code at all. These would be the only extant examples of a breach in Cricks dogma since the advanced control and feedback enzymes and cofactors allow DNA, RNA and polymerases, including ribosomes, to degrade and not be replenished. The relatively brief life of erythrocytes (115 days) and platelets (10 days) points to the essential nature of an archive for longevity.

The main reservations for the RNA world hypothesis is that there is no force to keep amino acids and nucleotides apart (at biological temperatures) if they have an affinity based on the force of electromagnetism and secondly, proteinoid catalyst formation by wet-dry cycling has been adequately demonstrated to be considered as a plausible prebiotic process.

This scenario claims that the protocell outlined is bacterial or archaean from their formation, has converged in their biochemical evolution and been subject to ongoing horizontal gene transfer. There are at least 14 pieces of evidence for this primordial divergence.

1. Battistuzzi, F. U. et al. (2004) supporting molecular clock studies indicating archaea and bacterial ancestors were the first biotic cells and diverged up to 4.1 Gya. This was followed up in 2017 by a more comprehensive study and more elegant circular branching phylogenetic tree. Potential systematic errors in logic or definitions in the algorithms raises the concern whether molecular clocks can be considered accurate at these great distances into the past.

2. The self-assembling nature of amphiphiles (sphingolipids, fatty acids, ketoacids and terpenoids) caused by Van der Waals, Debye and London forces resulting in archaea and bacteria having different cell membrane composition from the time of their primordial cell membrane formation; terpenoid vs fatty acid or ketoacid respectively.

3. The Lebrun et al. article 2003 on the arsenite oxidase enzyme phylogeny predating the modern cell and the archaea-bacteria split.

4. The phylogenetically different release factors (that bind a stop codon and hydrolyse the peptide chain from the last tRNA) of archaea and bacteria: if they diverged post the era of the modern cell, these would be related between the two domains. The Recycling Factors that separate the ribosomal subunits post translation are also evolutionarily distinct between the two domains, with the bacterial recycling factor sharing a domain origin with several aminoacyl-tRNA synthetases (Maxwell Burroughs A and Aravind L (2019) whilst the archaea use aIF2.

5. The structurally and functionally different flagella/archaella and pili for propulsion and adhesion and

6. the phylogenetically different primase and DNA repair enzymes.

Amazingly, the ACC adding enzyme of bacteria and eukaryotes is of class 2 while archaea use class1 ACC adding enzyme (Hou, Y. M. (2011) *IUBMB Life*, 62(4)). This appears to confound the notion that eukaryotes are descended from archaea that were infected by an aerobic bacterium but could plausibly be explained by the constant infection, predation (e.g. choanoflagellates consuming bacteria) and symbiosis of bacteria on archaea and eukaryotes (especially the mitochondrion forming endosymbiosis) which means gene transfer by mobile genetic elements resulted in this ACC adding enzyme similarity.

In unaffected archaea, the ACC adding enzyme continued to evolve away in its own direction. Since much of the 3' tRNA CCA end is coded on tRNA genes, the ACC adding enzyme, although ubiquitous, is a type of quality control molecule like RNAase P and therefore is likely to be of recent advent. Even this ubiquitous enzyme, RNAase P is dispensable in Nature as evidenced by Nanoarchaeon equitans that is the only species known that does not use it. Its small genome has dispensed with RNAase P by coding the CCA end of its tRNAs directly off the genes.

7. The different introns and protein encoding introns of archaea, which, except for some group 11 introns, are unrelated to any found in the other two domains of life (Zhao C and Pyle AM 2017). Following the endosymbiosis event, the eukaryotes had enough energy and genetic material to revive the spliceosome from pseudogenes and

8. is represented by the difference in amino acid sequence, structure and mode of action of the recombinase enzymes RecA (bacteria) and RadA (Archaea) (Seitz, E. M. et al. (1998) *Genes Dev.*) as well as the different Holliday Junction resolvases that cleave and ligate HJs to produce two double stranded DNA segments from the "crossroad" conformation of a HJ. This probably reflects a parallel evolution of two ancient groups of "dice and splice" enzymes essential for maintaining order from the chaos of biochemistry even though they are both ATPases. The chaos is compounded when scientists name a bacterial helicase involved in recombination RadA as well,

9. is the ATP synthase of the two domains of life which are considered different enough to have evolved separately even though individual proteins and electron transport chain complexes have been subject to significant horizontal gene transfer.

10. is the difference in techniques to unblock a stalled translation; archaea use the Pelota protein bound to IF2A whilst bacteria use tmRNA, a hybrid RNA bound to EF-Tu. Some of the above differences could have evolved post-modern cell but

11. a most telling difference is in the aminoacyl-tRNA synthetases which have a type 1 and type 11 in both prokaryotic domains based on protein domain morphology and tRNA binding conformation but a different phylogeny altogether between bacteria and archaea (Woese, C. R. et al. (2000) *Microbiol Mol Biol Rev*, 64(1), 202–236). This observation, fittingly by the discoverer of

the Archaea, Carl Woese, pushes the divergence between archaea and bacteria way before the modern cell.

12. The very rare presence of non-ribosomal peptide synthetases and polyketide synthetases in archaea has led to phylogenetic analyses indicating that they were likely acquired in archaea and eukaryotes by horizontal gene transfer (Wang, H. et al. (2014) *PNAS*, USA). This research finding ought to add weight to the primordial divergence hypothesis but convergent evolution is an alternative explanation and the authors concede that gene reduction with the great passage of time probably also occurred (i.e. the archaea have lost the need for them) thereby making 11 above the strongest evidence.

13. Out of 50–68 ribosomal proteins in archaea depending on species they are all represented in eukaryotic ribosomal proteins, whereas none are shared exclusively with bacteria (Londei, P. (2020) *Wiley Online Library*, doi.org/10.1002/). With proteins around the PTC and decoding channel being the most ancient and conserved, some should be similar between the two prokaryote domains if they diverged after the time of the modern cell.

14. The extant use of hypusine and dipthamide amino acids in archaeal initiation and elongation factors that probably reflect an ancient cytosolic de novo synthesis that has now evolved into a post translational in situ synthesis from lysine and histidine, respectively.

15. The presence of a peptidoglycan (polymers of N-acetylglucosamine linked to N-acetylmuramic acid by beta 1,4 glycosidic bonds interlinked by pentapeptide bridges of l- and d-amino acids) cell wall in nearly all bacteria whilst only some methanogenic archaea have a pseudopeptidoglycan wall composed of polymers of N-acetylglucosamine and N-acetyltalosaminuronic acid linked by beta 1,3 glycosidic bonds. This difference is probably the result of convergent evolution.

One striking similarity is the presence of Shine-Dalgarno sequence variations in both bacteria and archaea, possibly reflecting convergent evolution towards use of the extant genetic code, horizontal gene transfer and the many control mechanisms involving recombination, transposition and splicing outlined below.

Additionally, it is likely that the spliceosome has evolved in both domains as an offshoot of the ribosome around the time of the biotic cell with short, scattered RNA genes and spliced appropriate sequences into appropriate locations to produce both the Shine-Dalgarno sequence as well as the high sequence and individual base conservation (many with more than 98% conserved) of the prokaryotic PTC along a symmetry axis between the A and P centre near the PTC tunnel entrance reported by Ada Yonath in 2005 (Agmon, I. et al. *Biol. Chem. Vol.*, 386).

A 2015 analysis across the three domains of life found 23 conserved nucleotide sequences of 6 bases, each with 10 of those with >90% conservation (Doris, S. M. et al. (2015) RNA 21(10)).

Following intron removal, double stranded RNA was subject to base excision repair, nucleotide excision repair and base mismatch repair enzymes with repair polymerases then filling in the excised sequences and ligases closing the polymer.

Furthermore, those ribosomes with PTC nucleobases that did not extend away from the backbone of the RNA into the PTC were less effective so that the cells that contained them were selected against. This amazing likelihood was revealed by the findings in the distinguished GE Fox labs of this nucleobase arrangement exclusively in the PTC pore and no other RNA pores of the 23S ribosomal RNA. Following the advent of DNA these enzymes have now mostly transitioned to working on DNA except for some examples acting on rRNA.

Additionally, Holliday Junction Resolvase analogues have been found in eukaryotic spliceosomal RNA which hints at the plausible dating of both resolvases (that "resolve" the crossroad conformation of the Holliday junction into double strand DNA) and spliceosomes prior to the DNA era.

Subsequent loss of the spliceosome in prokaryotes following a period when reverse transcriptase faithfully archived the corrected RNAs of all types into DNA to then be ligated into chromosomes has led to great confusion regarding the origin of sequence conservation across domains.

Alternatively, the spliceosome ribonucleoproteins evolved into the Cas9 ribonucleoprotein of the CRISPR prokaryotic immune system that binds known phage DNA sequences, unwinds them and binds them to a complementary RNA sequence that Cas9 is bound to, then cleaves the double-stranded polynucleotide thereby inactivating the phage.

Within the Eukaryote domain ancient components of the spliceosome could variably form RNAase P, telomerase and the Dicer-Drosha-Pasha "microprocessor complex" enzymes that are not only involved in controlling gene expression by variably suppressing mRNA but are also involved in the DNA damage response. It is reasonable to surmise that this repair, control and defence was focused on RNA when it once comprised the archive of the cell.

The drastic reduction in nucleobase coding choices from 300 or so in the first protocell colonies to four by the end of the Archaean together with the work of the primordial spliceosome, aeons of horizontal gene transfer, repair enzymes and recombination controls together with RNA polymerases of high fidelity and the 29 types of DNA gene and gene product regulation listed below together with Darwinian molecular natural selection acting on molecular machines and cells is why these conserved sequences exist with gene duplication and replication slippage likely to be additional factors.

The spliceosome was lost for reasons of parsimony in prokaryotes following the evolution of the modern prokaryotic cell as the self-splicing introns (group 1) and maturase mediated introns (group 11) of bacteria and some archaea and the splicing endonuclease systems of archaea superseded the spliceosome by performing the same function cheaper regarding ATP and it likely also evolved into Cas9 of the CRISPR immune system.

There is an obvious question as to why archaea are almost always not predatory compared to some bacteria and many eukaryotes. Most superficially, one can point to the lack of a thick cell wall for self-defence. More deeply one can see predatory prokaryotes and protists along with multicellular life and its food chains with apoptosis encoded in their DNA as a symbiosis/endosymbiosis partner and a larder for non-predatory prokaryotes and plants thereby debunking the conceit that a predator is a superior being with the prey at their mercy.

Alternative hypotheses for the cytoplasmic membrane differences of the two domains is that the bacteria acquired an efficient fatty acid synthase early in evolution or that archaea evolved the efficient terpenoid synthases to deal with hostile environments. Both of these are less explanatory by far.

The timelines of this scenario could be expanded 10-fold for inclement conditions for life without changing the inevitable progression of the molecular evolution so 10 million years to form stable budding protocells and 200 million years to get to the 50 gene biotic cell stage still ends the scenario at 3.6 Gya (assuming life kept being extinguished by the Late Heavy Bombardment).

Once complexity began, however, there was a strong selective pressure for accuracy, control and catalytic efficacy in order to defeat degradation or dilution and later in evolution to compete with other biotic cells. Wherever there were the ideal Darwinian "warm little ponds" or "perfect storm" conditions, the scenario could progress very quickly. The possibility remains that molecular clocks are flawed on the basis of the potentially flawed assumption that the genetic code was always universal.

Conversely, with the fastest protein catalyst (Orotidine-5'-phosphate decarboxylase interestingly producing UMP) increasing the reaction rate by 16-23 orders of magnitude, some incredibly quick evolution can occur in the right conditions. This optimism is capped by the great difficulties in producing polymerase molecular machines, working helicases and the ubiquitous ATP synthase, which accounts for the enormous passage of time for complex unicellular life with mobility systems to arise and pave the way for multicellular life to arise.

The complexity of the biology that produces codons for leucine, serine and arginine (six each with variations in the first and/or second base) confounds any grand attempt at an elegant analysis of the code of life as do the wobble base rules which have been updated from those of Francis Crick. This analysis claims to be an exception by proposing a "first reallocation (reassignment) period" when the code was still 1+1 (1 fixed and 1 wobble base) gradually executed by the polymerases over millions of years at a time when nucleotide salvage pathways meant the nucleobase concentrations were maintained but choices were greatly reduced.

This firstly resulted in more than one amino acid with the same starting base and finally culminated in each of the four canonical bases being allocated to 16 amino acid codons and stop codons in the first position. Later when the codon transitioned to the 2+1 (2 complementary and 1 wobbly base), for the same reason (nucleobase variety scarcity compared to amino acids employed) codons or groups of codons that evolved for and belonged to extant or defunct proteinogenic, amino acids were reallocated by adaptor and control molecules (tRNA, aa-tRNA synthetases) to the "start" or "stop" function or to other extant proteinogenic amino acids during a time of amino acid depletion.

This was in addition to an ongoing selection at the polymerase-polynucleotide interface for the best substrates on the basis of available concentration x stereochemical affinity x functional advantage. This seemingly grand conjecture merely reflects the Collision Theory of Max Trautz from 1916 along with the principles of molecular evolution.

These substrates were not always nucleotides (Kool, E. T. (2002) *Annu. Rev Biochem.*) as pyrene, difluorotoluene, methylated nucleosides, ribose with side chains and other aromatic molecules could be incorporated by the DNA polymerases. What seemed to be errors was the variety that evolution could work on, constrained by the "functional value" part of the equation.

The survival advantage of having Methionine or N formyl Methionine as the first amino acid on a protein made reallocation of its codon a negative survival advantage and the reallocation to Stop simply meant that codon bound no amino acid and caused a disruption to translation, a known negative selection pressure if it comes too early in the gene.

By the time of the "second reallocation (reassignment) period" the four canonical bases were increasingly available at the adequate concentrations to be used by the fast acting polymerases which removed them from solution thereby shifting equilibria of synthesis and salvage pathways such that they were enhanced by Le Chateliere's principle.

These reassignments were driven by the inadequacy of the 1+1 codon length and by nucleotide concentration variations. Translational recoding was occurring at the tRNA-mRNA interface, which could be permanent if the amino acid depletions that caused them were lengthy and not fatal. They do not represent a violation of Cricks dogma because information is not flowing from the protein structure to the DNA. Cricks dogma, which he said was always meant to be a testable hypothesis, highlights the power of DNA in the translation process but it ought to be seen more as a team member in a genotype-phenotype-epigenetics-environmental nutrients functional tetralogy that has evolved into being.

It could be inferred that a defunct amino acid, possibly hypusine has recently had 2 groups of 2 codons (the 4 AG-codons) reallocated to arginine and serine which already had four each (they now have six each) and that Methionine has been allocated AUG from Isoleucine when it returned to translating as the best "start" amino acid after a period of diminished availability.

This return to translating for methionine occurred when bacteria evolved de novo synthesis pathways for it as natural selection proved N formyl methionine to be the best start codon for bacteria. It is significant to note that N-formyl Methionine is the "start" amino acid in bacteria, mitochondria and chloroplasts and it has its own special "initiator" tRNA, whereas Methionine is the start codon in archaea and eukaryotes suggesting that the coding system was complex and entrenched by the time the eukaryotes evolved more than 1.2 Gya as were the control and feedback molecules.

Hence, if de novo synthesis of Methionine led to its return as the best start amino acid for archaea and consequently eukaryotes, it began to bind a tRNA isoacceptor with anticodon UAC, possibly a former isoleucine anticodon with the mRNA codon AUG in an example of convergent evolution with bacteria except for the fact they use the N formyl methionine.

Indeed, if an alternative start codon is used in E Coli, it is often still translated as Methionine. Depletion of methionine would have constituted a survival crisis and could most efficiently be surmounted by the evolution of its de novo synthesis pathways, of which there are many, but could also be aided by predation. If Methionine returned to adequate levels in eukaryotes before its tRNA isodecoders and aminoacylator could evolve to not sterically bind it, then it would resume its former role with the same codon.

Some small evidence that methionine was allocated one of Isoleucines ' codons when it first returned to the coding system is the consistent bovine mitochondrial ribosomal translating of AUA, one of isoleucines' codons, as methionine (Suzuki, T. et al. 2014). The experiments and review by Battacharyya, S. et al. in 2017 indicate that methionine reflects the bioenergetic readiness of the cell to complete protein translation and its unique initiator tRNA composition is designed by molecular evolution to bind the initiation factors 1 and 2 as well as the P site of the ribosome whereas the other amino acid-tRNAs bind the A-site.

The authors found by experiments and review that the initiator tRNA was not crucial and could also work as an elongator and the elongator as an initiator. Phylogenetic analysis places the initiator tRNA met to be closest to the tRNA for proline so its advent is quite recent.

In 1975, Delk AS and Rabinowitz JC found that a folate depletion caused Strep. faecalis initiator tRNA to bind methionine and N formyl Methionine could not be formed nor could ribosylthymine as a post transcriptional modification on any tRNA tested. This was despite the authors supplying adequate methionine and highlights the crucial nature of nutrient levels in evolution.

It also suggests the possibility that N-formyl methionine in adequate concentration to be a substrate for an aaRS became toxic to bacteria as well as archaea and eukaryotes by interfering with methionine metabolism cycles resulting in the surviving bacteria evolving the in situ acting methionyl tRNA formylase as methionine returned to adequate levels. The negative selection pressure of maintaining an adequate cytosolic level of N formyl methionine at the expense of other metabolic cycles that needed methionine is also a factor.

As required methionine levels fell across the two domains due to its increasing use in metabolic cycles (especially the dUMP conversion to dTMP catalysed by thymidylate synthase in de novo nucleotide synthesis) the surviving bacteria were selected for on the basis of 1. De novo methionine biosynthesis and 2. Increased methionyl formylase activity (because it was needed for peptide initiation) until the enzyme evolved to act in situ on the tRNA (and is now termed methionyl tRNA formylase), in order to avoid the toxicity of high N formyl methionine levels.

The archaea had only to increase their de novo methionine biosynthesis since they never used N-formyl methionine.

The degeneracy of the coding ensures Cricks' dogma is obeyed and information flows from the DNA archive to RNA and then proteins so in the form it takes is a demonstration by life of the sophistication of extant control molecules and how they seem to have backup systems in the form of binding the next best stereochemical substrate when the usual one is unavailable.

In particular, it is apparent that the aa-tRNA synthetases add a correct amino acid to an appropriate tRNA isodecoder-isoacceptor, but it is the initiation factors and elongation factors that decipher whether that is the right amino acid for that mRNA codon and permit its binding to the A-site. As stated before, EIF5A even initiates the first peptidyl transferase catalysis before the ribosomal peptidyl transferase takes over.

With regards to the wobble base rules, it is far simpler to see the whole third base as "wobbly". If one uses the updated wobble base rules Methionine and tryptophan which have only 1 codon each (AUG and UGG respectively) have 9 possible anticodons each with C, pseudouridine, A, U, xO5U, xm5s2U, xm5Um, Um, xm5U in the wobble position (Murphy, F. V. et al. (2004) *Nature Struct.& Mol Biol.*).

Even if one uses the original Francis Crick wobble base rules, the Methionine codon AUG has two anticodons, UAC and UAU. This means it shares an anticodon with Isoleucine (UAU), thereby making the code ambiguous. This is the reason for the use of post transcriptional modifications lysidine (bacteria), pseudouridine (some archaea and all eukaryotes) and Agmatidine (some archaea) in the wobble position of isoleucine tRNAs that decode AUA, namely to defeat ambiguity with methionine.

Tryptophan, which has one mRNA codon, UGG, is also ambiguous because it shares an anticodon with stop codon UGA, namely ACC under the wobble base rules. Most of life does not have a tRNA with ACC anticodon, otherwise it would read through the Stop codon and the danger is avoided by a protein release factor binding in place of the tryptophan tRNA. An exception is the case of the several mycoplasma species where this UGA stop codon is consistently translated as tryptophan. What appears to be ambiguity is controlled and used to create flexibility. The amino acids with several mRNA codons have even more ambiguity at the anticodon level.

The discovered proofreading techniques of the aa-tRNA synthetases only tell part of the story since there are 13 domains with an unknown function to be explored and some do not need proofreading at all.

The inevitability of the scenario is only true if the raw substrates are in plentiful supply because salvage pathways and de novo synthesis pathways take a long time to develop; 300–800 million years, according to Caetano-Anollés, K. et al. 2013. Carbonaceous chondrite meteorites and cometary dust infall supplied those plentiful substrates along with subsequent physicochemical processes on Earth at a time when metabolism was slow and simple but varied.

The consequences of the Chicxulub carbonaceous chondrite bolide estimated to be 10 km in diameter were not sterilising for the Earth and indeed did not even wipe out multicellular eukaryotic life, let alone prokaryotes. The absence of oxygen in the Eoarchean and the hyperbaric carbon dioxide mean that a gigantic Chicxulub sized bolide would not cause the same destruction by fire, which will not take hold in these conditions.

In this scenario, the RNA world did not exist alone but together with some peptides and some DNA.

The use of four nucleobases and a 3-base codon in DNA does not reflect a great evolutionary bottleneck caused by extinction events but a path requiring the least energy to achieve in that four nucleotides are easier to synthesise reliably and quickly enough for polynucleotide synthesis (from two de novo synthesised bases Uridine Monophosphate and Inosine Monophosphate) when the evolved 3 base pair codon-anticodon-control and adaptor system of deciphering can make sense of it.

With the coevolution of the adaptor and control molecules (tRNA like molecule and the aminoacylating ribozyme or aminoacyl-tRNA synthetase) eventually they continued to improve fidelity and speed, which is crucial in the modern cell.

The biotic cell with modern genes started at 50 protein-coding genes plus tRNA and ribosomal RNA genes and about 60 kilobases that worked well rather than the previous multiple reading frames that gave great variations but at great cost in energy and waste. Each gene was therefore about 1,200 bases long, including introns with the exon averaging 1 kb and the post translational protein product about 330 amino acids.

A plasmid may be the closest extant clue to the size and characteristics of the biotic cells' DNA at the end of this scenario, with a polynucleotide ligase responsible for the circular shape. This genome has less than 50% of the genes of the obligate proteobacterial endosymbiont Tremblaya Princeps, 2% of the genes of a Pandoravirus (2,500 genes) and 1% of the smallest free-living eukaryotic genome found in Cyanidioschyzon merolae, a haploid unicellular red algae adapted to life in hot Sulfur containing springs with 16.5 Mbases, 5,331 genes of which only 26 have introns and 30 are tRNA genes (none of these with introns).

It has a complex life cycle with 20 chromosomes, production of gametes and five histone genes (Nozaki, H. et al. 2007). C. merolae has only one chloroplast and one mitochondrion, no vacuole or cell wall but has as many genes as E Coli and 100x the genes of this scenarios biotic cell.

The chemical systems of the biotic cell (receptors, membranes, enzymes and archiving molecules) were still developing which accounts for the far fewer genes than the minimal genome bacteria of today, such as Nasuia deltocephalinicola (a proteobacterium with 112 Kbases and 137 protein-coding genes), which is an obligate endosymbiont. Tremblaya princeps, an alpha proteobacterium mealy bug endosymbiont, has a larger genome but the fewest protein-coding genes at 110 (Lopez-Madrigal, S. et al. 2011).

The infancy of control and feedback mechanisms meant that any DNA polymerases of the biotic cell, at this stage only reverse transcriptase, allowed it to have several copies of its plasmid genome (polyploidy) on a nutrient dependent basis. This allowed it to have a copy in each daughter cell upon budding but the uncertainty of this outcome had driven the use of an actin homolog employed in budding, possibly ParM whose gene is currently located on plasmids, that attached to two plasmids and polymerised in an ATP or GTP dependent way (as does the extant ParM which can use either) until they were pushed to opposite ends of the cell (Shaevitz, J. W. and Gitai, Z. 2010).

The lack of sophisticated controls meant plasmids could vary in size and hence gene content from 1 kB to the full 60 kB, so equal distribution is crucial. In extant E Coli bacteria, this ParM induced polarisation of low copy R1 plasmids reduces plasmid loss during division by several orders of magnitude (Gerdes, K. et al. (1985) *J Bacteriol*, 161).

At 3.6 Gya, there were still enough meteorite borne organic substrates in the environment to prevent the need for complex predation or photosynthesis innovations. Some evidence for this is the geological discovery of a 3.46Gya giant meteorite impact evidenced by glass spherules found in Northwestern Australia between two volcanic layers that made their dating precise (Glikson and Hickman ANU Planetary Institute).

The 382 minimal genes proposed by Glass J I and C Venter for a free-living organism (mycoplasma genitalia) is true today due to the sophistication of a "modern" bacterium's needs (Glass, J. I. et al. 2006). A sophisticated computerised analysis that took endosymbionts into account proposed a minimum 206 essential protein-coding genes (Gil, R. et al. 2004).

This figure is falsified by Tremblaya princeps 110 protein-coding genes which is evidence that current estimates are too high because Eoarchean environments were likely to be more abundant and varied in nutrients than those possible in modern bacterial culture media and because of the promiscuous enzymes (act on several substrates or steps in a reaction pathway) of the biotic cell.

Each Tremblaya itself has several endosymbionts Moranella Endobia gamma proteobacteria in its cytoplasm whose genome is larger (>530 kb) (Lopez-Madrigal, S. et al. 2013). I believe this is the only known extant example of one prokaryote living in endosymbiosis with another with a recent genomic data entry reporting 406 protein-coding genes and 46 tRNA genes for Moranella.

Table 5 - Protein Coding Genes Of The Biotic Cell

1. Phosphokinase
2. Hydroxylase
3. Phosphatase
4. Phosphodiesterase
5. Phosphoribosyl transferase
6. Aminotransferase
7. ACC adding enzyme

8. Primordial ParM (actin homolog)
9. Helicase monomer1
10. Na+/K+ translocase
11. Helicase monomer2
12. Retinal binding H+ translocase
13. Methyl transferase
14. Carboxylase
15. Primordial FtsZ (tubulin homolog)
16. Hydrogenase
17. Dehydrogenase
18. Thiolase
19. Sulfur/sulfhydryltransferase
20. Glycerol synthase (from G-3-P)
21. Release factor
22. Primase
23. DNA dependent RNA polymerase
24. RNA dependant RNA polymerase
25. Reverse transcriptase
26. Simple (carbon monoxide) dehydrogenase
27. Simple Acetyl CoA synthase
28. Exonuclease
29. Primordial dynamin (DymA)
30. Transketolase
31. Polynucleotide ligase
32. Endonuclease
33. Primordial ferritin
34. Ribosomal protein 1
35. Ribosomal protein 2
36. Ribosomal protein 3
37. Pre Procollagen
38. Protease
39. Simple ferredoxin
40. Aminoacyl tRNA synthetase domain2
41. Aminoacyl tRNA synthetase domain1
42. Aminoacyl tRNA synthetase domain3
43. Topoisomerase

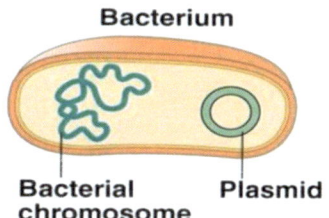

44. Initiation factor
45. NTP reductase
46. Aldolase
47. Hydrolase
48. Hydratase
49. Thioesterase
50. Lyase
51. Elongation factor
52. Amino acid isomerase   Simple Chromosome and Plasmid
53. Fibroin-like protein
54. Mutase

Nitrogen fixation is unnecessary at this stage due to ample supply of ammonia and ammonium from other physical (lightning) and chemical (Haber process in volcanoes, thermolysis of amino acids) sources as well as the lysed contents of colony members. The nitrogenase will evolve much later from the ferredoxin and reductase group of enzymes following the time of the modern cell when physicochemical and recycled sources of usable nitrogen are supplemented by the nitrogenase ability to overcome the high activation energy of $N_2 + 8 H + 16 ATP \longrightarrow 2NH_3 + H_2 + 16 ADP/P_i$.

In this scenario, the code was fully evolved by this stage, 200My after the end of the late heavy bombardment (3.6 Gya) but in reality, it could have taken more than 2Gy until the LECA forming endosymbiosis event for this to happen fully and could still be evolving to this day but so slowly we can't detect it or forecast its direction.

Despite the primitive nature of this cell many ribozymes, the protogene, some enzymes and the translatase have become extinct but it includes precursor proteins to pre-procollagen and fibroin (silk protein-see final chapter) and the most simple possible Acetyl CoA synthase and carbon monoxide dehydrogenase which are accreted assemblies of kinase, decarboxylase and Transferase enzymes.

The apparent inadequate number of protein products was enhanced to an adequate number by errors in transcription and translation as well as promiscuity of enzymes.

At this stage, primase exists as an initiator for the ancient reverse transcriptase by having DNA recognition motifs for ORI (origin of replication initiation) regions. Primase now has a certain conserved structure involving four antiparallel beta sheets stacked onto two alpha spirals, but these motifs may not have existed in our biotic cell yet. Without transcription factors, the biotic cell relied on a significantly increased affinity of its polymerases for promoter or Origin of Replication (ORI) regions on the DNA archives.

As similar polymerases evolved they worked to complement each other, culminating in the distant future in the multi-subunit holoenzyme DNA pol 111 seen in modern bacteria and the cooperation with primases. Even RNA replicases have this propensity to accrete with other (in this case host) proteins for full functionality as the Qbeta phage RNA replicase recruits both bacterial EF-Tu and EF-Ts for full function (Kidmose, E. T. et al. 2010).

Between the time of our biotic cell with 50 genes and the fully modern cell with binary fission and maybe 1000 genes this propensity to accrete and cooperate resulted in the RNA polymerases becoming multi subunit enzymes with two double psi beta barrels and the sandwich barrel hybrid motif that are present in all three domains of life. These beta barrel motifs serve to maintain the separation between the DNA strands in order for the mRNA to form on the template strand.

This evolution of RNA polymerase complexity is evidenced today by the mode of action of replicases which require a single NTP to bind to the template strand before binding and catalysing the polymerisation compared to DNA dependent RNA polymerases which bind promoter regions with transcription factors guided by sigma factors and which are capable of significant proof reading. Extant RNA ligases have evolved to work on single-stranded RNA employing an adenylation step where the ligase first binds and cleaves an ATP to form AMP. Extant DNA ligases have evolved to work on double strands.

DNA polymerase has not evolved yet but since dNTPs have attained a usable concentration in the cytosol, it will evolve from reverse transcriptases which themselves had evolved by this stage from ancient replicases bound to exonuclease. Alternatively, some repair DNA polymerases may have evolved from primases.

Initially replication of DNA must have been piecemeal, thus producing profuse circular plasmid-like structures until the lack of control inherent in such a system drove progressively larger replications and simultaneous lagging strand synthesis by the time of the eukaryotes culminating in whole genome replication prior to advanced cell division by mitosis.

ATP synthase has not evolved yet but its components, the Na+ pump and helicase, are included in the list.

Division occurs by budding involving simpler versions of ParM, MreB, FtsZ and dynamin when the cell has grown significantly.

The enzymes that catalysed the complex de novo UMP and IMP synthesis pathways are included in the generic enzymes listed above with the hopeful expectation that they were promiscuous in the sense that they were not confined to one set of substrates or one reaction (Khersonsky, O. and Tawfik. 2010) and that the original pathways were shorter (fewer steps).

Additionally, transcriptional errors, misacylation rates much higher than today, translation errors and random post translational alterations would provide more than 50 protein products of the genes and a host of ribozymes involved in splicing, RNA endonuclease, the peptidyl transferase ribozyme and tRNA added to the suite of genes available to the cell.

Furthermore, groups of the above enzymes could potentially self-assemble by simple electrostatic attraction at first to produce the enzyme complexes now recognised as the non-ribosomal peptide synthetases (NRPS), the fatty acid synthase (FAS) and the polyketide synthetases (PKS). The NRPSs could have added to the number of protein products of the small genome in a way that was not limited to the choice of amino acid types or their chirality.

The evolution of this type of multifunctional enzyme, albeit unrelated to NRPSs is now evidenced in eukaryotes, S. cerevisiae, in the form of the pentafunctional AROM protein of the Shikimate pathway that produces the aromatic amino acids Tyrosine, Phenylalanine and tryptophan. AROM catalyses steps 2-6 of the seven-step pathway and its domains are similar to mono functional E. coli proteins (Duncan, K. et al. 1987) thereby indicating that the ARO1 gene was formed by a linking of mono functional genes.

In the Eoarchean, the aromatic amino acids could be synthesised by a single promiscuous transferase enzyme catalysing a condensation reaction between serine and imidazole to produce histidine, serine and indole to produce tryptophan, serine and benzene to produce phenylalanine and serine with phenol to produce tyrosine. If this seems implausible to some, then one needs to keep in mind that a single enzyme selenocysteine synthase (with pyridoxal phosphate coenzyme) produces selenocysteinyl tRNA from serine bound to tRNA in bacteria, whereas an additional serine phosphokinase is used in archaea and eukaryotes.

These aromatic compounds were all present in the environment from breakdown products of kerogens and from the lysed contents of other cells until their biosynthesis was evolved. The circuitous nature of the Shikimate pathway has evolved for complex reasons, including availability of substrates and toxicity avoidance (e.g. of benzene). As a backup, the Diels Alder reaction provided the cell with cyclohexenes that it could convert into the range of aromatic amino acids in use in that era, with a second backup reaction being the Friedel Crafts reaction.

The spliceosome at this stage could be a homolog of the metaribosome and protoribosome. In this scenario leading to the 50 gene biotic cell, the spliceosome forms from accretions of proteins previously destined for the ribosome binding with endonuclease, ligase and reverse transcriptase to remove deleterious or useless mRNA sections.

This splicing had been occurring in a random manner for millennia on free floating cytosolic RNA but was acted upon by molecular natural selection favouring cells with useful splicing that resulted in enzymes and ribozymes of higher efficiency therefore it was a simple natural progression in our biotic cell of 50 protein-coding genes. Strong evidence for the possibility of this splicing is the extant existence of the Cre recombinase enzyme in bacteriophages that is ATP and cofactor independent and splices out certain DNA segments between two defined (LoxP) recognition sequences.

A phylogenetic analysis of the major and minor spliceosomes places them in the last eukaryotic common ancestor LECA in an advanced form but does not infer they were present in the "first eukaryote" (Collins, L. and Penny, D. 2005). Phylogenetic analysis is limited by the evolution of the genetic code so one can hypothesise that proteins destined for the ribosome in prokaryotes more than 3.5 billion years ago serendipitously bound splicing RNAs and found a functional niche in removing introns from RNA for reasons of parsimony and protection from harmful or useless, selfish genetic elements including mutated retroviruses, transposons and pseudogenes inserted by random ligase.

Supporting evidence comes in the finding of a helicase like protein PRP22 in yeast spliceosomes that shares RNA binding motifs with bacterial ribosomal protein S1 (Company, M. et al. (1991) *Nature*). PRP22 serves to mediate mRNA release from the spliceosome.

Introns type 1 and 11 and inteins have been found in phage viruses, in chloroplasts and mitochondria, in E. Coli, Cyanobacteria, Proteobacteria and in some archaea. Those in bacteria are self-splicing (group 1 introns) or use maturase (group 2 introns), a splicing, endonuclease and reverse transcriptase capable enzyme. Those in archaea use unique splicing endonucleases and ligases, thereby emphasising their uniqueness from the bacteria (Belfort, M. et al. 1995).

The presence of group 11 introns in some archaea is evidence enough that they could once have evolved and then lost a spliceosome. A recent study into maturase and group 2 introns has found they have an ancestor RNA molecule in common with spliceosomes and a protein component similar to flaviviral RNA dependent RNA polymerase and the Prp8 protein in spliceosomes (Zhao, C. and Pyle, A. M. 2017).

This could signify both a sharing and a recruitment of protein domains and RNA transcripts as well as a common ancestry. The assessment by some scientists that spliceosomes evolved from group 11 introns is ill conceived since there is strong evidence that mutations in the U12 introns on which minor spliceosomes act often result in their conversion to a U2 intron on which the major spliceosome acts.

This has resulted in a loss of the minor spliceosome in many closely related phyla (Turunen, J. J. et al. (2012) *Wiley Interdisciplinary Rev. RNA*) which is strong evidence that a large organelle can disappear in an evolutionary branch and leave behind the (altered) intron on which it acted. Since the catalytic core assembly and structure of the two types of spliceosome is practically identical, it was easy for nature to recruit subunits for the major and divert the subunits for the minor into other roles.

Indeed, the U5 protein is shared between the two spliceosomes. Introns can survive without spliceosomes but not vice versa due to recruitment into other roles, so the common ancestor hypothesis is far more plausible with a date range of 3.8–3.4 Gya. This means it recruited proteins destined for the ribosome together with endonuclease ribozymes and RNA ligases.

Parsimony of energy and size limitations may have precluded the prokaryotes from devoting such a complex system as a spliceosome to intron removal, especially as increasing reaction rate became important.

The laboratory observation that variation in organelle (e.g. ribosome, carboxysome, spliceosome) protein assembly in vitro and in vivo is highly dependent on temperature and pH is strong evidence for this variable primordial assembly process of organelles as is the large variety of proteins that can be used to make a U1-6 subunit of the spliceosome (>300 in humans) and the evolution of the alternative splicing system for tRNA in archaea and eukaryotes that involves a group of specific endonucleases, EndA, with different biochemistry whilst bacteria still employ group 1 introns (Hirata, A. (2019) *Frontiers in Genetics. RNA*).

It is plausible that these splicing introns and spliceosomes played a part in transcription termination and that the methods employed now in the three domains of life are a splicing endonuclease evolution involving some recognition of a repeating base (e.g. polyA) and cleavage facilitation.

The lack of clear homology between ribosomal proteins and spliceosome proteins or EndA endonucleases merely reflects the enormous passage of time since their divergence. Ribosomal proteins have been conserved on geological time scales whilst spliceosomal proteins and tRNA endonucleases in archaea and eukaryotes have gone down a different pathway of variability, hence flexibility so no homology is evident.

The result for complex humans is a far greater alternative splicing choice that brings the potential protein products of some single genes into the range of many thousands.

Walter Gilbert, who named introns following their discovery in 1977 by Sharp and Roberts (Gilbert, W. (1978) *Nature*) believes them, after decades of investigation, to be ancient if not primordial genetic elements. This view was backed up in 2001 by A Fedorov, with the assistance of Gilbert, in relating introns of ancient protein coding regions to the junctions of functional protein domains. This was not found to be true for "modern" protein domains (Fedorov, A. 2001).

Importantly, the actin ancestor molecule to ParM could have polymerised and depolymerised in response to variations in intracellular ATP levels and interacted with primordial FtsZ and primordial dynamin A domains and MreB to assist budding and the polarisation of the genome during budding.

Unlike extant mitochondria which sense lowered ATP levels via their RNA pol41-Mtf1 complex and increase the transcription rate of their products (ATP synthase, cyt C enzymes etc) our biotic cell had no such compensatory mechanism and slowed its metabolism by simple laws of equilibrium during low nutrition and ATP levels.

The multiple reading frame system is currently observed in some extant prokaryotes, viruses and mitochondria. Ribosomal translational frame shifting is currently observed to occur in a controlled manner for the enrichment of gene expression (Advani, V. M. et al. (2016) *Bioessays*) and transcriptional frame shifting on DNA is observed at "slippage prone sequences" with similar favourable outcomes for gene expression and products (Atkins, J. F. et al. (2016) *Nucleic Acids Research*).

In the biotic cell, the 50+ genes "suffered" similar slippages to provide variations that natural selection could work on. Previously, in the protocell, the uncontrolled nature of the frame shifting and overlap ought to have rendered the transcription process useless were it not for the lack of competition, absence of apoptosis, absence of predation and the simplicity of a protocells' needs.

Even at this biotic stage with metaribosomes and small versions of modern ribosomes producing both functional and useless proteins, it is likely that division was achieved by budding until natural selection and increasing complexity many years in the future favoured the biotic cells with accurate and equal division mediated by complex enzyme systems, (the Cyclin dependent kinase, Cyclin dependent kinase inhibitors and cyclins), cytoskeleton protein ancestor molecules to actin, tubulin and intermediate filaments (primordial MreB, FtsZ and FilP respectively) and regulating signals based on phosphorylation and phosphatase enzymes that cause the cell to replicate its' DNA for a division event (Lim, S. and Kaldis, P. (2013) *Development*).

This complexity also depends on productive and fast metabolic cycles. Even today, after 4 billion years of evolution, many yeast cells, the planctomycetes and L-form bacteria divide by budding, which suggests that a process that works can be retained by life indefinitely even if it is lacking in sophistication.

The carotenoids, phycobilins and heme were all present by this stage in catalysed assemblies of pyrrole rings derived from 5-aminolevulinic acid around Mg^{2+} or Fe^{2+} but not chlorophyll, a complex tetrapyrrole molecule that requires more than 17 enzymes to synthesise. Alternatively, the first chlorophyll synthesis pathway could have been less complex with a catalysed assembly of tetrapyrrole around Mg^{2+} with six types of bacteriochlorophyll molecules having evolved to date in addition to the chlorophyll a, b and c of plants, green Sulfur bacteria, cyanobacteria and dinoflagellates.

This catalysed assembly could have evolved from uncatalysed corrole synthesis from benzaldehyde and pyrrole in methanol, HCl and water to produce the terrapyrrole bilane (corrole) followed by ring closure with p-chloranil, a chlorinated benzene derivative. All of these molecules were plausibly present from the breakdown products of kerogens.

Oxygen could have been pumped into the atmosphere from 3.4 Gya for over a billion years by bacteriochlorophyll bacteria with an oxygen evolving complex, OEC, before the true cyanobacteria appeared 2.1 Gya with their chlorophyll-a and the extant Oxygen Evolving Complex. There is phylogenetic evidence that the OEC preceded Photosystem 11 so the extant lack of the OEC in all but the cyanobacteria is best explained by the likelihood that prokaryotes that couldn't split water used an alternative electron donor and the OEC became redundant in those biotic cells.

RuBisCo (>500kD) is too complex to be present so early and other less efficient carboxylase enzymes catalysed a primordial Calvin cycle, themselves superseding the inorganic carboxylases Zn^{2+}, Cu^{2+} and $Rhenium^{2+}$. The specific photosynthesis membrane-bound electron transport chains were continuously evolving to make use of porphyrins' resonating response to light, which later evolved into the biliverdin, bilirubin, haem and chlorophyll group of bilin chromophores.

The proteins to which these chromophores attached in the electron transport chains (phycobiliproteins and opsins) would not be possible without the already evolved archival, transcription and translation molecular machinery. A simpler carboxylase and other basic enzymes from the above list could have fixed carbon from CO_2 to start the Calvin cycle before the advent of RUBISCO enzyme by employing ATPs generated by a newly evolved ATP synthase in the cell membrane to produce glucose and other products for amino acid and sugar biosynthesis all beginning with phosphoenolpyruvate and glyceraldehyde 3 phosphate. Hyperbaric CO_2 levels would greatly aid the primordial Calvin cycle.

Before the advent of chlorophyll biotic cells may have used phycobilins and phycobilisomes to store and transfer light energy through cytoplasmic membrane-bound electron transport chains that pumped protons out of the cell. ATP synthase had evolved by this stage by a merging of ATP dependent helicase and a membrane bound ion channel or proton pump together with other proteins to generate ATP from ADP by using the energy of the proton motive force.

The evolution of Photosystem 11 and the OEC is of great interest to scientists as various bacteria use it as a serendipitous evolution that employs the chemical ability of manganese oxide to catalyse splitting of the water molecule by employing the porphyrin molecules (of which chlorophyll a, b and c, bacteriochlorophylls-a to d are derived) ability to absorb and convey light energy through resonance.

The evolution of the oxygen evolving complex fast tracks the expulsion of dioxygen and the capture of 4 electrons from H2O to replace those sent down the electron transport chain in this process and hence facilitates the manganate chemical process that had been active long before it ever evolved, namely the reverse of the common reaction, heat + 2MnO2 + 4KOH + O2—>2K2MnO4 + 2H2O.

A common ancestor protein to key oxygen evolving complex proteins, D zero, is estimated to have been present by 3.4 Gya (Cardona, T. et al. (2018) *Geobiology*, 17(2)).

Eukaryotes had yet to evolve and our humble biotic cell described here may represent the ancestors of aerobic proteobacteria that had yet to form an endosymbiosis with an archaean species (Lynn Sagan J Theor Biol 1967) to give us mitochondria (Davidov, Y. et al. 2006) and the eukaryotes. Before the advent of the eukaryotes, enough ligases and DNA replicases had evolved to result in long DNA polymers that were kept from supercoiling by ancient topoisomerase and gyrase that had themselves evolved from endo/exonuclease and polynucleotide ligases.

A plausible scenario for the endosymbiotic event that eventually led to the eukaryotes, based on phylogenetic studies of mitochondrial genomes, is afforded by a 2011 study by K Georgiades and Raoult, *Biology Direct* involving the failed predation by a proto-Rickettsiales, proto-Rhizobiales and proto-alpha proteobacterium of early pre eukaryotic cells on many occasions approximately 1.0Gya years ago which led to the wealth of genes for the eukaryotic cell.

This "strong evidence" based on phylogenetic studies could be accounted for by a prolonged failed predation by a common ancestor of the three classes of alpha proteobacteria proposed by the authors only much earlier, over 1.2Gya (Shih, P. M. and Matzke, N. J. (2013) *PNAS*, USA, 110(30)). Others are of the opinion that they have discovered fossil evidence of eukaryotes dating to 1.7Gya. Ongoing predatory behaviour and endosymbiosis events tend to cloud the earlier endosymbiotic event, which is of most interest.

If these figures are accurate, then it took 2.3 billion years of evolution to go from the biotic cell with a modern code and molecular machinery 3.5 Gya to this endosymbiotic period at 1.2 Gya. A review by Gray MW in 2012 describes this endosymbiotic gene transfer as a "hijacking" by the archaeon of the genes of the would be predator (Gray MW 2012).

This may reveal reasons why microscopic predators have evolved to kill their host after being transmitted to a new host: because the hosts are plentiful and a partial predation could result in resistance and domination by the host of the predators genes and products. A total eradication of the host is suicide for the predator, hence evolution has erred on the side of endosymbiosis.

This analysis suggests that predation, which most likely began with prokaryotes predating other prokaryotes by passively adhering to their plasma membrane, secreting proteases to breach the membrane and ingesting their nutrient contents (Davidov, Y. et al. 2006), is an ancient process driven by the gradual depletion of organic chemical resources following the end of the late heavy bombardment as they were ingested by biotic cells, turned into unreactive kerogens by the heat and pressure of rocks or simply diluted beyond the point of usefulness.

Predation, symbiosis, photosynthesis and de novo nutrient synthesis pathways were most likely all driven by this depletion but again the process was gradual and was effected by molecular evolution of enzymes. Whatever intercellular medium was used to share nutrients and buffer ionic, heat or nutrient fluxes now became the medium through which primordial predators could extend a filamentous creation (probably of type 111 secretion system in bacteria or type 4 secretion system in archaea i.e. syringe shaped pilus) to access nutrients from its neighbours.

These tiny appendages currently share homology with flagellum hook proteins and have eight homologs of the nine proteins found in the flagellar apparatus (Troisfontaines, P. et al. 2005). They inadvertently resulted in some exchange of polynucleotide material in the process. The ancestral proteins that led to the injectisome branched away into the flagella, pili, fimbria, cilia and cytoskeleton fibres of immense diversity and function using available proteins such as those of the ATPase (shares homology with Fil I of the flagellum) to begin building these complex, enormous structures long after the advent of the ATP synthase (Liu, R. and Ochman, H. (2007) *PNAS*, 104, 17, 7116–7121).

Predation began with biotic cells attacking adjacent members of their own colony until the obvious negative selection pressure of this course of action together with self-defence innovations such as the cell wall evolved chemical systems that focused the attack on other types of biotic cell.

Alternatively, the developing control circuits limited the attacks on other colony members to periods of starvation and limited their extent, as observed in extant Bacillus subtilis species during spore formation. Phylogenetic studies place the "injectisome" and the flagellum proteins in quite separate groups meaning that they have not shared lateral acquisition of genes but instead diverged from a common ancestor molecule (Gophna, U. et al. 2003) close to the time of our convergently evolving biotic cells.

The extreme complexity of the flagellum means it evolved from the type 111 secretion system and not vice versa. Importantly, Gophna et al. conclude 'The suggestion that Type 111 secretory system genes have evolved from genes encoding flagellar proteins is effectively refuted.' This refutes the concept of a spirochete being the endosymbiont ancestor of the centrosome and there is good evidence that the flagellum basal body and hook in gram-negative bacteria evolved from similar proteins to the type111 injectisome structure since they are homologous (Liu, R. and Ochman, H. 2007).

The eukaryotes have the unique use of microtubules and Dynein ATP powered molecular motors in their flagella whilst the archaea had gone down a similar evolutionary pathway towards the archaella that grows from the bottom and uses ATP but never evolved or else lost the type 111 secretion system and its genes and either abandoned or never acquired predation as a means of nutrition. Gram-negative bacteria use the proton motive force, the sodium motive force and also have an ATPase in their basal body.

Previous to the complex injectisome a simple symbiosis by cytoplasmic membrane adhesion and exchange of nutrients following proteolysis would have occurred since it is simpler. This is evidenced today by the Ignicoccus, a hyperthermophilic, chemolithotrophic archaeon that has a 400 nm diameter Archaeon symbiont Nanoarchaeum equitans attached to the outer membrane. This parasitic archaeon has lost the ability to biosynthesise most amino acids, lipids and nucleotides but is parasitic rather than predatory. It mimics the abundance that was available to protocells of the Eoarchean.

A second observation from this research is that predatory prokaryotes (either prokaryote-prokaryote or prokaryote-eukaryote) are vast in the minority of species. This observation indicates that the predatory eukaryotes have dominated this form of nutrient acquisition and the majority of prokaryotes, plants and fungi have reverted to symbiotic relationships and saprophytic-autotrophic means of obtaining their nutrients.

Pasternak, K. et al. in 2013 identified a bacterial "predatome" that involved heightened expression of proteolysis genes and adhesins and a loss of some vitamin, nucleotide and amino acid biosynthesis genes as well as a consistent use of the mevalonate pathway (Acetyl CoA—> isoprene) for isoprenoid synthesis while non-predatory bacteria use the DOXP (pyruvate + glyceraldehyde 3 phosphate—> isoprene) pathway.

With archaea known to have widespread use of the mevalonate pathway for the "ether linked isoprenyl lipids that constitutes their plasma membranes" (Lange, M. B. et al. (2000) *PNAS*, USA, 97(24)) the Pasternak et al. finding reflects the greater sophistication of the MVA pathway that uses CoA, a highly evolved molecule, to begin the pathway.

With this domain oriented view of predation, the herbivores of all sizes are themselves predators.

Chloroplast ancestors, the Cyanobacteria were yet to evolve due to a lack of true speciation but by 3.4 Gya at the earliest, 200Myears after our humble cell of 50 protein-coding genes, oxygen producing bacteria had evolved according to a review and phylogenetic-molecular clock study (Falcon, L. I. et al. (2010) *The ISME Journal*).

This complex evolution of photosynthesis was driven by a depletion of nutrients available from predation, scavenging lysed cell contents and absorbing environmental organic chemicals of meteorite origin and began with the phycobilin based photosystems, which are now accessory pigments to chlorophyll. This could be another example of Nature maintaining a backup system that potentially works.

More recent phylogenetic analysis of photosystem 11 place it in the early Archaean, over a billion years before the common ancestor of cyanobacteria 2.1Gya and it is logical that many photosynthesising bacteria could not split water and hence used alternative electron donors to H2O.

Protein D0, the common ancestor of two ancient oxygen evolving complex proteins D1 and D2 dated to 3.4Gya (Cardona T et al. 2018 Geobiology 17(2). This finding is consistent with the finding of non-oxygenic PS11 complexes in other extant bacterial phyla, including the proteobacteria, they simply lost the OEC by using other electron donors instead of water.

It suggests some biotic cells could have become oxygenic in the Palaeoarchean period (3.60–3.20 Gya) from 3.40Gya when D zero evolved and it took nearly a billion years for saturation of mineral oxides, mainly iron, before atmospheric oxygen levels could rise significantly. At the genomic level, it took over a billion years for true cyanobacteria (with chlorophyll-a to evolve 2.1 Gya which opens up the question of variable criteria on which species definition is made.

The attempted predation by cyanobacteria of mitochondrion bearing endosymbiont archaeukaryotes to start the photosynthesising eukaryote line, probably comprising freshwater green algae, occurred over 1.1 Gya (Shih, P. M. and Matzke, N. J. (2013) *PNAS*, USA, 110(30)). This date is 1 billion years after the cyanobacteria evolved and suggests that photosynthesis was not the only strategy that cyanobacteria used to get the energy they needed.

The extensive thylakoid membranes of cyanobacteria, if present 1.1 Gya, are a plausible source of the extensive membrane systems of eukaryotes, including the nuclear envelope, the endoplasmic reticulum and the Golgi bodies. One hundred million years is more than enough time for redundancy of the cyanosome-phycobilisome electron transport system in Protozoa through lack of use. With protozoan Choanoflagellates being predatory (feed on bacteria) ancestors of multicellular sponges, they are excellent candidates for this route to the Animalia.

More precisely, workers in the field conclude from phylogenetic and molecular clock studies a common ancestry with Metazoa in the Tonian epoch 720–850 Mya and have detected significant gene loss in Choanoflagellates. Photosynthetic gene reduction by 800Mya together with further collagen and chitin development could then plausibly pave the way for the rise of the multicellular heterotrophic phyla, the Animalia and Fungi, the earliest fossils of which are the sponges of the Ediacran (>620Mya) according to the fossil record followed closely by Charnia.

These were hundreds of millions of years later than the multicellular photosynthetic algae such as Proterocladus at 1Gya which presumably began the multicellular plant line of organisms and this is more than enough time for the protist thlakoid membranes to unravel into the internal membranes of all Eukaryotes.

It is hypothesised in this scenario that Porifera, Cnidaria, Charnia, Molluscs, Kimberella, Arthropoda and Picaia, all of the animalia kingdom and fungi, their own kingdom, derived from a common heterotrophic protist ancestor ~800Mya that became multicellular, mobile in all but the sponges, sea pens and mature fungi, lost photosynthetic metabolism but left no fossil record. The fungi are also immobile as adult organisms but motile in gamete stages.

If the failed predation by or of the cyanobacteria was compounded by transient endosymbiosis effectively, the Cyanobacterial genes for membrane building would be gained by endosymbiotic gene transfer to the host.

Extant Melainabacteria are a phylum of cyanobacteria that have lost their photosynthetic mode of nutrition by being predatory, thereby supporting this hypothesis.

In the distant future, in evolved chloroplasts the stromal (layered) thylakoids would evolve further in some areas of the chloroplast into grana, stacked and connected discs of membranes whose evolved purpose is almost certainly the enhancement of a potential difference across the "stack" by the Voltaic pile effect increasing the electromotive force (voltage).

With PS11 concentrated in the grana and PS1 concentrated in the stromal thylakoids, the enhanced electromotive force hurries electrons through the membrane associated electron transport chain from PS11 to PS1 and then Ferredoxin-NADP reductase and hurries protons from the grana lumen into the stroma of the chloroplast via the ATP synthase.

This voltaic pile is also evident in the stacked phycobiliproteins in the phycobilisome antennae attached to Cyanobacterial thylakoid membranes which are estimated to have a 95% efficiency in converting light energy to chemical energy. Thylakoids are similar in structure to smooth and rough endoplasmic reticulum, thereby making it evident that eukaryotes are a product of both endosymbiotic events, alpha proteobacterium and cyanobacterium.

Snowball Earth put a great pressure on living organisms towards predatory behaviour, increasing size for warmth (lower surface area to mass ratio), cooperation and self-defence, efficient photosynthesis, oxidative phosphorylation by seconding mitochondria and towards oceanic habitation to the point that when it ended, multicellular Metazoa (e.g. sponges, charnia, picaia), algae (e.g. seaweeds) and sexual reproduction had evolved considerably in the ocean and deep lake habitats that could support their increasing weight whilst the land was mostly inhabited by prokaryotes.

The endosymbiosis of the alpha proteobacterium within the archaea to produce the eukaryotes had many benefits: 1. Acquisition of oxidative phosphorylation genes 2. Acquisition of sphingolipid and ceramide synthesis genes that increasingly free the organism to grow without being as dependent on phosphorus for phospholipids and 3. Acquisition of genes for synthesis of fatty acid synthesising molecular machines. Following the Cyanobacterial endosymbiotic event on archaeukaryotes they also acquired internal membrane building genes.

Even though meiosis can occur in single-celled organisms, it would seem that multicellularity drove the requirement for meiosis (using variations of enzymes that had evolved to create the orderly mitotic process) as budding became an impractical way of propagating colony individuals with enough gene diversity to allow Darwinian evolution to work well.

It is noteworthy that, in prokaryotes, the predator is almost always smaller than the prey. Some evidence that this was possible is the extant predatory cyanobacterium Vampirovibrio Chlorellavorus that has a flagellum but is immotile. It attaches to the periplasm of single-celled algae (Chlorella) and divides while siphoning the cytoplasmic contents through a type 4 secretion system apparatus (Hugenholtz, P. et al. 2015).

Vampirovibrio is not photosynthetic but genome studies place it in the Cyanobacteria phylum and Melainabacter class of bacteria. It has over 2800 genes which is about half the genes of free-living Cyanobacteria. By being predatory, it has lost many metabolic synthesis pathways including photosynthesis which demonstrates that a similar gene reduction in algal protists could have begun the protists that would give rise to the Eumetazoa namely the common ancestor of Chordates, sponges (Porifera), Cnidaria, Nematodes, Molluscs and Arthropoda.

Several examples of true endosymbiosis by a cyanobacterium exist with a Cyanothece derived species of 1,720 open reading frames that lives in the diatom species Rhopalodiaceae, losing its photosynthetic ability over the 12 Mya estimated endosymbiosis and containing hundreds of pseudo genes indicative of host domination and suppression of its genome (Nakayama, T. et al. (2014) *PNAS*, USA). This proves that photosynthesis can be lost quickly on a geologic time scale.

Another true cyanobacterial endosymbiont of a protist is the alpha Cyanobacteria derived chromatophore of protist Paulinella chromatophora, a non-phagotrophic protist that harbours Cyanobacteria with only 867 protein-coding genes, the smallest known to date. They provide the host with energy from photosynthesis (Nowack, E. C. M. and Melkonian, M. 2010), thereby demonstrating that drastic gene reduction does not necessarily eradicate a useful function.

More genomic evidence lies in the larger genomes of chloroplast DNA compared with mitochondrial DNA (~100 genes vs an average of 37 genes respectively). This fact reflects a shorter time over which chloroplast genes have had to transfer to the nuclear genome by endosymbiotic gene transfer, a process which occurs almost exclusively in the direction of the host genome.

This endosymbiotic gene transfer from the mitochondria to the host nucleus is virtually total in two Dinoflagellata (eukaryote) species Cryptosporidium Parvum and Hematodinium which have only minute mitochondrial fragments that lack genes (Gornick et al. (2015) *PNAS*).

The transfer is total in the protist eukaryote Monocercomonoides, an intestinal parasite of chinchillas and other animals that have no mitochondrion or remnants. With eukaryotes lacking cell membrane ATP synthase, this means Monocercomonoides lacks any ATP synthase and has adequate ATP synthesis from enzymatic breakdown of nutrients (e.g. the ATP producing arginine deiminase pathway) to sustain its energy needs without the proton motive force. This proves that, in a nutrient rich environment, the ATP synthase is redundant.

The sum of this evidence and that of mitochondrial evolution points to an endosymbiosis that is based on competition for nutrients, hence energy and that is dominated in the long term by the host to the point that the endosymbiont may be employed as an organelle (e.g. mitochondrion), slowly deleted as in Monocercomonoides, used to store and possibly express numerous genes gained by horizontal gene transfer (as in the case of the extant plant Amborella Trichopoda) or accommodated as a true endosymbiont. At the organelle stage, they no longer have enough control and feedback genes in their archives to be independent, even in their fusion and fission functions.

This means that the endosymbionts' long term survival depends on the health and survival of the host of which it may eventually become an indistinguishable part. During a period of chaos, destruction and plenty, such as a giant carbonaceous chondrite meteorite strike, there should be a survival advantage to endosymbiont relationships compared to independent organisms.

Transposase genes (transposable DNA gene elements) and retrotransposons would appear to be beyond the era of this simple scenario but could be a molecular fossil of this pre-histone and pre-chromosome era where the genome was scattered in the cell and was short in length. In the distant future, from the era of this scenario, transposons, retrotransposons and DNA recombination events would occasionally result in gene fusions that led to multi domain, multifunctional versions of previous enzymes.

To begin with, on the protogenes, the absence of start codons meant the start of translation occurred anywhere and continued synthesising the protein in the 5' to 3' mRNA template direction until the end of the polynucleotide molecule or a physicochemical interruption. For transcription, the template is read in the 3'-5' direction, a situation that exists to this day whether the template is DNA or RNA to form an RNA transcript from the 5' to 3' direction.

As the RNA became invariably double stranded with a drop in temperature, the polymerases still bound the 3' end of the template strand which represents the (-ve) antisense strand now that is bound to the 5' of the (+ve) sense strand. Then, as protoribosomes evolved, direction was established by the "steric gate" of the channel architecture from the 5' end of the polynucleotide in a 5' to 3' direction and continued until the 3' terminus for translation.

Some evidence for this early method of translation termination is the observed phylogenetic difference between archaean and bacterial release factor 1 which evolved separately after the two domains separated but then converged in their evolutionary morphology to resemble tRNA (in order to bind the "stop" codon in the A-site of the ribosome) and acquire the GGQ (glycine-glycine-glutamine) motif that hydrolyses the forming polypeptide in order to effect its release from the tRNA in the P position of the ribosome.

This would suggest that release factors were not present in the original protoribosome biotic cells but may have been present by the time the modern ribosome had evolved fully. The GGQ peptide cleavage motif of release factors intimates that, for primordial transcription, similar proteins bound the archival strand at polyU analogous regions and cleaved the forming mRNA strand at polyA tail analogues until the current similar but varied termination systems evolved.

Logic would suggest that the start and stop codons evolved after the three base codon had evolved and there was enough of a polynucleotide archive to allow this new system to work. Multiple reading frames thence became rarer and frame shifting evolved towards a fine tuning role for the biotic cells' functions as it is today. The use of Methionines' codon AUG as a start codon is consistent with a scenario in which start and stop codons were selected for after the 3 base codon was in effect (Belinky, F. et al. 2017).

It is the assertion of this scenario that AUG was reallocated to N-formyl Methionine and methionine from Isoleucine, as the trial and error of natural selection chose N formyl Methionine to be the best start codon for bacteria and methionine for archaea. Methionine is rare in protein sequences, as S-adenosyl Methionine it is a cofactor in several reactions and by being a central molecule in many metabolic cycles including the important plant hormone ethylene (the Methionine or Yang cycle) and thymidine synthesis its adequate availability reflects a fitness of the cell to begin translation.

Subsequently, it became the best stereochemical fit for ribosome and initiation factors alike. This means Methionines' original codons were reallocated during a period of methionine depletion and it acquired the same AUG codon, from Isoleucine, as its formylated molecule when it returned as methionine de novo synthesis pathways (there are several different pathways, some more direct than others) were selected for. The dedicated formylating enzyme methionyl tRNA formyl transferase must have existed by this stage.

There is evidence that other (mutated) codons can work as start codons even though another amino acid is laid down in place of Methionine (Drabkin, J. H. and Bhandary, R. 1998). The authors concluded AUG Methionine was selected over other choices by being the most effective.

Additionally, the UUG codon (leucine) was found to be selected against most of all but none of the alternative start codons were selected against as much as a mutation in other sequences in the gene presumably because of the assistance of the Shine Dalgarno sequence in the accuracy of the "start" command in bacteria. There are variations in results between prokaryotes and eukaryotes, but the finding that some of these alternative start codons are translated as Methionine or formyl Methionine is evidence that the aaRSs, initiation and elongation factors can override the genetic code by "reading" the D arm and T arm of the tRNA.

The highly conserved sequence preservation of tRNAs reflects their central role in the evolution of the genetic code, highlighted by an identical genetic sequence of all vertebrate initiator tRNAs tested to date.

Paradoxically, however, the ancient flexibility of RNA is highlighted in tRNA with the provision of isodecoders and isoacceptors for each amino acid, 85 post transcriptional modifications available, approximately double the tRNA genes to tRNA types ratio (i.e. not all available genes are expressed) and a large backup supply of suppressor tRNAs that can allow a read through of early STOP codons or other types of gene regulation.

More than 3.6 billion years later, some prokaryote mycoplasma species have assigned UGA stop codon to tryptophan with a specific tRNA, while some eukaryotes (e.g. paramecium) have reallocated some of their stop codons to Cysteine or glutamine (Bertram, G. et al. (2001) *Microbiol*).

In the case of cysteine, one of its possible isoacceptor anticodons ACU fits perfectly with UGA stop codon whereas glutamine does not fit perfectly with any STOP codons but its GUU anticodon can still hydrogen bond with the UAA Stop codon since Guanine and Uracil can hydrogen bond at two points to make this stereochemically favourable. In effect, these tRNAs outcompete release factors for the STOP codon.

Programmed read through (viruses) or unprogrammed read through occurs regularly, often depending on upstream individual nucleotides or sequences. Presumably these proteins can be trimmed by proteases later since the mutations are often not lethal.

It was only after all this infrastructure was laid down that DNA could be selected for by Nature via the polymerases that could recognise a difference between dNTPs and NTPs and a difference between Thymine and Uracil. Some evidence is the 4-point mutation of bacterial Taq DNA polymerase that rendered it equally fast but non-specific for NTPs or dNTPs (Ong, J. L. et al. 2006).

An example of a single mutation changing a DNA polymerase into a non-specific polymerase is the Murine myeloma leukaemia virus with Phe155 replaced by Valine (Joyce, K. M. (1997) *PNAS* and Guangxia, G. A. O. et al. (1997) *PNAS*). This is in addition to the Baogen Duan article of 2012 that reported changing a T7 phage RNA polymerase to a non-specific nucleotide polymerase with a mutation at Tyr 639 to Phe 639.

The sum of this evidence is that discrimination is a complex, acquired capability and the primordial polymerases were most likely to be non-specific for rNTPs or dNTPs. It also hints at the ease with which a single mutation could potentially have begun the era of DNA only to be selected for over aeons for reasons already mentioned.

Despite the importance of genomics and DNA directed dogma several control and feedback mechanisms have evolved to influence its biochemistry.

1. TRANSCRIPTION FACTORS binding PROMOTER regions of DNA genes probably evolved from proteins binding RNA sequences upstream of the RNA gene before the differentiation epoch but evolved later to

regulate transcription by the binding of protein transcription factors to facilitate polymerase binding to the promoter of the DNA gene thereby to accelerate cellular speciation.

This scenario is supported by Deshpande, A. P. et al. (2013), who report, 1. a 10,000 fold increased binding affinity of T7 phage RNA pol. for the promoter over other regions of DNA and 2. an induced fit mechanism in yeast mitochondrial RNA pol. effected by the Rpo41-Mtf1 transcription factor complex, which could sense and respond to ATP levels by increasing or decreasing mitochondrial transcription rates.

2. ENHANCER sequences in 5' untranscribed regions of a gene which can be bound by REPRESSOR molecules and their COREPRESSORS that blocks RNA polymerase binding and thereby blocks gene expression until an INDUCER molecule binds to it and either inactivates the repressor or induces the ACTIVATOR molecules essential for transcription. Before the advent of DNA genes, this function was achieved by

3. RIBOSWITCHES, which are RNA sequences found on 5' non-coding regions of bacterial mRNA that bind their own effector molecule e.g. glucosamine 6 phosphate which causes a conformational change to create a ribozyme-like entity that terminates transcription of the gene by cleaving mRNA and releasing the polymerase or inhibits the translation of the mRNA for its synthase by inducing a mRNA conformational change that hides the ribosomal binding site, the Shine-Dalgarno sequence. Riboswitches come under the ATTENUATOR (LEADER SEQUENCE) mode of gene regulation.

4. SMALL INTERFERING RNAs, ~24 nt long formed by cytoplasmic DICER cleaving of short RNA sequences which bind proteins to form RNA INDUCED SILENCING COMPLEXES (RISC). These bind mRNA to inhibit or cleave it, mainly in the 5' untranslated region, thereby rendering it ineffective. In eukaryotic RNA, the former promoters became non-coding regions whilst their 3' untranslated regions became binding regions for.

5. MICRO RNA's of ~60 nt long formed by DROSHA with DGCR8 protein. These bind ARGONAUT ribonucleoproteins that are also part of RISC complexes that silence mRNA by binding and cleaving, which added a further layer of control to gene expression.

Mi-RNA are produced by the DICER DROSHA PASHA group of RNA endonucleases, which protect eukaryotic and prokaryotic cells from viral infection and tumorigenesis by providing a system of cleaving recognisable harmful gene sequences. Clearly, the additional epigenetic control by

6. acetylation-deacetylation, methylation-demethylation or biotinylation of HISTONES to ravel-unravel DNA from NUCLEOSOME structure for transcription or replication thereby playing a significant role in gene silencing, cell proliferation and DNA repair. This epigenetic process is arguably the most influential extant control of gene expression augmented by others, such as

7. complex phosphorylation-phosphatase enzymatic action on enzymes to switch them on or off. In the distant future, these KINASES could themselves be modulated by

8. phosphorylation-phosphatase action on KINASE INHIBITOR proteins to add another level of epigenetic control and the evolution of

9. CHAPERONES to guide correct protein folding whilst

10. SIGMA FACTORS and their inhibitors that bind bacterial RNA polymerase transcription factors to guide them to the appropriate promoter region constitutes a tenth without falsifying Cricks dogma.

11. A recent review into INTEINS, self-splicing proteins that are found in all three domains of life indicates that they have a role in regulating gene expression in times of stress by being localised to transcription polymerases and to DNA repair and recombination enzymes (Pavankumar TL (2018). Microorganisms.

12. Walter Gilbert in his famous 1978 paper "Why Genes in Pieces" indicates that VARIATIONS IN GENE SPLICING by splicing ribonucleoproteins, type 1 or type 11 introns or spliceosomes constitutes a mode of variability to the expression of an organism's genome. This phenomenon is highlighted in eukaryotes, including humans with ALTERNATIVE SPLICING by spliceosomes potentially resulting in many different alternative protein products from a single gene. Introns themselves have been found to code for.

13. INTRON ENCODED PROTEINS with gene regulating function whilst

14. RECOMBINATION events on chromosomes during division and damage repair feedback favourably on DNA to maintain fidelity. These could not have arisen as repair orders by the genetic code but have arisen by natural selection of cells that had enzymes that recognised and restored cognant sequences, often working with RecA, RadA, Rad51, LIGASES or RESOLVASES (that cleave Holliday Junction crossover points) and specialised DNA polymerases.
15. POST TRANSCRIPTIONAL MODIFICATION enzymes acting on mRNA, tRNA and on
16. RIBOSOMAL RNA (often methyltransferases or acetyltransferases) alter their affinity for mRNA processing with human ribosomes being subject to over 200 post transcriptional modifications (in number, not variety) (Sloan, K. E. et al. (2017) *J RNA Biol.*) whilst RNA in general is subject to several different types of modification.

    It must be emphasised that most post transcriptional modifications have no known enzymes, probably being catalysed by nonspecific methylators or formylators. With the transition to DNA one of these modifications can work on DNA to protect cells from their own RESTRICTION ENZYMES (endonucleases that recognise and cleave both strands of DNA at certain sequences), namely
17. DNA METHYLATION catalysed by the enzyme DNA methyl transferase
18. Proteins are also subject to a range of POST TRANSLATIONAL MODIFICATIONS (e.g. glycosylation, phosphorylation, palmitoylation) that affects their function, including the spectacular examples of hypusine and dipthamide synthesis in situ from lysine and histidine, respectively. These PT modifications include the precise cleaving of pre proteins into one or more fully functional proteins by PROTEASES which have evolved into being alongside the endonucleases, exonucleases and splicing ribonucleoproteins, including the spliceosome.
19. The DEGRADATION OF DEFECTIVE PROTEINS following UBIQUITINATION or proteolysis tags in proteasomes analogous to the
20. DEGRADATION OF DEFECTIVE mRNA in exosomes of eukaryotes and degradosomes of prokaryotes.

21. The existence of numerous aminoacylated SUPPRESSOR tRNAs that are able to bind premature Stop codons and thereby cause a read-through that creates a variation to what was coded for.
22. The FORMATION OF OPERONS, assemblies of genes of complementary function in one open reading frame. They are transcribed and translated as one by an overlap of the upstream stop codon and the downstream start codon (Price, M. N. et al. (2006) *PLoS Genetics*, 2(6):e96), which cause the DNA dependent RNA polymerase to recognise neither Start nor Stop.
    The great significance of this molecular evolution is that when the mRNA for that operon is translated as one fused multiple unit and then cleaved by proteases into individual proteins they are in close proximity to 1. be assembled by chaperones into multimers in the case of structural proteins or enzyme complexes in the case of enzymes or 2. have a discrete but sequential effect in the case of enzymes.
23. A suite of DNA MISMATCH and DNA REPAIR ENZYMES that repair mismatches, insertions and deletions as well as using polymerases and ligases to complete the repair. These are coded for by DNA but had to have arisen by molecular natural selection of enzymes and their mRNAs when fidelity became important following the full biotic cell in the RNA-protein world and their RNA sequences were subsequently laid down in the DNA archives by reverse transcriptase.
24. The synthesis of Non-Ribosomal Peptide Synthetases by bacteria, fungi (which acquired the genes from the eukaryote forming endosymbiosis event) and rarely in archaea indicates an indirect peptide synthesis mode that is not directly coded by mRNA and ribosomal decoding of mRNA. The non-ribosomal peptides are comprised of such a variety and number of canonical and exotic amino acids of both d and l form that it cannot be said they are directed by the genetic code.
25. Alterations to the genetic code by elevations or depletions of nucleotide triphosphate substrates causing MISINCORPORATIONS. These can also potentially be caused by poisoning, e.g. caffeine overdose.
26. Alterations to the genetic code by TRANSLATIONAL RECODING caused by elevations or depletions of proteinogenic amino acid levels in the cytoplasm. This mechanism in practice is fleeting on a geological

time scale and is often harmful, but in a prolonged elevation or depletion in amino acid concentration would cause a RECODING and hence, a genuine breach of Cricks' dogma and a major mechanism of evolution.
27. Transcriptional slippage during DNA transcription to mRNA that creates an altered exon that may or may not have a deleterious effect.
28. Translational slippage of correctly transcribed mRNA at the ribosome that can cause a frame shift that may or may not have a deleterious effect.
29. A suite of RNA BINDING PROTEINS that are controlled by phosphorylation or dephosphorylation to inactivate the mRNA until it arrives at a target location.

These complex chemical circuits could only have arisen by natural selection on a molecular level with increased mortality and reduced growth and division rates of cells and colonies that could not evolve good control and feedback reactions that allowed them to evolve in order to meet environmental challenges. The presence of the archive molecule, DNA, in that loop is undeniable but its role as "supreme commander" should be seen in some perspective and not all the above gene expression and control methods are employed by all three domains of life.

Additionally gene duplications, whole (e.g. polyploidy or multiple alleles) or part (e.g. caused by replication slippage), horizontal gene transfer (conjugation, transduction and transformation) and retrotransposition are all mediated by enzymes and cellular processes that act as feedback and control on DNA not as servants of it. Replication slippage is a simple plausible explanation for tandem repeats with reverse transcription and ligation of short RNAs is a plausible alternative.

All of these processes are in addition to the mutations caused by physical or chemical factors on the archives content and sequence. Furthermore, as complexity increased reflexes and subsequently behaviours and preferences such as turning towards a food source, away from toxins or appearance preferences (animalia) all feedback on the archive without necessarily being driven by it.

Pursuant to these facts, it appears that the notion of DNA sequence being a supreme commander of the living cell is overtly accurate but fails to take into account this was not always the case and that it is controlled by much feedback chemistry. Sequence importance and the extant genetic code have evolved into being and were not always present.

The conclusion is that the above processes explain the plasticity of phenotype within much shorter time frames than mutation alone could possibly account for with Darwinian natural selection occurring at an enzyme, ribozyme, molecular machine and cellular level.

The homing endonucleases which precisely cleave the original site of an intein coding region in a gene to then be filled in by repair DNA polymerases is a potential assault on Cricks dogma but not a breach. Some bacterial species are known to possess two or more genome copies. The repair process itself in all three domains of life appears to be dominated and directed by proteins, including polymerases whose competence can only have evolved by decreased survival, growth and division rates of those cells with incompetent repair proteins.

Heritable prion diseases do not contradict Cricks dogma because information is not flowing from protein to nucleic acid.

This analysis suggests that the code for life has always been relatively accurate for replication and transcription but always "wobbly" for translation. Indeed, the error rates of some of the aa-tRNA synthetases is 1 in several hundred before proofreading, yet 1 in 10,000 afterwards compared to transcription error rates of 1:100,000 and DNA replication error rates after proofreading of 1: 100,000,000.

Proofreading was most unlikely in the Eoarchean so the high error rate of tRNA aminoacylation was part of the variety that Nature could work on. This signifies that the work of DNA is almost purely the supply and storage of a simple and accurate coding method analogous to the 0 and 1 (plus hard drive) available to computer science. The only reasons it didn't evolve to this point is the limited rates of 1. UMP and IMP nucleotide synthesis, 2. replication, 3. transcription and 4. translation and the wider availability of nucleotide varieties from recycling and ingestion.

The control, messenger and feedback molecules are the sophisticated readers, relays, networks and software that uses it to achieve survival and procreation. The great accuracy and, in some cases, speed of DNA replication (up to 1000 nt/sec in E Coli) has been acquired and was not always present.

From the era of the protocell, there was a selective pressure to give each of the two daughter cells an equal chance for survival. It is not effective procreation to bud into one well-equipped daughter cell and one daughter cell doomed by inadequate size and cell components, hence the selective pressure for binary fission.

A need, however, does not mean a solution is available and a crude budding facilitated by ATPase and GTPase domains on primordial cytoskeleton proteins sufficed until this selective pressure was eventually met by the complexity of a biotic cell with 350 to 1000 genes which developed several cytoskeleton components with complementary control pathways.

It should be concluded of LUCA that it is an erroneous construct that should be termed "the modern cell" already consisting of great variety and represents a great convergence in the evolution and dominance of the coding system, translation and transcription apparatus that makes life forms on Earth today, from viruses to humans, uniquely bound to each other by the advent of the polymer dependent polymerases culminating in the sophisticated translating machinery of the ribosome.

This dominance is highlighted by the loss of non-ribosomal peptide synthetases in higher eukaryotes. The modern two subunit ribosome is the polymer dependent polymerase that, together with those acting on RNA and DNA, interrelates all life on Earth and was likely formed by the initiation factors bringing a metaribosome with a blocked channel together with a protoribosome with a blocked decoding channel.

The non-ribosomal peptide synthetase archives were created by the reverse translatase acting on polypeptide synthetase sequences and were propagated by non-specific replicases to then be translated by protoribosomes. Later, with the evolution of specialist polynucleotide polymerases, their gene sequences, along with those of the fatty acid synthase domains and polyketide synthase domains, were laid down in the DNA archives by reverse transcriptases to be used as required.

These domains would assemble in the far distant future driven by DNA gene fusions to give life the multi domain non-ribosomal peptide synthetases, the fatty acid synthases (up to 2.6 MD in the fungal FAS with 48 domains) and the polyketide synthetases (Bukhara HST et al. 2014 Structure 23:12). The presence of FAS type1 multifunctional multi domain enzymes in mycobacterium, corynebacterium and nocardia suggests gene fusions in these species but demonstrates that bacteria are not confined to the type2 monofunctional FAS enzymes but have reverted to them, possibly for reasons of parsimony.

The glaring absence of a multi domain terpenoid synthase akin to the type 1 FASs may hint at one reason why Eukaryotes have fatty acid membranes when the evidence points to an Archaean ancestor that had isoprenyl phosphate based membranes. A review by Bohlmann et al. in 1998 PNAS 95(8) on the mechanism of action of terpenoid synthases would suggest that on a molecular level the branched terpenoid chains with a propensity for forming cyclic molecules, even at the C10 length (to form limonene) and their easy diversion into numerous primary and secondary metabolic pathways may have precluded an effective multidomain terpenoid synthase.

This means terpenoid membrane substrates could not be guarded and guided into membrane forming roles as easily as the fatty acids.

Furthermore, there are more than 10 steps in producing a C20 terpenoid and only six in producing C16 Palmitic acid. This was in addition to the endosymbiotic gene transfer over many years from the invading proteobacterium in the direction of the Archaean host, meaning the host thereby acquired the archives for additional fatty acid synthase domains to those it may have had previously. Gene fusions and operon formation subsequently led to the multi domain synthases being transcribed together.

Evolution has favoured fatty acid synthase products, especially palmitate (C16), for the ever-growing cell membrane of Eukaryotes (currently ~100x the surface area of prokaryotes) for reasons of availability in adequate concentrations than survival advantage. With phosphates being limited in the environment, the eukaryotes, with their greater demands for size and energy, increasingly employed sphingolipids that are amino alcohol-fatty acid molecules bound to choline, ethanolamine or glycosides thereby freeing the requirement for phosphate which is limited in the environment.

The greater energy of a mitochondrion bearing cell could accommodate either fatty acids or terpenoids but the fewer steps of palmitate synthesis means this course is more parsimonious. This scenario does not mean terpenoids were suppressed in eukaryotes since cholesterol and phytosterols derived from cycloartenol form up to 30% of their cell membranes and their biosynthesis follows the mevalonate pathway to squalene, a triterpene, before cyclisation to the sterols.

Sterols (lanosterol and phytosterol) are almost exclusively eukaryotic, with the exception of the Planctomycetes so it could be inferred that their biosynthesis continued to evolve in this direction following the major endosymbiosis event.

Therefore, on a molecular level, this would make this phenomenon, following a path of availability and parsimony, an additional influence on evolution to that of Darwinian natural selection.

A phylogenetic study by Boucher, Y. et al. in 2004 in *Molecular Microbiol.* into isoprenoid biosynthesis in extant archaea which outlines several "evolutionary processes" involved. These were "1. Co-option of ancestral enzymes 2. Modification of enzyme specificity 3. Homologous and non-homologous gene displacement 4. Integration of components from eukaryotes and bacteria and 5. Lateral gene transfer within and between archaeal orders".

This complexity is probably relevant to eukaryotic membrane evolutionary processes without altering the plausibility of the above scenario. Boucher et al. refer to a great plasticity of the terpenoid synthase enzymes highlighted by a single amino acid substitution converting a geranylgeranyldiphosphate (C20) synthase into a farnesylgeranyldiphosphate (C25) synthase in Sulfolobus acidocaldarius.

Inferences regarding phylogeny in these circumstances are more unsafe and this finding hints at another reason why multidomain terpenoid synthases are not feasible; minor mutations in one domain are more liable to render the whole product dysfunctional by disrupting the synthetic sequence, hence eukaryotes went down the path of fatty acid membrane synthesis.

The complex phenomena of binary fission, mitosis, meiosis, sexual reproduction, apoptosis, the fully functioning flagellum, Dynein, kinesin, microtubules and multicellularity are beyond the era of our biotic cell and require highly sophisticated reaction cascades, protein accretions and feedback loops involving many gene products and much energy.

The simplest of these, apoptosis, involved exapting elements of controlled metabolic cycles to self-defence and attack adaptations following the end of the late heavy bombardment and was later employed by members of cell colonies in altruistic apoptosis to outcompete not only their enemy colonies (predators or prey), but their rival colonies of the same species with colonies that exhibited this phenotype prevailing over those that didn't.

Following the advent of collagen-like proteins in bacteria (Yu, Z. et al. (2014) *J Struct Biol.*, 186(3)) and eukaryotes and subsequently true multicellularity in eukaryotes this apoptosis was used to provide extracellular matrices and for multicellular (e.g. embryo) morphogenesis. The lack of adequate energy (ATP) production in bacteria, together with their cell walls, precluded them from developing true multicellularity and they employed apoptosis in areas of self-defence and altruism.

Myxococcus colonies display this altruism when a proportion of a colony will self-destruct and lyse upon finding a food source whilst the remainder energise and become actively mobile to take advantage of the food source.

Hence, what people always saw as a noble sacrifice for the good of humanity that signified the highest human principles may be an offshoot of apoptosis 3 G years old coevolved by competing bacteria and archaea, only to undergo further sophistication in the eukaryotes. A thorough and up to date phylogenetic analysis by Klim, J. et al. in G3 2018 has supportive data for these inferences, but the authors focus on the "arms race" between the mitochondria and the early eukaryote ancestors as well as issues to do with the effects of oxidation levels on apoptosis.

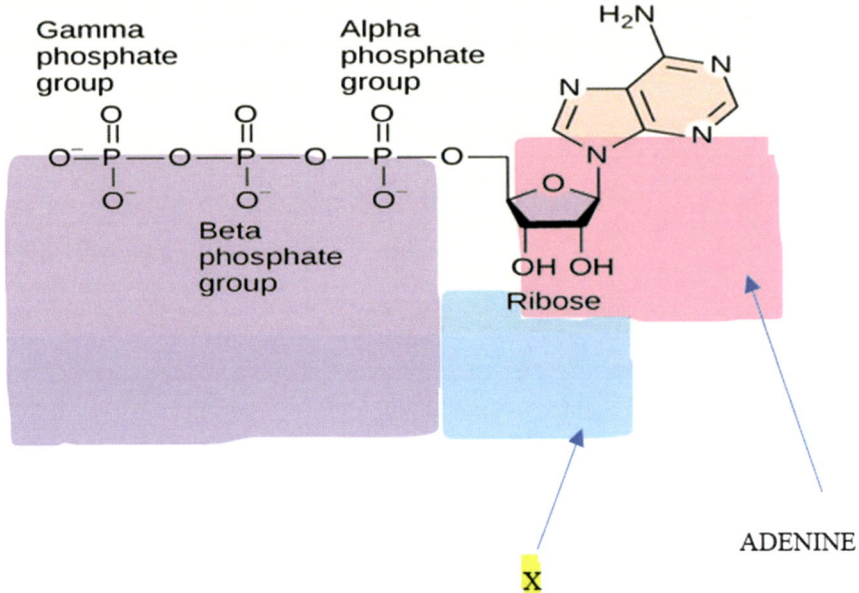

ABOVE - ATP. The molecular natural selection formula has been working inexorably over billions of years on the three components of nucleic acids as well as on the polymer as a whole. ATP is a coding information molecule as well as having a major role in metabolism and as a signal (cAMP) or deoxy ATP precursor so it has a high F (functional value) score. together with a high concentration of its precursors, ADP & Pi, and high stereochemical affinity its' MNS score is very high in all 3 domains of life as well as in replicating viruses.

NB - O ATOM INDICATED BY X IS MISSING IN DNA MONOMERS BY THE REDUCTION CATALYSED BY THE RIBONUCLEOTIDE REDUCTASE ENZYME

Table 6 - Primordial Nucleotide Component Alternatives

NUCLEOBASE POSITION - modified canonical bases eg thiouridine >300, pyrene, pyridines, quinones, pyrroles, benzaldehydes, imidazolidinones, pyrazines, flavins, nicotinamides

RIBOSE POSITION- amino acid, glucose, mannose, tetrose, ribulose, ribose with side chains

PHOSPHATE- dimethylene sulfone, sulfide, borate , arsenate, imidazolides, amino acids

2 diagrams of Phycobilisomes (note also PS1, PS11, ATP synthase) on Cyanobacterial Thylakoid membranes and their voltaic pile protein structure.

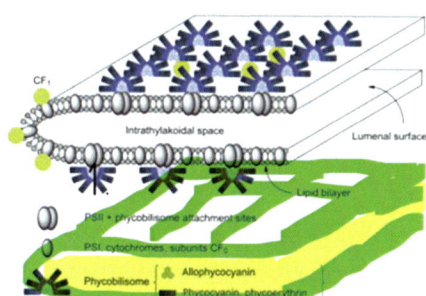

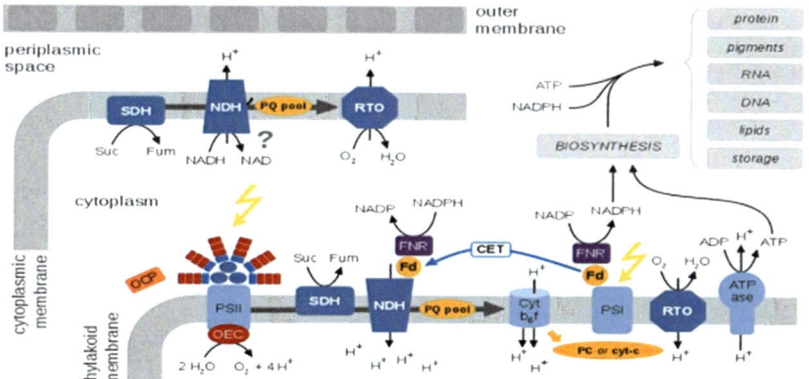

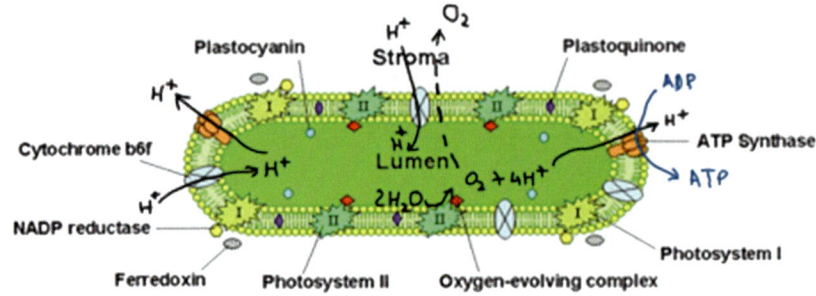

ABOVE - Single granum found in stacks in plant, algae and Dinoflagellate chloroplasts, Zooxanthellae and Zoochlorellae. electron carriers (Plastoquinone and Plastocyanin) and molecular complexes involved in oxygen and atp synthesis are shown. cytochrome B6F is the only proton pump whilst the oxygen evolving complex in the lumen produces 4H+ and 1O_2 in the lumen for every 2 H_2O molecules split. O^2 then diffuses out for respiration by the plant cells' mitochondria or diffuses into the environment.

Chlorophyll is found in PS1, PS11 and in Quantasomes (230-250 Chlorophyll a molecules each) on the inner surface of the granum membrane.

BELOW - Chloroplast, a functional endosymbiotic cyanobacterial remnant, depicting stacked grana for voltaic pile voltage enhancement. DNA(~100 genes) and ribosomes shown. Mitochondria which are of proteobacterial origin are found in the surrounding cytoplasm. CO^2 is used in the stroma in the calvin cycle for sugars.

NB - Chlorophyll not found on outer chloroplast membrane.

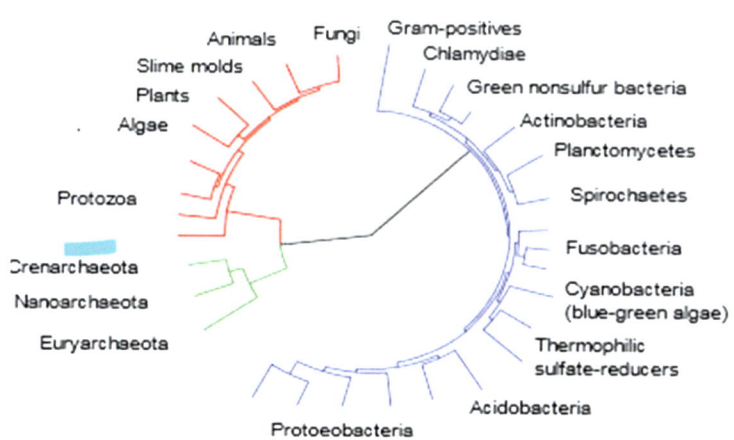

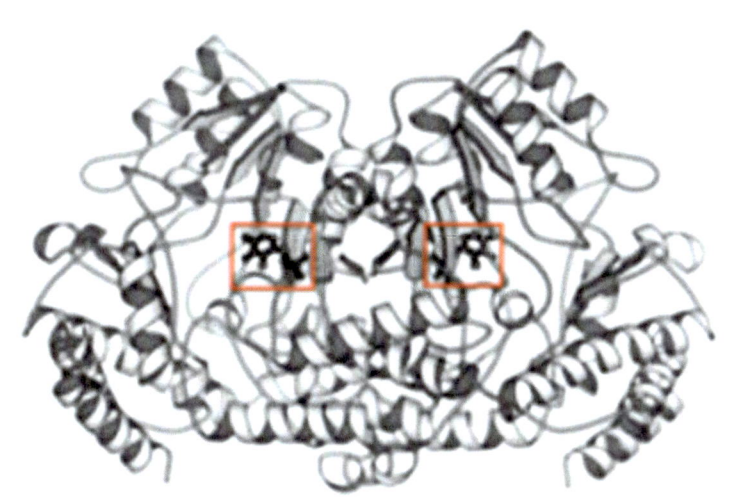

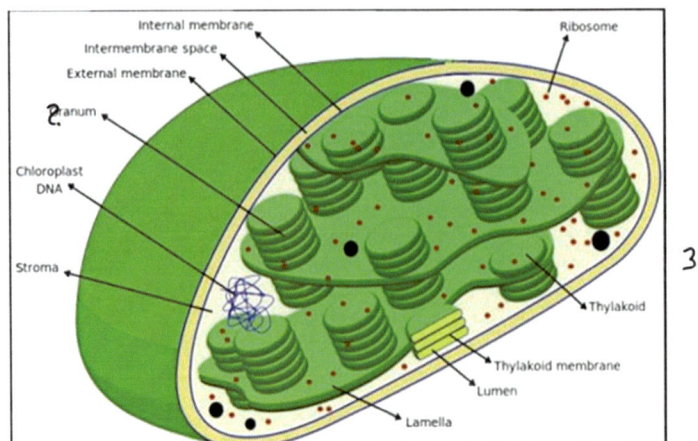

1

3

Top Tree of Life supported by molecular clock, phylogenetic and biochemical studies. Archaea 1. and bacteria 3, evolved separately from 4 billion years ago but with significant horizontal gene transfer and endosymbiotic events that led to the eukaryotes 2. At about 1.2 Gya - each of the 2 central arms represent ~1018 diverse cells.

ABOVE - Serine Hydroxymethyltransferase with 2 pyridoxal Pi coenzymes shown in red boxes on either side of the central aperture. A similar enzyme was significant in the molecular evolution of pre- procollagen and fibroin (silk) sequences as well as biosynthesis of Phenylalanine, Tyrosine, Tryptophan and Histidine from Serine reacting with Benzene, Phenol, Indole and Imidazole respectively. The extant synthesis pathways for these 4 amino acids (Shikimate + Histidine) are a modern evolution. Before Folate biosynthesis evolved SHMT catalysed the reaction. Serine ←→ Glycine + Methanol

Perplexing Collagen and Silk

Collagen is the foundation for true multicellularity in animals, along with the sophistication of gene control that led to the speciation of single-celled organisms. Without it, many beginnings towards multicellularity in Animalia, more than 50, encountered great limitations and stalled.

Unlike lignin and cellulose polymers in plants and chitin in fungi and Arthropoda, its flexibility and strength allowed directed motion to be added to the support of a larger bulk. Arthropods have both collagen (muscles and connective tissues) and chitin (exoskeleton or squid gladius and beak) but could not achieve directed motion without the strength and flexibility of collagen in their connective tissue.

How could such a complicated molecule, as pre-procollagen with a glycine at every apical turn, every third amino acid residue, have possibly been created by the coding and control system outlined in this manuscript? How could proline and its post translational product hydroxyproline comprise ~20% in specific locations?

Pre-procollagen is possibly a coil variation of the wavy beta sheet. A major difference from the alpha spiral which is marred by glycine and proline in its sequence (often leading to breaks in the spiral) is the Gly-Xaa-Yaa motif of pre procollagen with Yaa most often being proline or hydroxyproline and Xaa being more varied. The ordered content of procollagen leads to the formation of a left-handed helix, unlike the right-handed alpha spiral.

The simplest hypothesis that solves this perplexing phenomenon is the existence of an Eoarchean transferase of a helicase structure and promiscuous nature (could catalyse different reactions of a similar type) that was produced by the protoribosome and cleaved all apical amino acid side chains from any wavy beta sheets to produce glycine at that point in the chain as it traversed the central aperture in which was located a pyridoxal phosphate coenzyme.

The closest extant approximation is serine hydroxymethyl-transferase which has a large central aperture. Presumably, the side chains of residues that were not at the apex were too far from the active site or were protected by other interactions. Amino acids in folded proteins were not exposed but free amino acids could be affected by this enzyme to result in a maintenance of glycine concentration from serine, alanine and other few amino acids by the equilibrium directives of Le Chateliere's principle.

Upon exiting the aperture, the wavy beta sheet morphology was transformed to a left-handed helix. That this is plausible is evidenced by the extant enzyme prolyl hydroxylase that also has a helicase morphology and hydroxylates, any prolines in the Yaa position of animal collagens which have a Gly-Xaa-Yaa repeating sequence with X being any amino acid and Yaa most often represented by proline (Yu, Z. et al. 2014).

A sequential degradation of the side chains instead of a single pass cleavage could also be plausibly achieved by the same promiscuous transferase, which would be most closely approximated today by serine hydroxymethyltransferase. This enzyme produces glycine from serine in solution by cleaving serines' hydroxymethyl side chain and has a sizeable central aperture with a pyridoxal phosphate coenzyme on either side of it. In the above list of 50 essential genes, this enzyme is represented by 13. Methyltransferase.

Without a prevalence of proline and hydroxyproline in the Yaa position, however, the scenario is incomplete. Proline itself was retained by molecular natural selection favouring its role in strengthening beta spirals and sheets and by being available in adequate concentration for proteinogenesis.

Hydroxyproline could have been a proteinogenic amino acid in the Archaean or was selected for by evolution following the action of a hydrogenase. Additionally, a promiscuous lyase enzymatic action of proline, an established organocatalyst, on glutamate, arginine, ornithine (could have been a proteinogenic amino acid in the Eoarchean), glutamate-5-semialdehyde or 1-pyrroline-5 carboxylic acid in the Yaa position to produce a pyrrolidine ring could have acted over time to strengthen the pre procollagen with a post translational synthesis of proline.

Three of these molecules today can be converted into proline in a single step, each catalysed by a specific enzyme, pyrroline-5-carboxylase, prolyl hydroxylase and ornithine cyclodeaminase. Glutamate-5-semialdehyde requires a dehydrogenase as well.

If this is actually what happened, it would explain the presence of proline, an otherwise problematic amino acid member, in the 20 proteinogenic amino acid list, namely that one proline catalysed the synthesis of an adjacent proline from the amino acids mentioned above.

Additionally, the supply of proline could be supplemented from the environment with Pyrrolidine reacting with formate catalysed by gamma rays to proline and Pyrrolidine 3 carboxylate in a 1:5.5 ratio (Davidson, A. et al. (1976) *Australian Journal of Chemistry*). The gamma rays were produced by lightning passing through the atmosphere and from radioactive rocks. The Pyrrolidine itself is formed by 1,4 butane diol + ammonia catalysed by Zn^{2+}.

Subsequent reverse translation of the preprocollagen left an RNA copy in the archives for use in intracellular strengthening.

Such a post translational aetiology for procollagen synthesis could not have occurred more recently, otherwise it could not be laid down in the archives following the extinction of the translatase.

By occurring during the era of the translatase the pre-procollagen spiralled through the translatase to produce an RNA archive with a one or two nucleotide codon of its existence and the replicase amplified its number. Later, during the era of the modern cell outlined in chapter 21, the codons had evolved into three nucleotide lengths and reverse transcriptase laid this RNA archive into the DNA archive and later the DNA polymerases continued to propagate it.

There was no negative selection pressure on the pre procollagen due to a perennial structural advantage to the biotic cells that would become the bacteria. Archaea may have never evolved procollagen or fibroin since their genomes show no sign of it. If this were true, then it is another indication of an early divergence hypothesis between bacteria and archaea and helps to explain their saprophytic means of nutrition. Alternatively, they have lost these genes through lack of use and need.

Cells did not have the need, the energy or ability to produce fully formed collagen, a triple helix of procollagen molecules bound by hydroxyl groups and disulfide until the advent of the eukaryotes and the sustained rise in the levels of atmospheric oxygen that allowed the necessary post translational hydroxylation of proline and lysine side chains together with glycosylations that made the fibre both tough and flexible.

Hundreds of bacterial species, both pathogenic and non-pathogenic, have collagen-like sequences in their genomes but most are not expressed and the products have only been isolated following expression in E Coli by laboratory techniques. Why do archaea lack these sequences? Possible answers include:

1. They never acquired this protein or this gene, a primordial aetiology.
2. They lost the protein and its distinct gene sequence when it lost its usefulness (following the loss of predation in archaea) a primordial aetiology.
3. Bacteria acquired the gene sequences by horizontal gene transfer from animal predators or prey, a recent aetiology which does not explain how animals acquired collagen.

All of these possibilities are consistent with the primordial divergence hypothesis, with HGT being the least plausible aetiology since Archaea are also prey items and are subject to HGT. How could eukaryotes develop such an intricate gene so late in evolution?

Fibroin, the silk protein fibre of famous delicacy has repeating units of [glycine-serine-glycine-alanine-glycine-alanine] coated with a gummy protein called sericin whose glue-like properties come from the 32% serine levels that form hydrogen bonds.

A scenario identical to that of procollagen synthesis with alanine organocatalysing the in-situ synthesis of adjacent alanine and serine is the only plausible explanation for the coded synthesis of fibroin even though its sequence motifs have not been found in prokaryotes yet. If they do not exist, they may have been lost with gene deletion over time.

The RNA codons that coded for glycine, alanine, serine and proline before the advent of DNA were morphed over the aeons in the manner already described previously and eventually reverse transcribed into the DNA archives when reverse transcriptase was the only DNA producing and replicating enzyme: around the time of the basic modern cell described in chapter 21.

Pre procollagen and fibroin gave rise to many modern variations in the category of Intermediate Filaments which are sequence variations of these two progenitors derived from much feedback chemistry.

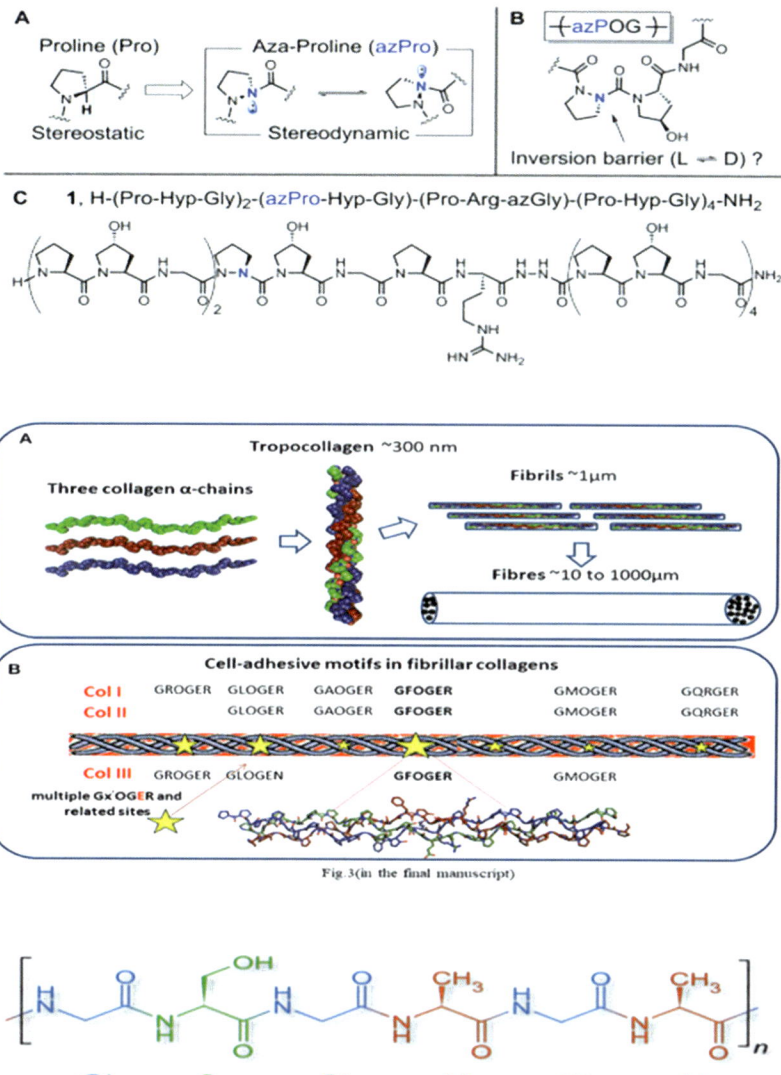

TOP - Preprocollagen amino acid sequence with experimental Azaproline in place of some Prolines and experimental Azaglycine for one Glycine. Note Pyrrolidine ring of Proline forming part of the Peptide chain. **MIDDLE** - diagram of typical collagen fibre organisation (O_2 dependent). **BOTTOM** - amino acid sequence of silkworm fibre (Fibroin). Both needed enzymes, Serine Hydroxymethyltransferase, asymmetric Organocatalysis and the Translatase to achieve these long repeating sequences in the coding archive (RNA in the Eoarchaen).

Epilogue

If one was to accept this account of the origin and evolution of life as plausible then it follows that grandiose attempts to create a modern cell in the laboratory are hopeless due to the constraints of materials, time and work compared with the abundance of these in nature.

With Avogadro's number at 6.022 x 1023 number of molecules per litre of solution it follows that the great passage of time for reproducible life to emerge on Earth had much to do with cells acquiring and maintaining stable levels of functional chemicals and catalysts even with some, such as the dNTP's in micromolar concentrations. A glance at the proposed molecular natural selection formula would suggest that a long time must pass for enzyme and ribozyme levels to rise adequately, for their efficiency to adequately increase, for RNA-DNA feedback mechanisms to evolve adequately and for nutritional acquisition and energy storage mechanisms to evolve adequately to permit coded speciation, mitosis, sexual reproduction and multicellularity.

Ingestion of nutrients does not negate the proposed molecular evolution formula. Analogous to panspermia it just shifts the focus to wherever the relevant molecule is biosynthesised and naturally many inorganic molecules or elements are provided by Nature in processes that don't rely on living entities.

In effect it was inorganic and organic abiotic catalysts, ribozymes, proteinoid catalysts and subsequently enzymes that changed rate limited, apparently zero order slow reactions into first, second and higher order fast reactions where higher reactant concentration significantly increased the reaction rate. This could still lead to equilibrium and hence death if not for a. the constant ingestion and excretion into the environment, b. the evolved feedback mechanisms and c. organisms of all sizes using their own organelles and other reserves of energy as food sources.

The axiom in chemistry that bond formation releases energy and bond breaking uses energy led to polymers within and between cells evolving into larger molecules and molecular machines thereby favouring anabolism over catabolism and hence life over death and degradation. This does not mean that accretion or growth defines life since celestial bodies and Earthly structures can accrete and thereby accumulate entropy therefore Schrodinger's definition of life should be regarded as one that does not define life by failing to distinguish it from other entropy accretions such as forming stars, planets or asteroids.

The scenario herein extends an explanatory theory of Darwinian natural selection down to the molecular level and allows new research findings to be added and corrections of fact to be made.

References

1. Lupas, A. N. et al. (2017) 'Ribosomal Proteins as Documents of the Transition from unstructured polypeptides to folded proteins', *Journal of Structural Biology*. Vol. 198, Issue 2, 74–81.
2. Miller, S. L. and Urey, H. C. (1959) 'Organic Compound Synthesis on the Primitive Earth', *Science* 130 (3370), 245–51.
3. Turk, R. M. and Yarus, M. (2010) 'Multiple translational products from a five nucleotide ribozyme', *Process Natl Acad Sci USA*, 107(10):4585–9.
4. Yarus, M. et al. (2009) 'RNA-amino acid binding: a stereochemical era for the genetic code', *J Mol Evol*, 69(5), 406–29.
5. Carvunis, A. R. et al. (2012) 'Protogenes and de novo gene birth', *Nature*, 487(7407): 370–4.
6. Yanagawa, H. et al. (1990) 'Synthesis of Polypeptides by Microwave Heating 1: Repeated Hydration-Dehydration Cycles', *Journal of Molecular Evolution*, Vol. 31, Issue 3, 180–186.
7. Ito, M. et al. (1990) 'Synthesis of Polypeptides by Microwave Heating: 11. Function Cycles', *J Mol Evol,*. 31: 187–194.
8. Schmitt-Kopplin, P. et al. (2010) 'High molecular diversity of extra-terrestrial organic matter in Murchison meteorite revealed 40 years after its fall', *PNAS*, 107(7):2763–8.
9. Bahadur, K. (1954) 'Photosynthesis of amino acids from paraformaldehyde and potassium nitrate', *Nature, alone*, 173, 1141.
10. Bahadur, K. (1964) 'Synthesis of Jeewanu, units capable of growth, multiplication and metabolic activity', II, *Zbl. Bakt*, 117, 575–587.
11. Blank, J. G. et al. (2001) 'Experimental shock chemistry of aqueous amino acid solutions and the cometary delivery of prebiotic compounds', *Origins of Life and Evolution of Biospheres*, Vol 32, Issue 1–2, 15–51.

12. Waddell, T. G. and Austin, S. M. (1999) 'Prebiotic Synthesis of vitamin B6 type compounds', *Origin of Life and Evolution of Biospheres*, 29(3):287–296.
13. Oro, J. (1960) 'Synthesis of Adenine from ammonium cyanide', *Biochem. Biophys. Res. Commun.* 2, 407–412.
14. Ritson, D. and Sutherland, J. D. (2012) 'Prebiotic synthesis of simple sugars by photoredox systems chemistry', *Nature Chemistry* 4, 895–899.
15. Patel, B. H. et al. (2015) 'Common origins of RNA, proteins and lipid precursors in a cyanosulfidic protometabolism', *Nature Chemistry*, 7, 301–307.
16. Reusch, R. N. (1999) 'Polyphosphate/Poly-B-(R)-3-Hydroxybutyrate ion channels in cell membranes. In: Schroder HC, Muller WEG Inorganic Polyphosphates', *Progress in Molecular and Subcellular Biology,* Vol. 23, Berlin/Heidelberg: Springer.
17. Breslow, R. and Appayee, C. (2013) 'Transketolase reaction under credible prebiotic conditions', *PNAS*, 110(11):4184–4187.
18. Srivatsan, S. G. And Verma, S. (2001) 'Nucleobase containing metallates polymeric resins as artificial phosphodiesterases: Kinetics of hydrolysis, pH dependence and catalyst recycling', *Chem Eur J*, Vol. 7, Issue 4, 828–833.
19. Astbury, W. T. (1947) 'X-ray studies of nucleic acids', *Symp Sic Exp Biol*, (1):66–76. PMID: 20257017.
20. Lee, H. D. Et al. (1996) 'A self replicating peptide', *Nature*, 382, 525–528.
21. Gull, M. (2014) 'Prebiotic phosphorylation reactions on the early Earth', *Challenges*, 5, 293–212.
22. Nashimoto, M. (2001) 'The RNA/Protein symmetry hypothesis: Experimental support for reverse translation of primitive proteins', *Journal of Theoretical Biology*, Vol 209, Issue 2, 181–187.
23. Tamura, K. (2015) 'Origins and early evolution of the tRNA molecule', *Life*, 5(4), 1687–1699.
24. Ritson, D. J. and Sutherland, J.D.(2014) 'Conversion of biosynthetic precursors of RNA to those of DNA by photoredox chemistry', *J. Mol. Evol*, 78(5):245–250.

25. Srinivasan, V. And Morowitz, H. J. (2009) 'Analysis of the intermediary metabolism of a reductive chemoautotroph', *The Biological Bulletin*, Vol. 217, Issue3, 222–232.
26. Powner, M. W. and Sutherland, J. D. (2009) 'Synthesis of activated pyrimidine ribonucleotides in prebiotically plausible conditions', *Nature*, 459, 239–242.
27. Ferus, M. et al. (2017) 'Formation of nucleobases in a Miller-Urey reducing atmosphere', *PNAS*, USA, 114(17):4306–4311.
28. Yamagata, Y. et al. (1991) 'Volcanic production of polyphosphates and its relevance to prebiotic evolution', *Nature*, 352(6335):516–9.
29. Joyce, G. F. And Horning, D. P. (2016) 'Amplification of RNA by an RNA polymerase ribozyme,' *PNAS*, Vol. 113, no. 35, 9786–9791.
30. Hazen, R.H. and Sverjensky, D. A. (2010) 'Mineral surfaces, Geochemical complexities and the origins of life', *Cold Spring Harb Perspect Biol*, 2(5): a002162, doi:10.1101/cshperspect.a002162.
31. Sussman, J. L. et al. (1978) 'Crystal Structure of Yeast Phenylalanine Transfer RNA 1. Crystallographic Refinement', *J. Mol. Biol*, 123, 607–30.
32. Xu, H. et al. (2017) 'Vesicles of 2 Ketooctanoic Acid in Water', *Soft Matter*, 13, 2246–2252, DOI:10.1039/c65M02665F.
33. Hammer, P. G. Et al. (2017) 'Thermal Studies of Ammonium Cyanide Reactions: A Model for Thermal Alteration of Prebiotic Compounds in Meteorite Parent Bodies', *Lunar and Planetary Science*, XLVIII.
34. Oreille, C. et al. (2015) 'Synthesis of Ribosomes With Tethered Subunits', *Nature*, 524(7563):119–24, doi:10/1038/nature 14862.Epub2015Jul 29.
35. Sagan, L. (1967) 'On the Origin of Mitosing Cells', *Journal of Theoretical Biology*, 14, 225–74.
36. Parisien, M. et al. (2013) 'Diversity of human tRNA genes from the 1000-genome project', *RNA Biol*, 10(12):1853–186, doi:10.4161/rna.27361.
37. Berg, J. M. et al. (2002) *Biochemistry*, 5th edition, WM Freeman.
38. Stirling, A. et al. (2016) 'Prebiotic NH3 Formation: Insights from Simulations', *Inorganic Chemistry*, Vol 55, Issue 4, 1934–1939.

39. Szymanski, M. et al. (2001) 'Aminoacyl-tRNA Synthetases database', *Nucleic Acids Research*, 29(1):288–290, PMID:11125115.
40. Nakatani, Y. et al. (2014) 'Search for the Most "primitive" Membranes and Their Reinforcers: A Review of the Polyprenyl Phosphates Theory', *Orig Life Evol Biosph*, 44(3), 197–208.
41. Tamura, K. and Schimmel, P. (2004) 'Non-enzymatic Aminoacylation of an RNA Minihelix with an Aminoacyl phosphate Oligonucleotide', *Nucleic Acids Symp Ser (Oxf)*, 48, 269–70.
42. Nam, I. Et al. (2018) 'Abiotic synthesis of purine and pyrimidine ribonucleosides in aqueous microdroplets', *PNAS*, USA, 115(1), 36–40.
43. Lim, S. and Kaldis, P. (2013) 'CdKs, cyclins and CKIs: Roles Beyond Cell Cycle Regulation', *Development 2013,* 140:3079–3093.
44. Duan, B. et al. (2014) *A Critical Residue Selectively Recruits Nucleotides for T7 RNA Polymerase Fidelity Control Biophys J*, 107(9), 2130–2140.
45. Joyce, C. M. (1997) 'Choosing the right sugar: How Polymerases select a nucleotide substrate', *PNAS*, 94(5), 1619–1622.
46. Gao, G. et al. (1997) 'Conferring RNA polymerase Activity to a DNA polymerase: A single residue in reverse transcriptase controls substrate selection', *PNAS*, 94(2), 407–411.
47. Battistuzzi, F. U. et al. (2004) 'A genomic timescale of prokaryote evolution', *BMC Evolutionary Biology*, 4, 44.
48. Ong, J. L. et al. (2006) 'Directed evolution of DNA polymerase', *J Mol Biol*, 361(3), 537–50.
49. Bertram, G. et al. (2001) 'Endless Possibilities; translation termination and stop codon recognition', *Microbiology*, 147, 255–269.
50. Belinky, F. et al. (2017) 'Selection of Start Codons in Prokaryotes and Potential Compensatory Nucleotide Substitution', *Scientific Reports*, 7, Article no: 12422.
51. Drabkin, J. H. and RajBhandary, U. L. (1998) 'Initiation of Protein Synthesis. Other than Methionine', *Mol Cell Biol*, 18(9), 5140–5147.
52. Baeza, A. et al. (2007) 'Solvent Free Synthesis of Alpha Aminonitriles', *Synthesis*, 1230–1234.

53. Johnson, H. G. and Crosby, D. G. 'Alpha Amino Acid Amides: a Convenient Synthesis', *The Journal of Inorganic Chemistry*, Vol. 27, Issue 3, 798–802.

54. Samanta, B. and Joyce, G. F. (2017) 'A reverse transcriptase ribozyme', *eLife*, 6:e31153.

55. Redrejo-Rodriguez, M. et al. (2017) *Primer Independent DNA Synthesis by a Family B DNA Polymerase from Self Replicating Mobile Genetic Elements Cell Rep*, 21(6), 1574–1587.

56. Cantara, W. A. et al. (2011) 'The RNA modification database, RNAMDB:2011 update', *Nucleic Acids Research*, Vol 39, Issue Suppl 1, D195–D201.

57. Chawla, M. et al. (2015) 'An atlas of RNA base pairs accurate energies', *Nucleic Acids Research*, Vol 43, Issue 14, 6714–6729.

58. Schwendinger, M. G. and Rode, B. M. (1992) 'Investigation on the mechanism of the salt induced peptide formation', *Orig Life Evol Biosphere*, 22, 349–59.

59. Da Silva, L. et al. (2014) 'Salt promoted synthesis of RNA-like molecules in simulated hydrothermal conditions', *J Mol Evol*, 80(2).

60. Ferris, J. P. (2006) 'Montmorillonite-catalysed formation of RNA oligomers: the possible role of catalysis in the origins of life', *Philos Trans R Soc Lond: B. Biol Sci*, 361(1474), 1777–1786.

61. Yarus, M. (2017) 'The Genetic Code and RNA-Amino Acid Affinities', *Life*, 7(2), 13.

62. Caetano-Anolles, G. and Sun, F. J. (2014) 'The Natural History of Transfer RNA and its interactions with the Ribosome', *Frontiers in Genetics. RNA*, doi.org 10/3389/fgene.2014.

63. Keller, M. A. et al. (2014) 'Non-enzymatic glycolysis and pentose phosphate pathway-like reactions in a plausible Archaean ocean', *Molecular Systems Biology*, Vol. 10, Issue 4.

64. Tamura, K. (2011) 'Molecular Basis for Chiral Selection in RNA Aminoacylation', *Int. J. Mol. Sci*, 12, 4745–4757.

65. Englander, M. T. et al. (2015) 'The ribosome can discriminate the chirality of amino acids within its peptidyl transferase centre', *PNAS*, USA, 112(19), 6038–43.

66. Murphy, F. V. and Ramakrishnan, V. (2004) 'Structure of a purine-purine wobble base pair in the decoding center of the ribosome', *Nature Structural& Molecular Biology*, 11, 1251–1252.

67. Furukawa, Y. et al. (2013) 'Selective stabilisation of ribose by borate', *Origin of Life and Evolution of Biospheres*, 43(4–5), 353–361.

68. Ma, B. et al. (2010) 'Why Does Binding of Proteins to DNA or Proteins to Proteins Not Necessarily Spell Function?', *ACS Chem Biol*, 5(3), 265–272.

69. Buddhue, J. D. (1942) 'Nitrogen and its Compounds in Meteorites', *Contributions of the Society for Research on Meteorites,* 3 (8), 59–61.

70. Cooper, G. et al. (2011) 'Detection and formation scenario of citric acid, pyruvic acid and other metabolism precursors in carbonaceous meteorites', *PNAS*, 108(34), 14015–14020.

71. Fox, S. W. and Harada, K. (1958) 'Thermal Copolymerisation of Amino Acids to a Product Resembling Protein', *Science*, Vol. 128, Issue 3333, 1214.

72. Fox, S. W. (1973) 'Molecular Evolution to the First Cells', *Pure Appl Chem,* 34 (3), 641–69.

73. Advani, V. M. and Dinman, J. D. (2016) 'Reprogramming the genetic code', *Bioessays*, Vol. 44, No.15, 7007–7078.

74. Atkins, J. F. et al. (2016) 'Ribosomal frame shifting and transcriptional slippage', *Nucleic Acids Research*, Vol.44, No.15, 7007–7078.

75. Oremland, R. S. et al. (2009) 'Arsenic in the Evolution of Earth and Extraterrestrial Ecosystems', *Geo microbial J*, 26, 522–536.

76. Kulp, T. R. (2014) 'Early Earth: Arsenic and primordial life', *Nature Geoscience*, 7(11), 785–6.

77. Lebrun, E. et al. (2003) 'Arsenite oxidase, an ancient bio energetic enzyme', *Mol Biol Evol*, 20, 686–693.

78. Wolfe-Simon, F. et al. (2011) 'A Bacterium That Can Grow by Using Arsenic Instead of Phosphorus', *Science,* Vol. 332, Issue 6034, 1163–1166.

79. Rogne, P et al. (2008) 'Molecular Mechanism of ATP versus GTP selectivity of adenylate kinase', *PNAS.org*, doi/10.1073/PNAS.1721508115.

80. Scott, K. A. et al. (2008) 'Coarse-Grained MD Simulations of Membrane Protein-Bilayer Self Assembly', *Science Direct,* Vol.16, Issue 4, 621–30.
81. Dingermann, T. et al. (1980) 'Functional Role of Ribosyl-Thymine in Transfer RNA', *Eur. J Biochem*, 104, 33–40.
82. Amin, M. R. et al. (2018). 'Re-annotation of 12,495 prokaryotic 16s rRNA 3' ends and analysis of Shine-Dalgarno and anti Shine-Dalgarno sequences', *PLoS ONE*, 13(8):e0202767.
83. Varma, S. J. et al. (2018) 'Native iron reduces CO_2 to intermediate and end-products of the Acetyl-CoA pathway', *Nature Ecology & Evolution*, 2, 1019–1024.
84. Raven, J. A. et al. (2008) 'The evolution of inorganic carbon concentrating mechanisms in photosynthesis', *Philos Trans R Soc Lond B Biol Sci*, 363 (1504), 2641–50.
85. Yeates, T. O. et al. (2008) 'Protein-based organelles in bacteria: Carboxysomes and related microcompartments', *Nature Reviews: Microbiology*, Vol. 6, 681–92.
86. Kim, E. Y. et al. (2014) 'The effects of time, temperature and pH on the stability of PDU bacterial microcompartments', *Protein Science*, Vol. 23, Issue 10.
87. Goodman, G. et al. (2012) 'Fullerenes and the Origin of Life', *Isr Med Assoc J*, 14(10), 602–6.
88. Glass, J. I. et al. (2006) 'Essential genes of a minimal bacterium', *PNAS*, 103(2), 425–430.
89. Gil et al. (2004) 'Determination of the Core of a Minimal Bacterial Gene Set', *Molecular Microbiology Reviews*, 68, 3, 518–537.
90. Caetano-Anolles, K. et al. (2013) 'Structural Phylogenomics Reveals Gradual Evolutionary Replacement of Abiotic Chemistries by Protein Enzymes in Purine Metabolism', *PLoS ONE*, 8(3):e59300.
91. Striepen, B. et al. (2004) 'Gene transfer in the evolution of parasite nucleotide biosynthesis', *PNAS*, USA, 101(9), 3154–3159.
92. Davidov, Y. et al. (2006) 'A new alpha proteobacterial clade of Bdellovibrio-like predator implications for the mitochondrial endosymbiont theory', *Environmental Microbiology*, doi:10.1111/j.1462-2920.2006.01101.x.

93. Fox, G. E. (2010) 'Origin and Evolution of the Ribosome', *Cold Spring Harbour Perspectives in Biology*, 2(9);a003483.
94. Spirin, A. S. (2002) 'Ribosome as a molecular machine', *FEBA Lett*, 514(1), 2–10.
95. Takyar, S. et al. (2005) 'mRNA helicase activity of the ribosome', *Cell*, 120(1), 49–58.
96. Amunts, A. et al. (2015) 'The structure of the human mitochondrial ribosome', *Science*, 6230, 95–98.
97. Chain, P. et al. (2003) 'Complete Genome Sequence of the Ammonia-Oxidizing Bacterium and Obligate Chemolithoautotroph Nitrosomonas', *Europaea J Microb Physiol*, 1989, 30, 125–81.
98. Prosser, J. I. 'Autotrophic nitrification in bacteria', *Adv Microb Physiol*, 1988, 30, 125–81.
99. Hao, Y. M. (2010) 'CCA Addition to tRNA: Implications for tRNA Quality Control', *IUBMB Life*, 62(4), 251–260.
100. Raina, M. et al. (2014) 'Reduced Amino Acid Specificity of Mammalian Tyrosyl-tRNA Synthetase Is Associated With Elevated Mistranslation of Tyr Codons', *J Biol Chem*, 289(25), 17780–17790.
101. Neumann, H. et al. (2010) 'Encoding multiple unnatural amino acids via evolution of a quadruplet-decoding ribosome', *Nature*, 464(7287), 441–4.
102. Parker, J. (1989) 'Errors and alternatives in Reading the universal genetic code', *Microbiol Rev*, 53(3), 273–298.
103. Lundin, D. et al. (2015) 'The Origin and Evolution of Ribonucleotide Reduction', *Life,* 5, 604–636.
104. Case, A. J. (2017) *On the Origin of Superoxide Dismutase: Antioxidants (Basel)*, 4, 82.
105. Lopez-Madrigal, S. et al. (2011) 'Complete genome sequence of "Candidatus Tremblaya princeps" strainPCVAL, an intriguing translational machine below the living-cell status,' *J Bacteriol*, 193(19), 5587–8.
106. Lopez-Madrigal, S. et al. (2013) 'How Does Tremblaya princeps Get Essential Proteins from its Nested Partner Moranella endobia in the Mealybug Planoccocus citri?', *PLoS ONE*, 8(10):e77307.

107. Troisfontaines, P. and Cornelis, G. R. (2005) 'Type 111 secretion: more systems than you think', *Physiology (Bethesda)*, 20, 326–39.

108. Gophna, U. et al. (2003) 'Bacterial type 111 secretion systems are ancient and evolved by multiple horizontal-transfer events', *Gene*, Vol:312, 151–163.

109. Hugenholtz, P. et al. (2015) 'Back from the dead: the curious tale of the predatory cyanobacterium Vampirovibrio Chlorellavorus', *DOE JGI. Peer J*, 3:e968.

110. Petrov, A. S. et al. (2015) 'History of the ribosome and the origin of translation', *PNAS*, 112(50), 15396–15401.

111. Lafontaine, D. L. J. (2010) 'A "garbage can" for ribosomes: how eukaryotes degrade their ribosomes', *Trends Biochem Sci*, 35(5), 267–77.

112. Suzuki, T. et al. (2014) 'A complete landscape of post-translational modifications in mammalian mitochondrial rRNAs', *Nucleic Acids Res,* 42(11), 7346–57.

113. Rohlfing, D. L. and Fox, S. W. (1969) 'Catalytic Activities of Thermal Polyanhydro-a-Amino Acids', *Advances in Catalysis*, Vol 20, 373–418.

114. Gornik, S. G. et al. (2015) 'Endosymbiosis undone by stepwise elimination of the Plastid in a parasitic dinoflagellate', *PNAS,* 112(18), 5767–5772.

115. Shaevitz, J. W. and Gitai, Z. (2010) 'The Structure and Function of Bacterial Actin Homologs', *Cold Springs Harb Perspect Biol*, 2(9):a000364.

116. Olek, A. T. et al. (2014) 'The Structure of the Catalytic Domain of a Plant Cellulose Synthase and it's Assembly into Dimers', *The Plant Cell*, Vol. 26, 2996–3009.

117. Vanholme, R. et al. (2010) 'Lignin Biosynthesis and Structure', *Plant Physiol*, Vol. 153, 110–119.

118. Gerdes, K. et al. (1985) 'Stable inheritance of plasmid R1 requires two different loci', *J Bacteriol*, 161, 292–298.

119. Bienstock, R. J. et al. (2014) 'Phylogenetic analysis and evolutionary origins of DNA polymerase X-family members', *DNA Repair (Amst)*, 22, 77–88.

120. Guilliam, T. A. et al. (2015) 'Primase/polymerases are a functionally diverse superfamily of replication and repair enzymes', *Nucleic Acids Res*, 43(14), 6651–6664.

121. Inoue, M. et al. (2019) 'Structural and Phylogenetic Diversity of Anaerobic Carbon Monoxide Dehydrogenase', *Front. Microbiol*, 9, 3353.

122. Becerra, A. et al. (2014) 'A phylogenetic approach to the early evolution of autotrophy: the case of the reverse TCA and reductive acetyl-CoA pathways', *Int. Microbiol*, 17(2), 91–7.

123. Medrano-Soto, A. et al. (2018) 'Bioinformatic characterisation of the Anoctamin superfamily of Ca2+ activated ion channels and lipid scramblases', *PLoS ONE*, 13(3):e0192851.

124. Forterre, P. et al. (2007) 'Origin and evolution of DNA topoisomerases', *Biochimie*, Vol. 89, Issue 4, 427–446.

125. Collins, L. and Penny, D. (2005) 'Complex Spliceosomal Organization Ancestral to Extant Eukaryotes', *Molecular Biology and Evolution*, Vol. 22, Issue 4, 1053–1066.

126. Belfort, M. et al. (1995) 'Prokaryotic Introns and Inteins: a Panoply of Form and Function', *Journal of Bacteriology*, Vol. 177, No. 14, 3897–3903.

127. Zhao, C. and Pyle, A. M. (2017) 'The group 11 intron maturase: a reverse transcriptase and splicing factor go hand in hand', *Curr Opinion Struct Biol*, 47, 30–39.

128. Gilbert W. (1978) 'Why genes in pieces', *Nature*, 271(5645), 501.

129. Gilbert, W. and Glynias, M. (1993) 'On the ancient nature of introns', *Gene*, 135(1–2), 137–44.

130. Fedorov, A. (2001) 'Intron distribution difference for 276 ancient and 131 modern genes suggests the existence of ancient introns', *PNAS*, 98(23), 13177–13182.

131. Yan, C. et al. (2015) 'Structure of a yeast spliceosome at 3.6 angstrom resolution', *Science*, Vol. 349, Issue 6253, PDBj:3jb9.

132. Robart, A. R. (2014) 'Crystal structure of a eukaryotic group 11 intron lariat', *Nature*, 51, 4(7521), 193–197.

133. Srinivasan, G. et al. (2002) 'Pyrrolysine encoded by UAG in Archaea: charging of a UAG decoding specialised tRNA', *Science*, 296(5572), 1459–1462.

134. Xu, X. M. et al. (2007) 'Biosynthesis of selenocysteine on its tRNA in eukaryotes', *PLoS Biology*, 5(1):e4.

135. Rogalski, M. et al. (2008) 'Superwobbling facilitates translation with reduced tRNA sets', *Nat Struct Mol Biol*, 15(2), 192–8.

136. Nozaki, H. et al. (2007) 'A 100%-complete sequence reveals unusually simple genomic features in the hot spring red algae Cyanidioschyzon merolae', *BMC Biol*, 5, 28.

137. Potapov, V. et al. (2018) 'Base modifications affecting RNA polymerase and reverse transcriptase fidelity', *Nucl Acids Res*, Vol 46, Issue 11, 5753–63.

138. Kunz, B. A. (1982) 'Genetic effects of deoxyribonucleotide pool imbalances', *Environment Mutagenesis*, Volume 4, Issue 6.

139. Steer, A. M. et al. (2017) 'Prebiotic synthesis of 2-deoxy-D-ribose from interstellar building blocks promoted by amino esters or aminonitriles', *Chem Commun*, 53, 10362–65.

140. Nowack, E. C. M. and Melkonian, M. (2010) 'Endosymbiotic associations with protists', *Philos Trans R Soc Lond B Biol Sci*, 365(1541), 699–712.

141. Ulrich, S. and Kool, E. T. (2012) 'The Importance of Steric Effects on the Efficiency and Fidelity of Transcription by T7 RNA Polymerase', *Biochemistry*, 50(47), 10343–49.

142. Lee, I. and Berdis, A. J. (2010) 'Non-natural nucleotides as probes for the mechanism and fidelity of DNA polymerases', *Biochim Biophys Acta*, 1804, 1064–80.

143. Kool, E. T. (2002) 'Active site tightness and substrate fit in DNA replication', *Annu Rev Biochem*, 71, 191–219.

144. Bedford, E. et al. (1997) 'The thioredoxin binding domain of bacteriophage T7 DNA polymerase confers processivity on E Coli DNA polymerase', *PNAS*, 94(2), 479–84.

145. Bhattacharyya, S. et al. (2016) 'Evolution of initiator tRNA and selection of methionine as the initiating amino acid', *RNA Bio*, 13(9), 810–819.

146. Kyrpides, N. C. and Woese, C. R. (1998) 'Universally conserved translation initiation factors', *Proc Natl Acad Sci*, USA, 95(1), 224–228.

147. Buan, N. R. (2018) 'Methanogenesis: pushing the boundaries of biology', *Emerg Top Life Sci*, 2(4), 629–46.
148. Lie, T. J. et al. (2012) 'Essential anaplerotic role for the energy-converting hydrogenate Eha in hydrogenotrophic methanogenesis', *Proc Natl Scad Sci USA*, 109, 15473–8.
149. Brautaset, T. (2007) 'Bacillus methanococcus: a candidate for industrial production of amino acids from methanol at 50 degrees C', *Appl Microbiol Biotechnology*, 74(1), 22–34.
150. Weiss, I. M. et al. (2018) 'Thermal decomposition of the amino acids glycine, cysteine, aspartic acid, asparagine, glutamic acid, glutamine, arginine and histidine', *BMC Biophys*, 11, 2.
151. Falcon, L. I. et al. (2010) 'Dating the cyanobacterial ancestor of the chloroplast', *ISME J*, 4, 777–783.
152. Gray, M. E. (2012) 'Mitochondrial Evolution', *Cold Spring Harb Perspect Biol*, 4(9), a011403.
153. Schmeed, E. D. and Bourne, P. E. (2005) 'Structural Evolution of the Protein Kinase Superfamily', *PLoS: Comput Biol*, 1(5):e49.
154. Hill, J. M. et al. (2014) 'miRNAs and viroids utilise common strategies for genetic signal transfer', *Front Mol Neurosci*, 7, 10.
155. Ataman, G. et al. (1978) 'Clay mineralogy of Turkish clay deposits', *Chem Geol*, Vol. 22, 233–247.
156. Rufo, C. M. et al. (2014) 'Short peptides self-assemble to produce catalytic amyloids', *Nat Chem*, 6(4), 303, DOI: 10. 1038/nchem 1894.
157. Allamandola, J. L. (2008) 'Chemical Evolution in the Interstellar Medium: Feedstock for Solar Systems', *ACS Symposium Series*, 981, 10.1022/bk-2008-0981.ch005.
158. Dean, P. et al. (2016) 'Microsporidia: Why Make Nucleotides if You Can Steal Them?', *PLoS Pathog*, 12(11):e1005870.
159. Heinz, E. et al. (2014) 'Plasma Membrane-Located Purine Nucleotide Transport Proteins Are Key Components for Host Exploitation by Microsporidian Intracellular Parasites', *PLoS Pathog*, 10(12):e1004547.
160. Parker, E. T. et al. (2011) 'Primordial synthesis of amines and amino acids in a 1958 Miller H2S-rich spark discharge experiment', *Proc Natl Acad Sci USA*, 208(14), 5526–5531.

161. Sousa, R. and Padilla, R. (1995) 'A mutant T7 RNA polymerase as a DNA polymerase', *EMBO J*, 14(18), 4609–4620.

162. Zhang, X. V. and Martin, S. T. (2006) 'Driving Parts of Krebs Cycle in Reverse through Mineral Photochemistry', *J Amer Chem Soc*, 128(50), 16032–3.

163. Muchowska, K. B. et al. (2017) 'Metals Promote Sequences of the Reverse Krebs Cycle', *Nature Ecology and Evolution*, 1, 1716–21.

164. Keller, M. A. et al. (2017) 'Sulfate radicals enable a non-enzymatic Krebs cycle precursor', *Nat Eco Evo*, 1, 0083.

165. Lehmann, J. et al. (2009) 'Emergence of a Code in the Polymerisation of Amino Acids Along RNA Templates', *PLoS ONE*, 4(6):e5773.

166. Lee, N. et al. (2000) 'Ribozyme-catalysed tRNA aminocylation', *Nat Struct Biol*, 7, 28–33.

167. Yarus, M. and Kumar, R. K. (2001) 'RNA-catalysed Amino Acid Activation', *Biochemistry*, 40(24), 6998–7004.

168. Georgiades, K. and Raoult, D. (2011) 'The rhizome of Reclinomonas americanus, Homo sapiens, Pediculus humanus and saccharomyces cerevisiae mitochondria', *Biol Direct*, 6, 55.

169. Khersonsky, O. and Tawfik, D. S. (2010) 'Enzyme Promiscuity: A Mechanistic and Evolutionary Perspective', *Annu Rev Biochem*, 79, 471–505.

170. Bukhari, H. S. T. et al. (2014) 'Evolutionary Origins of the Multienzyme Architecture of Giant Fungal Fatty Acid Synthase', *Structure,* 23(12), 1775–85.

171. Bohlmann, J. et al. (1998) 'Plant terpenoid synthases: Molecular biology and phylogenetic analysis', *PNAS,* 1993, 95(8), 4126–33.

172. Boucher, Y. et al. (2004) 'Origins and evolution of isoprenoid lipid biosynthesis in archaea', *Molecular Microbiol*, Vol. 52, Issue 2.

173. Niu, Y. et al. (2017) 'Phylogenetic Profiling of Mitochondrial Proteins and Integration Analysis of Bacterial Transcription Units Suggest Evolution of F1Fo ATP Synthase from Multiple Modules', *J Mol Evol*, 85(5), 219–233.

174. Gibard, C. et al. (2018) 'Phosphorylation, oligomerization and self assembly in water under potential prebiotic conditions', *Nat Chem,* 10, 217–223.

175. Koumandou, V. L. and Kossida, S. (2010) 'Evolution of the FoF1 ATP Synthase Complex', *PLoS Comput Biol,* 10(9):e1003821.

176. Dibrovna, D. V. et al. (2010) 'Characterization of the N-ATPase', *Bioinformatics,* 26, 1473–6.

177. Fuerst, J. A. and Sagulenko, E. (2014) 'Towards understanding the molecular mechanism of the endocytosis-like process in the bacterium Gemmata obscuriglobus', *BBA-Molecular Cell Res*, 1843(8), 1732–1738.

178. Jakubowski, H. (2016) 'Aminoacyl tRNA synthetases and the Evolution of Coded Peptide Synthesis: the Thioester World', *FEBS Letters*, Vol 590, Issue 4.

179. Jakubowski, H. (2000) 'Amino Acid Selectivity Synthetases', *JBC Papers,* DOI: 10.1074/JBC.c000 577200.

180. Company, M. et al. (1991) 'Requirement of the RNA helicase like protein PRP22 for release of mRNA from spliceosomes', *Nature,* 349, 487–93.

181. Vasilyev, N. N. et al. (2013) 'Ribosomal protein S1 functions as a termination factor in RNA synthesis by Qbeta phage replicase', *Nat Commun,* 4, Article No: 1781.

182. Klim, J. et al. (2018) 'Ancestral State Reconstruction of the Apoptosis Machinery in the Common Ancestor of the Eukaryotes', *G3:Genes, Genomics, Genetics,* vol. 8, no. 6, 2121–34.

183. Fica, S. M. et al. (2013) 'RNA catalysed nuclear pre-mRNA splicing', *Nature*, 503(7475), 229–34.

184. Ekland, E. H. et al. (1995) 'Structurally Complex and Highly Active RNA ligases derived from random RNA sequences', *Science,* 269(5222), 364–70.

185. Josephson, K. et al. (2007) 'Ribosomal synthesis of unnatural peptides', *J Am Chem Soc*, Vol. 127, Issue 33, 11727–11735.

186. Hartman, M. C. T. et al. (2007) 'An expanded set of amino acid analogs for the ribosomal translation of unnatural peptides', *PLoS One*, (2):10 e972.

187. Narrowe, A. B. et al. (2018) 'Complex Evolutionary History of Translation Elongation Factor2 and Dipthamide Biosynthesis in Archaea and Parabasalids', *Genome Biol Evol,* Vol. 10, Issue 9, 2380–93.

188. Pavankumar, T. L. (2018) 'Inteins: Localized Distribution, Gene Regulation and Protein Engineering for Biological Applications', *Microorganisms*, 6(1), 19.
189. Escudero, J. A. et al. (2016) 'Unmasking the ancestral activity of integron integrases reveals smooth evolutionary transition during functional innovation', *Nat Commun,* 7, Article No:10937.
190. Siskind, L. J. et al. (2002) 'Ceramide Channels Increase the Permeability of the Mitochondrial Outer Membrane to Small Proteins', *J Biol Chem*, 277 (30), 26796–03.
191. Perera, M. N. et al. (2012) 'Ceramide channels: Influence of molecular structure on channel formation in membranes', *BBA-Biomembranes*, Vol. 1818, Issue 5, 1291–1301.
192. Nakayama, T. et al. (2014) 'Complete genome of a nonphotosynthetic cyanobacterium in a diatom reveals recent adaptations to an intracellular lifestyle', *PNAS*, USA, 111(31), 11407–11412.
193. Lambert, J. B. et al. (2004) 'Silicate Complexes of Sugars in Aqueous Solutions', *J Am Chem Soc*, 126, 31, 9611–25.
194. Steger, G. and Riesner, C. (2018) 'Viroid research and its significance for research technology and basic biochemistry', *Nucl. Ac Res*, 46(20), 10563–76.
195. Plateau, P. et al. (2017) 'Exposure to selenomethionine causes selenocysteine misincorporation and protein aggregation in Saccharomyces cereviae', *Nat Sci Rep*, 7, Article number: 44761.
196. Yakunin, A. F. et al. (2004) 'The HD Domain of Escherichia coli tRNA Nucleotidyltransferase Has 2', 3'-Cyclic Phosphodiesterase, 2'-Nucleotidase and Phosphatase Activities', *J Biol Chem*, Vol. 279, No. 35, Issue of Aug 27, 36819–27.
197. Breslow, R. (1959) 'On the Mechanism of the Formose Reaction', *Tetrahedron Letters*, 1(21), 22–26.
198. Seitz, E. M. et al. (1998) 'RadA protein is an archaeal RecA protein homolog that catalysed DNA strand exchange', *Genes Dev*, 12(9), 1248–53.
199. Duncan, K. et al. (1987) 'The pentafunctional arom enzyme of Saccharomyces cerevisiae is a mosaic of mono functional domains', *Biochem J*, 246(2), 375–386.

200. Bandurski, E. L. et al. (1976) 'The polymer-like organic material in the Orgueil meteorite', *Geochim Cosmochim Acta*, 40(11), 1397–1406.

201. Martins, Z. (2018) 'The Nitrogen Heterocycle Content of Meteorites and Their Significance for the Origin of Life', *Life (Basel)*, 8(3), 28.

202. Brudno, Y. et al. (2010) 'An in vitro translation, selection and amplification system for peptide nucleic Acids', *Nat Chem Biol*, 6(2), 148–155.

203. Zhang, C. J. et al. (2018) 'Precise synthesis of Sulfur-containing polymers via cooperative dual organocatalysts with high activity', *Nat Commun*, 9, Article number: 2137.

204. Sharma, S. and Lafontaine, D. L. J. (2015) 'View from a bridge: A new perspective on rRNA base modifications', *Perspect Biochem Sci*, 40 (10).

205. Sloan, K. E. et al. (2017) 'Tuning the ribosome: The influence of rRNA modification on eukaryotic ribosome biogenesis and function', *J RNA Biol*, Vol. 14, Issue 9.

206. Fedoseev, G. et al. (2017) 'Formation of Glycerol Through Hydrogenation of CO ice under prestellar core conditions', *Astrophys J*, Vol. 842, No. 1.

207. Sorensen, H. P. et al. (2001) 'Remarkable conservation IF2/eIF5B and IF1/eIF1A markers', *IUBMB Life*, 51(5), 321–7.

208. Leman, L., Orgel, L. and Ghadir, M. R. (2004) 'Carbonyl Sulfide-Mediated Prebiotic Formation of Peptides', *Science*, Vol. 306, Issue 5694, 283–6.

209. Moore, P. B. and Steitz, T. A. (2003) 'After the ribosome structures: How does peptidyl transferase work?' *RNA*, 9(2): 155–9.

210. Hou, Y. M. (2011) 'CCA Addition to tRNA: Implications for tRNA quality control', *IUBMB Life*, 62(4), 251–260.

211. Kobayashi, K. et al. (2010) 'Structural basis for mRNA surveillance by archaeal Pelota and GTP-bound EF1a complex', *PNAS*, USA, 107(41), 17575–9.

212. Janssen, B. D. and Hayes, C. S. (2012) 'The tmRNA ribosome rescue system', *Adv Prot Chem Struct Biol*, 86, 151–91.

213. Yu, Z. et al. (2014) 'Bacterial collagen-like proteins that form triple helical structures', *J Struct Biol*, 186(3), 451–61.

214. Keiler, K. C. and Ramadoss, N. S. (2012) 'Bifunctional transfer-messenger RNA', *Biochimie,* 93(11), 1993–7.
215. Watanabe, K. (2010) 'Unique Features of Animal Mitochondrial Translation Systems', *Proc Jpn Acad Ser B Phys Biol Sci*, 86(1), 11–39.
216. Delk, A. S. and Rabinowitz, J. C. (1975) 'Biosynthesis of Ribosylthymine in the tRNA of Strep. faecalis: A folate-dependent Methylation Not Involving S-Adenosylmethionine', *Proc Nat Acad Sci*, USA, 72(2), 528–30.
217. Tenson, T. et al. (1996) 'A functional peptide encoded in the E Coli 23S rRNA', *Proc Natl Acad Sci*, USA, Vol. 93, 5641–6. May 1996 Biochemistry
218. Pasternak, Z. et al. (2013) 'By their genes Ye shall know them: genomic signatures of predatory bacteria', *ISME J*, 7(4), 756–69.
219. Beringer, M. and Rodnina, M. V. (2007) 'The Ribosomal Peptidyl Transferase', *Molecular Cell*, Vol. 26, Issue 3, 311–321.
220. Mankin, A. S. et al. (1999) 'The Peptidyl Transferase Activity of Naked 23S Ribosomal RNA remains elusive', *RNA*, 5(5), 605–8.
221. Torres, A. G. (2019) 'Enjoy the Silence: Nearly Half of Human tRNA Genes are Silent', *Bioinform Biol Insights*, 13.
222. Price, M. N. et al. (2006) 'The Life Cycle of Operons,' *PLoS Genetics*, 2(6): e96.
223. Woese, C. R. et al. (2000) 'Aminoacyl-tRNA Synthetases, the Genetic Code and the Evolutionary Process', *Microbiol Mol Biol Rev*, 64(1), 202–36.
224. Kolitz, S. E. and Lorsch, J. R. (2011) 'Eukaryotic Initiator tRNA: Finely Tuned and Ready for Action', *FEBS Lett*, 584(2), 396–404.
225. Geslain, R. and Pan, T. (2010) 'Functional Analysis of Human tRNA Isodecoders', *J Mol Biol*, 396(3), 821.
226. Agmon, I. (2018) 'Sequence Complementarity at the ribosomal PTC implies self replicating origin', *FEBS Letters*, Vol 591, Issue 20.
227. Weisbeek, P. J. et al. (1977) 'Bacteriophage phiX174: gene A overlaps geneB', *PNAS*, USA, 74(6), 2504–8.
228. Hansen, J. L. et al. (1997) 'Structure of the RNA Dependent RNA Polymerase of poliovirus', *Structure*, 5(8), 1109–1122.

229. Pabis, A. et al. (2018) 'Cooperativity and flexibility in enzyme evolution', *Curr Opin Struct Biol*, 48, 83–92.

230. Kennelly, P. J. (2003) 'Archaeal protein kinases and protein phosphatases: insights from genomics and biochemistry', *Biochem J*, 370(2), 373–89.

231. Lilley, D. M. J. (2011) 'Mechanisms of RNA Catalysis' *Philos Trans R Soc Lond B Biol Sci*, 366(1580), 2910–17.

232. Ganai, R. A. and Johansson, E. (2016) 'DNA Replication - A Matter of Fidelity', *Molecular Cell*, 62, 745–755.

233. Wong, E. H. et al. (2018) 'Amino Acid Misacylation Propensities Revealed Through Systematic Amino Acid Starvations', *Biochem*, 57, 49, 6767–79.

234. Sesmero, E. and Thorpe, I. F. (2015) 'Using the Hepatitis C Virus: Viral Polymerase Structure, Function and Dynamics', *Viruses*, 7(7), 3974–94.

235. Oertell, K. et al. (2016) 'Kinetic selection vs free energy of DNA base pairing in control of polymerase fidelity', *PNAS*, 113(16), E2277–85.

236. Huber, S. M. et al. (2015) 'Formation and abundance of 5-Hydroxymethyl cytosine in RNA', *ChemBioChem*, 16(5), 752/55.

237. Reed, C. J. et al. (2013) *Protein Adaptations in Archaeal Extremophiles*, Vol. 2013, Article ID 373275.

238. Zhang, X. C. and Han, L. (2016) 'How does a beta barrel integral membrane protein insert into the membrane?' *Protein Cell*, 7(7), 471–7.

239. Kidmose, R. T. (2010) 'Structure of the Qbeta replicase, an RNA dependent RNA polymerase consisting of viral and host proteins', *PNAS*, USA, 107(24), 10884–9.

240. Lange, M. B. et al. (2000) 'Isoprenoid biosynthesis: The evolution of two ancient and distinct pathways across genomes', *PNAS*, USA, 97(24), 13172–77.

241. Lindahl, P. A. and Chang, B. (2001) 'The Evolution of Acetyl CoA Synthase', *OLEB*, 31, 403–434.

242. McGaughey, G. B. et al. (1998) 'Pi Stacking. Alive and Well in Proteins', *J Biol Chem*, 273(25), 15458–63.

243. Wilson, K. A., Kellie, L. and Welmore, S. D. (2014) 'DNA-protein Pi-interactions in nature', *Nucl Acids Res*, 42(10), 6726–6741.
244. Kondo, J. and Westhof, E. (2011) 'Classification of Pseudopairs between nucleotide bases and amino acids by analysis of nucleotide-protein complexes', *Nucl Acids Res*, 39(19), 8628–37.
245. Seeman, N. C. et al. (1976) 'Sequence specific recognition of double helical nucleic acids by proteins', *PNAS*, USA, 73, 804–8.
246. Cheng, A. C. et al. (2003) 'Recognition of nucleic acid bases and base pairs by hydrogen bonding to amino acid side chains', *J Mol Biol*, 327, 781–791.
247. 247. Arnold J.J et al. (2012). Human Mitochondrial RNA Polymerase: Structure, Function, Mechanism and Inhibition.Biochimie Biophys Acta 1819 (9-10): 930-938
248. Pizzarello, S. and Holmes, W. (2009) 'Nitrogen containing compounds in two CR2 meteorites:15N composition, molecular distribution and precursor molecules', *Geochim Cosmochim Acta*, 73(7), 2150–2162.
249. Emana, A. N. and Chand, S. (2015) 'Alkylation of benzene with ethanol over modified HZMS-5 zeolite catalysts', *Appl Petrochem Res*, 5, 121–34.
250. Agmon, I. et al. (2005) 'Symmetry at the Active Site of the Ribosome: Structural an Functional Implications', *Biol Chem*, Vol. 386, 833–844.
251. Doris, S. M. et al. (2015) 'Universal and Domain-Specific Sequences in 23s-28s Ribosomal RNA Identified by Computational Phylogenetics', *RNA*, 21(10), 1719–30.
252. Tharp, J. M. et al. (2020) 'Initiation of Protein Synthesis With Non-Canonical Amino Acids in Vivo', *Angew Chem Int Ed*, 59(8).
253. Ponnamperuma, C. et al. (1963) 'Ultraviolet Synthesis of ATP Under Possible Primitive Earth Conditions', *SAO Special Reports*, #128.
254. Rittenberg, S. C. (1972) 'The Obligate Autotroph – The Demise of a Concept', *Antonie van Leeuwenhoek*, 38, 457–478.
255. Cheng, K. et al. (2019) 'Short RNA ligation: T4 RNA ligase to form short circular RNA chains', *RSC Advances*, Issue 15.

256. Fujita, Y. et al. (2010) 'Generation and Development of RNA ribozymes with Modular Architecture Through "Design and Selection"', *Molecules*. 15(9), 5850–5865.

257. Hayatsu, R. et al. (1977) 'Origin of Organic matter: carbonaceous chondrites', *Geochim et Cosmoch Acts*, Vol. 41, Issue 9, 1325–1339.

258. Nomura, Y. and Yokobayashi, Y. (2019) 'Systematic minimisation of RNA ligase ribozyme through large scale design-synthesis-sequence cycles', *Nucl Ac Res*, 47(17), 8950–60.

259. Cornell, C. E. et al. (2019) 'Prebiotic amino acids bind to and stabilise prebiotic fatty acid membranes', *PNAS*, 116(35), 17239–44.

260. Dora-Tang, T. Y. et al. (2014) 'Fatty acid membrane assembly on coacervates as a step towards a hybrid protocell model', *Nat Chem*, 6, 527–33.

261. Kalra, P. et al. (2018) 'Simple Methods and Rational Design for Enhancing Aptamer Sensitivity and Specificity', *Front Mol Biosci*, 5, 41.

262. Vosseberg, J. and Snel, B. (2017) 'Domestication of self-splicing introns during eukaryogenesis: the rise of the complex spliceosomal machinery', *Biol Direct*, 12, Article No. 30.

263. Turunen, J. J. et al. (2012) 'The significant other: splicing by the minor spliceosome', *Wiley Interdiscipl Rev*, 4(1), 61–76.

264. Cardona, T. et al. (2019) 'Early Archaean origin of Photosystem 11', *Geobiology*, Vol. 17, Issue 2.

265. Burroughs, M. A. and Aravind, L. (2019) 'The Origin and Evolution of Release Factors: Implications for Translation Termination, Ribosome Rescue and Quality Control Pathways', *Int J Mol Sci*, 20(8), 1981.

266. Wang, H. et al. (2014) 'Atlas of NRPS and PKS pathways reveals common occurrence of non-modular enzymes', *PNAS*, USA, 111(25), 9259–64.

267. Shih, P. M. and Matzke, N. J. (2013) 'Primary endosymbiosis events date to the later Proterozoic with cross-calibrated phylogenetic dating of duplicated ATPase proteins', *PNAS*, USA, 110(30):12355–60.

268. Yanagawa, H. et al. (1988) 'Construction of protocellular structures under simulated primitive earth conditions', *OLEB*, 18, 179–207.

269. Ikeuchi, Y. 'Agmatidine-conjugated Cytidine in a tRNA anticodon is essential for AUA decoding in archaea', *Nat Chem Biol*, 6(4), 277–282.
270. Scintilla, S. et al. (2016) 'Duplications of an iron-Sulfur tripeptide leads to formation of a proto ferredoxin', *Chem Comm*, 52(92), 13456–9.
271. Kanavarioti, A. et al. (2001) 'Eutectic phases in ice facilitate nonenzymatic nucleic acid synthesis', *Astrobiology*, 1(3), 271–81.
272. Panevska et al. (2019) 'Ceramide phosphoethanolamine, an enigmatic cellular membrane sphingolipid', *Biochemica Biophysica Acta. Biomembranes*, Vol. 1861, Issue 7, 1284–92.
273. Liu, R. and Ochman, H. (2007) 'Stepwise formation of a bacterial flagellation system', *PNAS*, 104, 17, 7116–7121.
274. Londei, P. (2020) *Archaeal Ribosomes*, Wiley Online Library, doi.org/10.1002/9780470015902.a0000293.
275. Hirata, A. (2019) 'Recent Insights Into the Structure, Function and Evolution of the RNA Splicing Endonucleases: Frontiers in Genetics', *RNA*, doi.org/10.3389/frenetic.2019.0013
276. Deamer, D. and Ross, D. S. (2016) 'Dr/wet cycling and the Thermodynamics and Kinetics of Prebiotic Polymer Synthesis', *Life*, 6, 28, doi:10.3390/life6030028.
277. Budin, I. and Szostak, J. W. (2011) 'Physical Effects Underlying the Transition From Primitive to Modern Cell Membranes', *PNAS*, vol. 108, no.13, 5249–5254.
278. Adamala, K. and Szostak, J. W. (2013) 'Competition Between Model Protocells Driven by an Encapsulated Catalyst', *Nat Chem*, 5(6), 495–501.
279. Bialek, M. et al. (2019) 'Physiological effects of boron compounds for animals and humans: A review', *J Anim Feed Sci*, 28, 307–320.
280. Degrado, W. F. et al. (2014) 'De novo design of a Zn^{2+} Transporting 4 Helix Bundle Peptide', *Science*, Vol. 346, Issue 6216, 1520–1524.
281. Davison, A. et al. (1976) 'Gamma Radiation Induced Carboxylation of Proline', *Austral J Chem*, 29(12), 2603–2606.

282. Becker, S. et al. (2019) 'Unified prebiotically plausible synthesis of pyrimidine and purine RNA ribonucleotides', *Science*, Vol. 366, Issue 6461, 76–82.
283. Oba, Y. et al. (2022) 'Identifying the wide diversity of extraterrestrial purine and pyrimidine nucleobases in carbonaceous meteorites', *Nature Communications*.
284. Gasiorek, M. and Schneider, H. J. (2015) 'Unwinding DNA and RNA with Synthetic Complexes', *Chem Eur J*, 21(50), 18328–32.
285. Jerome, C. A., Benner, S. et al. (2022) 'Catalytic Synthesis of Polyribonucleic Acids on Prebiotic Rock Glasses', *Astrobiology*, 22(6).
286. Müller, F. and Carell, T. (2022) 'A prebiotically plausible scenario of an RNA-peptide world', *Nature*, 605, 279–84.
287. Bose, T. et al. (2022) 'Origin of life: proto-ribosome worlds', *Nucleic Acids Research*, 50(4), 1815–28.
288. Gresser, M. J. (1981) 'ADP-arsenate', *J Biol Chem*, Vol. 256, No. 12, 5981–3.
289. Wochner, A. et al. (2011) 'Ribozyme Catalysed Transcription of an Active Ribozyme', *Science*, 332, 209, DOI: 10.1126/science 1200752.
290. Traut TW. Physiological Concentrations of Purines and Pyrimidines. Mol Cell Biochem. 1994 Nov.9; 140 (1): 1-22